Langston Hughes and the *Chicago Defender*

Langston Hughes and the *Chicago Defender*

Essays on Race, Politics, and Culture, 1942–62

Edited by
Christopher C. De Santis

University of Illinois Press
Urbana and Chicago

Library of Congress Cataloging-in-Publication Data

Hughes, Langston, 1902–1967.
Langston Hughes and the Chicago defender : essays on race,
politics, and culture, 1942–62 / edited by Christopher C. De Santis.
p.   cm.
Includes bibliographical references and index.
ISBN 0-252-06474-7 (paper)
I. De Santis, Christopher C., 1966–   . II. Title.
PS3515.U274A6   1995
814'.52—dc20   94-45656
                                                              CIP

To John F. Callahan

Contents

Part 3: Fair Play in Dixie

Part 4: Nerve of Some White Folks

Part 9: Here to Yonder

Acknowledgments

In many ways, this book represents a collaborative effort over a period of several years. I would like to acknowledge those people who, at various stages of the project, generously gave me their time and expertise.

John F. Callahan, to whom this book is dedicated, introduced me to Langston Hughes's poetry when I was an undergraduate at Lewis and Clark College; he remains a limitless source of scholarly encouragement and a valued friend. While I was doing graduate work at the University of Wisconsin-Madison, Sandra Adell, Nellie McKay, and Craig Werner provided sound advice and criticism as I began to formulate my opinions about Hughes. It was at Wisconsin, too, that I first realized the importance of Hughes's *Defender* columns, and the need for a collection of them.

At the University of Kansas, William L. Andrews was instrumental in helping this project to be realized. From a note scrawled on a tiny piece of paper that I dropped in his mailbox at the Hall Center for the Humanities, he recognized the potential of the project and has guided me through to its completion. His comments on various drafts of my introduction, as well as on the project as a whole, have been invaluable.

Also at the University of Kansas, many faculty members and graduate students aided the project in general and specific ways. Anis Bawarshi proved to be a highly competent and enthusiastic research assistant, tirelessly pursuing obscure references for the annotations. Philip Barnard, Jill Franklin, Cheryl Lester, and David Ryan read and commented on various drafts of the introduction; and G. Douglas Atkins, Bernard Hirsch, Michael L. Johnson, and Haskell Springer provided encouragement and sound advice on preparing a scholarly edition.

Many others have contributed to this project in various ways. Arnold Rampersad, whose brilliant biography of Hughes informs much of my introduction, read and commented on the entire manuscript. For their help in securing permissions to reprint Hughes's columns, I thank Michael Brown at *The Chicago Defender,* and Patricia Powell and Craig Tenney at Harold Ober Associates. It was a sincere pleasure working with Richard L. Wentworth, Karen M. Hewitt, Janice Roney, Lisa Warne-Magro, Theresa L. Sears, and Michael Boudreau at the University of Illinois Press, each of whom was incredibly prompt in responding to my many inquiries throughout this project.

I am grateful to the staffs at the Wisconsin State Historical Society, the University of Wisconsin-Madison libraries, and the University of Kansas libraries for their help in locating and photocopying Hughes's *Defender* columns from microfilm.

Finally, I thank my mother and father, my sisters, and my grandmothers. They are inexhaustible sources of support and encouragement, and exemplify the generosity of spirit found everywhere in the writings of Langston Hughes.

Editorial Method

In the tradition of two important volumes of Hughes's writings that were published after his death in 1967, Faith Berry's *Good Morning Revolution: Uncollected Social Protest Writings by Langston Hughes* (1973) and Edward J. Mullen's *Langston Hughes in the Hispanic World and Haiti* (1977), this collection, too, is intended to introduce readers to a body of work that has been relatively overlooked by readers and critics. Although Hughes is perhaps best known for his poetry, it was in the genre of nonfictional prose that his most searing, ironic, and powerful critiques of American and international race relations were generated. Referred to by one critic as "the poet low-rate of Harlem," in his essays Hughes belied the deceptively simple nature of his verses through a profoundly broad and intellectually engaging understanding of twentieth-century American culture and world affairs. At the same time, Hughes retained in his nonfictional writing the same traits that endeared him in the 1920s to the African American community and later to a broad, international readership: clear, unaffected language; imagery that vividly depicted the lifestyles and concerns of common, working-class people; subtle, witty, yet sharply pointed commentary on the oppression of the African American community by racism, prejudice, and Jim Crow laws; and finally an enormous generosity of spirit that encompassed all people, and through which his prolific body of work has survived and continues to have a profound impact on students and scholars of African American culture.

I have made every attempt to present Hughes's columns from the *Defender* as they originally appeared, with only slight alterations. For the reader's convenience, I have provided dates of original publication under the title of each column. I have italicized the titles of books and periodicals appearing in the columns, although Hughes or the typesetter randomly alternated between italics, boldface type, and simply enclosing titles in quotation marks. In the original columns, Hughes or the typesetter alternated between all capital letters for the first few words in a paragraph and normal usage; for consistency, I have changed all paragraph openings to the latter. The column dated September 16, 1961, was not titled; I have assigned the final line of the column as a title. Finally, I have made silent corrections of misspellings and typographical errors, unless Hughes intentionally altered standard spelling and usage to convey African American vernacular. These alterations are not substantive, but are rather attempts to regularize inconsistent typesetting.

Readers should be aware that these essays were chosen from the hundreds of columns written by Hughes during his lengthy relationship to the *Defender.* The thematic divisions of the text are not intended to suggest a natural unity inherent in the body of columns as a whole; with the exception of several series of columns addressing such disparate topics as religion in the United States, Jamaica, Africa, and the Soviet Union (the latter of which is included in its entirety in part 7), Hughes would often present thematically unrelated topics week by week. The thematic divisions of this volume are intended to suggest those topics that most consistently informed Hughes's writing throughout his career: international race relations, Jim Crow, the South, white supremacy, imperialism and fascism, segregation in the armed forces, the Soviet Union and communism, and African American art and culture. The final section, which begins with the inaugural "Here To Yonder" column, is intended to suggest the wide-ranging nature of Hughes's interests and concerns. The themes implicit in this final series of columns are, however, very much in the spirit of the themes made explicit in the other sections.

Of the many essays that accumulated during his relationship with the *Chicago Defender,* approximately a quarter were devoted to accounts of Hughes's fictional character, Jesse B. Semple. Because Hughes collected many of these pieces in various volumes, I have not included them in this edition.

For the reader's convenience, I have provided annotations to these essays. Frequently cited names are annotated upon their initial appearance in the text; readers are encouraged to consult the index for subsequent references.

Langston Hughes and the *Chicago Defender*

Introduction

After reading *Langston Hughes and the* Chicago Defender: *Essays on Race, Politics, and Culture, 1942–62,* readers familiar with Hughes's work will again be struck by the democratic voice that resounds everywhere in his writings. Deeply committed to an American democracy that, in his own lifetime, never quite delivered in actuality what it promised in theory, Hughes nevertheless dedicated his life to capturing in print the triumphs, dreams, and frustrations of blacks everywhere, always retaining the youthful hope that "we have tomorrow / Bright before us / Like a flame."[1] This early vision was both an act of defiance and a call to action. On one hand, Hughes defied a nation that sought to keep the African American community in perpetual bondage through legal segregation and the fostering of racial prejudice. On the other hand, he challenged black artists to cultivate the rich culture of the African American community in music, paintings, sculptures, poems, and fiction. Now, twenty-eight years after his death, the defiance and challenge that Langston Hughes evoked on the page during his long career retain a sense of immediacy for modern readers. While the themes of these essays from the *Chicago Defender* were timely to Hughes and his contemporaries, their implications can everywhere be seen and felt as we move toward the twenty-first century.

Hughes was certainly no stranger to the painful experiences that African Americans suffered on a daily basis in the United States, and the Jim Crow laws and other forms of racial prejudice that he witnessed in his early years would later find an outlet in a prolific writing career that spanned nearly five decades. Born in Joplin, Missouri on February 1, 1902, Hughes spent most of his childhood living with his maternal grandmother, Mary Langston, in Lawrence, Kansas. His loving identification with the African American community, which he would spend a lifetime nurturing, came at high emotional cost and with much difficulty. His father, James Hughes, estranged himself from his family early in Langston's childhood and lived mostly in Mexico. In his early years, Hughes harbored visions of his father as a powerful man, one who lived a life of freedom and did great things for the black community. This idealistic vision was shattered, however, in 1919, when his father returned to the United States and Langston accompanied him back to Mexico. Hughes writes of this incident and of his painful awareness about the ideas of his father in *The Big Sea:* "My father hated Negroes. I think he hated himself, too, for being a Negro. He disliked all of his family because they were Negroes."[2]

Despite the scorn for the African American community displayed by his father, several people in Hughes's life provided enough insight into black culture to overshadow the older Hughes's harsh views. While his mother was largely unhappy about her personal situation, having been left a single parent and also quite poor, she was, at times, able to provide Hughes with a sense of what was possible in black culture. Indeed, Carrie Hughes was responsible for her son's first visit to the Kansas City music halls and instilled a love of reading in the boy with frequent trips to the Topeka public library (Rampersad 1, 12).

It was his maternal grandmother, however, who was able to provide Hughes with a sense of a positive African American identity. Though she was past seventy, Mary Langston took steps to ensure that Hughes had a strong notion of an heroic consciousness within the black community. Excursions to hear Booker T. Washington speak and to witness the dedication of the John Brown Memorial Battlefield in Osawatomie, Kansas, perhaps gave Hughes the sense that he ought to be proud of his race (Rampersad 1, 13). As Hughes notes in *The Big Sea,* his grandmother's stories of slavery and freedom, and the heroism that marked the people of these stories, served to reinforce the effects of these excursions: "Through my grandmother's stories always life moved, moved heroically toward an end. Nobody ever cried in my grandmother's stories. They worked, or schemed, or fought. But no crying" (17). Moreover, Mary Langston instilled in Hughes her own hatred of racial segregation and refused to attend any church because of the discrimination of the all-white ones (Rampersad 1, 13).

Hughes found that Jim Crow and other forms of racial prejudice affected African Americans no matter where they traveled or in whatever activity they were engaged. During his brief tenure as a student at Columbia University in the early 1920s, school officials attempted to bar Hughes from the campus dormitories (Rampersad 1, 52). A trip to Africa in 1923 further provided him with a sense of the universality of racial distrust and of the often ridiculous confusion that it propagates. Hughes's first impressions of Africa, recorded in *The Big Sea,* were filled with a childlike sense of wonder: "My

Africa, Motherland of the Negro peoples! And me a Negro! Africa! The real thing, to be touched and seen, not merely read about in a book" (10). Hughes failed to predict, however, that the Africans would see him not as a black man but as an American, perhaps there to exploit them as countless other Americans had done. Later in *The Big Sea* he writes: "They looked at my copper-brown skin and straight black hair—like my grandmother's Indian hair, except a little curly—and they said: 'You—white man'" (103). To be considered a white man was a crushing blow to Hughes, for, as Arnold Rampersad points out in his biography, the love and approval of the black community was to become the obsession of Hughes's life. This obsession would often be expressed in writing, as Hughes sought to expose and criticize the many forms of oppression African Americans faced on a daily basis and, at the same time, to celebrate the contributions of black people to American culture.

The celebratory aspects of Hughes's writing were nowhere more profound than in "The Negro Speaks of Rivers," the poem that helped establish his early reputation within the African American community. First published in 1921 in the NAACP's *Crisis,* the poem's unique blend of self-revelation and historical consciousness revealed a young poet with firm control of the English language and a deep appreciation of the people on whom he chose to focus his talents:

> I've known rivers:
> I've known rivers ancient as the world and older than the flow of human
>   blood in human veins.
>
> My soul has grown deep like the rivers.[3]

The poem also served to introduce Hughes to several important contacts in New York City. Invited by Jessie Fauset of the *Crisis* to visit the offices of the NAACP and to meet W. E. B. Du Bois, Hughes had, upon publication of "The Negro Speaks of Rivers," arrived both literally and spiritually in the city he would henceforth call home.

Hughes wrote poetically about entering New York harbor for the first time, innocently clouding the darker side of city life behind a veil of grandeur: "New York is truly the dream city,—city of the towers near God, city of hopes and visions, of spires seeking in the windy air loveliness and perfection."[4] Equally magnificent to Hughes was the group of intellectuals and artists gathering in Harlem during the 1920s, people who, according to historian Nathan Irvin Huggins, "wanted to be where, to the greatest effect, they might convert their skills and minds into personal and racial success."[5] Hughes embraced these people and the intellectual and artistic goals they were achieving and accepted the philosophy of the "New Negro" as defined by

Alain Locke, who proudly announced that "the day of 'aunties,' 'uncles' and 'mammies' is . . . gone. Uncle Tom and Sambo have passed on, and even the 'Colonel' and 'George' play barnstorm roles from which they escape with relief when the public spotlight is off."[6]

Though Hughes reveled in the splendor of Harlem, he was certainly not blind to the plight of the poor, working-class people of the city. Hughes was as much a part of this community as he was of the elite group that comprised the members of the Harlem Renaissance, a cultural movement of international significance that generated an outpouring of African American art, literature, and music. Hughes immersed himself in the culture of the working class, fascinated by its actions, music, and patterns of speech. In *The Weary Blues* (1926), Hughes's first volume of poetry, he began to record elements of working-class culture and patterns of speech on the page. A year later, the publication of *Fine Clothes to the Jew* showed that Hughes had mastered the blues idiom in poetry.

In rejecting elitist notions of what constituted "literature," Hughes embraced a literary language that enabled him to give voice to the people in whom he was most interested. This language could not be regulated by the older intellectuals of the Harlem Renaissance, such as W. E. B. Du Bois and Alain Locke, for they subscribed to a notion of literacy that was deeply entrenched in Eurocentric tradition. Hughes increasingly understood the limitations of this tradition when applied to the African American experience, as Margaret A. Reid notes in "Langston Hughes: Rhetoric and Protest": "As Hughes and others after him were to discover, the rhymed abstractions of the classical poetic tradition were not always suited to the portrayal of the concrete hardships borne by the oppressed Negro. The conventional, often stilted, literary language often lacked emotional power."[7] Hughes reclaimed this emotional power by first embracing and finally immersing himself in the culture of the people he loved most, folks who were "workers, roustabouts, and singers, and job hunters on Lenox Avenue in New York, or Seventh Street in Washington or South State in Chicago—people up today and down tomorrow, working this week and fired the next, beaten and baffled, but determined not to be wholly beaten, buying furniture on the installment plan, filling the house with roomers to help pay the rent, hoping to get a new suit for Easter—and pawning that suit before the Fourth of July" (*BS* 264).

Hughes chose to focus most of his attentions on these people, assimilating their painful but colorful lifestyles and in the process creating his own standards of literacy. In "The Negro Artist and the Racial Mountain" (1926), an article that brilliantly displayed his own sense of a black aesthetic and that later became a proud theme for many of the younger writers of the Harlem Renaissance, Hughes wrote:

We younger Negro artists who create now intend to express our individual dark-skinned selves without fear or shame. If white people are pleased
we are glad. If they are not, it doesn't matter. We know we are beautiful.
And ugly too. The tom-tom cries and the tom-tom laughs. If colored people
are pleased we are glad. If they are not, their displeasure doesn't matter
either. We build our temples for tomorrow, strong as we know how, and
we stand on top of the mountain, free within ourselves.[8]

The artistic truth and integrity that Hughes evoked during the Harlem
Renaissance was at no time more necessary than during the American Depression, a period that marked an increase in racial violence against and
economic hardship for the African American community. The beatings,
lynchings, and daily humiliation of segregation that African Americans suffered in the South and elsewhere outraged Hughes, and he accepted the
responsibility to speak out against these injustices in his writing and to fight
them in his daily life. Hughes's writings of this period, while adhering to his
basic artistic ideals established in the 1920s, were far removed from the
optimism generated by the artists of the Harlem Renaissance. The sense of
hope that resulted in lines such as "we have tomorrow / Bright before us /
Like a flame" was supplanted by the immediacy of hunger, oppression, and
racial hatred. These facets of American life were certainly not new to Hughes,
but during this period he sensed something more evil and more dangerous
with which African Americans had to contend. Not content to see the African American community merely endure, Hughes felt that revolution was a
necessary end.

Several incidents and experiences shaped Hughes's writings of the 1930s,
perhaps the most influential being the Scottsboro case and trips to the Soviet Union and Spain in 1932 and 1937, respectively. The Scottsboro incident
of 1931 set the tone for much of Hughes's radical poetry and prose that would
emerge in the years leading up to his relationship to the *Chicago Defender,*
writings that would later haunt him when he was required to testify before
Joseph McCarthy's Senate Permanent Sub-Committee on Investigations. The
incident involved nine African American teenagers who were jailed in Scottsboro, Alabama, for allegedly raping two white women in an open railroad
freight car. After a trial in Scottsboro, eight of the youths were sentenced to
the electric chair and the ninth to life imprisonment. Ruby Bates, one of the
women involved in the incident, later recanted her rape testimony and admitted that she fabricated the entire story.[9]

While Hughes was lecturing and fund-raising on behalf of the youths
involved in the Scottsboro Case, he also took a firm stand on the incident
in his writing. Essays and poems, often searing and ironic in tone, respond-
ed to the call of the nine teenagers imprisoned at Kilby State Penitentiary in

Montgomery, Alabama. One of the most powerful essays to come out of the incident, which he wrote after visiting the boys while on a speaking tour through the South, evokes the fear and desperation Hughes felt in the face of Dixie justice: "For a moment the fear came: even for me, a Sunday morning visitor, the doors might never open again. WHITE guards held the keys. (The judge's chair protected like Pilate's.) And I'm only a nigger. Nigger. Niggers. Hundreds of niggers in Kilby Prison. Black, brown, yellow, near-white niggers. The guards, WHITE. Me—a visiting nigger."[10]

During the years that followed the Scottsboro trials, Hughes made two important trips that influenced both his creative writings and his nonfictional columns for the *Defender*. In 1932, he traveled to the Soviet Union with a group of twenty-two young African Americans to make "Black and White," a motion picture commissioned by the Meschrabpom Film Corporation. Although the film was not completed, Hughes remained in Russia for one year. His experiences in the Soviet Union, like the Scottsboro incident, found an outlet in some of Hughes's most powerful and controversial poems. In "Goodbye, Christ," a poem that right-wing reactionaries would hold against him for many years after its initial publication in the *Negro Worker*, Hughes embraced Soviet government and dismissed what he believed to be the hypocritical state of organized religion in the United States:

> Goodbye,
> Christ Jesus Lord God Jehova,
> Beat it on away from here now.
> Make way for a new guy with no religion at all—
> A real guy named
> Marx Communist Lenin Peasant Stalin Worker ME—
>   (*GMR* 37)

Like his experiences in the Soviet Union, which he would later document in a series of seven columns for the *Defender*, Hughes's six-month tenure in Spain as a correspondent for African American newspapers during the Spanish Civil War enabled him to draw connections between the situation of black people in America and the ways of life of oppressed people throughout the world. As biographer Arnold Rampersad has pointed out, the time spent in Spain reinvigorated Hughes's sense of himself as a poet for the people, a vulnerable position given the dehumanizing racial situation in the United States: "Langston's spirit, dulled and blunted by poverty and disappointment in America, became honed again under the pressure of the antifascist struggle in wartime Spain. As the foreboding grew that an even greater war was coming to Europe, he would begin to feel life with an intensity he had not known since his first weeks in the Soviet Union" (1, 341). That intensity found an outlet in Hughes's creative writings, in his nonfictional prose, and in his speeches, the latter represented most powerfully in July 1937, shortly before he left for Spain. Addressing the Second International Writers Congress in Paris, Hughes was both impassioned and optimistic in his critique of fascism around the world: "The Fascists know that we long to be rid of hatred and terror and oppression, to be rid of conquering and of being conquered, to be rid of all the ugliness of poverty and imperialism that eat away the heart of life today. We represent the end of race. And the Fascists know that when there is no more race, there will be no more capitalism, and no more war, and no more money for the munition makers, because the workers of the world will have triumphed" (*GMR* 99).

While Hughes retained his commitment to representing the dreams and frustrations of oppressed people in the pages of the *Defender* during the 1940s, his creative work lost much of the radical edge that poems such as "Goodbye, Christ" had exemplified in the 1930s. During the 1940s, too, Hughes ultimately abandoned his support of communism, though his love for the Soviet Union and its people remained. Arnold Rampersad has noted, however, that Hughes's renunciation of communism did not result in a break with all organizations on the Left, and that he continued to support groups that fell under the scrutiny of Senator Joseph McCarthy's investigations (2, 95). Retaining these ties, it seems, made Hughes amply suspect. On March 26, 1953, Hughes appeared before McCarthy's Senate Permanent Sub-Committee on Investigations to explain and account for his "anti-American," radical past. At the hearing, Hughes offered a prepared statement that effectively repudiated his radical writings and saved him from serious charges by the committee. When asked by Roy Cohn, the head examiner, to describe the period in which he sympathized with the Soviet form of government and when that period ended, Hughes replied:

> There was no abrupt ending, but I would say, that roughly the beginnings of my sympathies with Soviet ideology were coincident with the Scottsboro case, the American depression, and that they ran for some 10 or 12 years or more, certainly up to the the Nazi-Soviet Pact, and perhaps, in relation to some aspects of the Soviet ideology, further, because we were allies, as you know, with the Soviet Union during the war. So some aspects of my writing would reflect that relationship, that war relationship.[11]

Satisfied with his testimony, the committee quit badgering Hughes. Seven months after the hearings, however, Hughes would continue to attack in the pages of the *Defender* the governmental practices that had caused him so much trouble: "Some white liberals thought we were complaining to be complaining. When their own books get banned, their own ideas barred from publication for being too liberal, their own reputations attacked, more and more nice white folks get some little inkling as to what it has meant to be colored, over a whole life time."[12]

Despite the formidable obstacles that incidents such as the McCarthy hearings posed, Hughes continued to live up to the early goal he had set for himself after winning the 1931 Harmon Foundation prize for literature: "I'd finally and definitely made up my mind to continue being a writer—and to become a professional writer, making my living from writing" (*BS* 335). During the last decade of his life, Hughes could look back proudly on the honors that resulted from this important decision: fellowships from the Guggenheim Foundation and the Rosenwald Fund, first prizes in literary competitions sponsored by *Opportunity* magazine and the Poetry Society of America, the coveted Spingarn Medal, and honorary doctorates from Lincoln, Howard, and Western Reserve universities. Hughes did not, however, look back quietly or without anger. Though he was getting on in age, the turbulent 1960s saw no decrease in the prolific creative output that had always distinguished Hughes's professional writing career. With several collections of short fiction and two powerful books of poems—*Ask Your Mama: Twelve Moods for Jazz* and *The Panther and the Lash*—published during the last decade of his life, Hughes added a significant and influential voice to American literature up to the time of his death in 1967.

· · ·

In many ways, the *Defender* columns collected in this volume provide readers with a continuation of the autobiographical information that Hughes recorded in *The Big Sea* (1940) and *I Wonder As I Wander* (1956). To a greater extent, though, the columns represent a significant social, political, and cultural record of a turbulent and transitional period in American history. When Hughes accepted the offer to write a weekly column for the *Chicago Defender,* the country was well into the war with the Axis powers. Several events preceding the declaration of war on the United States in 1941, however, signified that the fighting abroad was very much connected to the African American struggle for justice in this country. Although the United States War Department issued a statement in 1940 declaring that "Negroes would be received into the army on the general basis of the proportion of the Negro population of the country," army units remained segregated, a glaring irony given the country's involvement in a war against international racism and fascism.[13]

Racialist policies were maintained not only in the armed forces preceding and during World War II, but also in United States war industries. According to a report issued by the National Urban League, employers questioned about hiring practices admitted "that they barred Negroes not because they themselves personally were opposed to them, but because they were afraid that the white workers in their plants would resent it, and 'it might lead to serious labor trouble, or at least sufficient ill will to interfere with efficient production.'"[14] In response to such overt discrimination, A. Philip Randolph, the president of the Brotherhood of Sleeping Car Porters, met with several prominent African American leaders and intellectuals in 1941 to organize a march on Washington, in which thousands of black activists would gather to protest inequitable treatment in the war industries and the armed forces. Although the march was eventually called off, the efforts made by Randolph and others to suppress such unfair treatment directly resulted in President Roosevelt's issuance of Executive Order 8802, which was designed to prevent "discrimination in the employment of workers in defense industries or Government because of race, creed, color, or national origin" (Franklin 388). The Committee on Fair Employment Practices (FEPC), established under the auspices of the Office of Production Management and directed by Louisville *Courier-Journal* publisher Mark Ethridge, sought to ensure compliance by investigating conditions that contravened Roosevelt's order.[15]

Although the efforts of black leaders and activists and the relatively progressive agenda established by the Roosevelt administration partially alleviated some of the more glaring injustices with which African Americans were faced during the war years, World War II failed to rid the United States of the Jim Crow laws that virtually guaranteed second-class citizenship to the black community. According to the sociologist E. Franklin Frazier, however, the war signified an important turning point in this country: "The Negro was no longer willing to accept discrimination in employment and in housing without protest."[16] In 1948, two important decisions reflected this ongoing struggle within the African American community for equitable treatment under the law. President Truman's Fair Deal policy, which mandated fair employment opportunities in the federal service, and a Supreme Court decision that prohibited the enforcement of racially based restrictive covenants in public housing signaled a progression on the national level toward ending the Jim Crow laws that had been in effect for over fifty years (Franklin 412–13).

One of the most important events of the postwar period was the United States Supreme Court's 1954 decision in *Brown v. Topeka Board of Education,* which historian Raymond Wolters has called "a landmark that separates Jim Crow America from modern America."[17] Overturning the 1896 Court decision in *Plessy v. Ferguson* that sanctioned racial segregation as long as separate facilities were equal, *Brown* exposed the inequities inherent in a social order based on the subjugation of one group of people by another. Regarding the Court's decision, Chief Justice Earl Warren stated: "We conclude that in the field of public education the doctrine of 'separate but equal' has no place. Therefore, we hold that the plaintiffs and others similarly situated for whom the actions have been brought are, by reason of the segregation complained of, deprived of the equal protection of the laws guaranteed by the Fourteenth Amendment."[18]

Despite the shortcomings of the *Brown* decision that resulted from the gradualist posture of the Warren Court, the issue nevertheless underscored E. Franklin Frazier's earlier prediction that the African American community would no longer accept racial discrimination without protest. One important manifestation of this activist spirit was the Montgomery, Alabama, bus boycott of the mid-1950s. Instigated by the arrest of Rosa Parks following her refusal to comply with Jim Crow laws and relinquish her bus seat to a white man, the boycott, led by Dr. Martin Luther King, Jr., and other activists from the Montgomery community, resulted in the local bus company's loss of sixty-five percent of its income and over one million dollars in losses to downtown merchants. In April 1956, Montgomery City Lines conceded to the protesters and announced that it would cease to enforce segregation. In response, the city of Montgomery, unwilling to revoke Jim Crow, obtained a court order that prevented the company from desegregating its buses. Despite this setback, however, the Supreme Court upheld an earlier ruling by the U.S. District Court in Alabama and maintained in November 1956, that segregation on the state's buses violated the constitution of the United States.[19]

While Montgomery remained a largely segregated town following the bus boycott, the victory over segregated buses marked an important step on the state level of the African American community's struggle for civil rights. On the national level, the late-1950s also gave rise to substantial changes in the sociopolitical status of blacks. Despite the reluctance of some legislators to make civil rights a matter of federal policy, Congress approved President Eisenhower's civil rights bill on August 29, 1957. The Civil Rights Act of 1957—the first civil rights legislation to be passed by Congress since 1875—created the United States Commission on Civil Rights and "authorized injunction relief in cases of proven voting irregularities."[20] More important, however, the 1957 act provided a precedent for subsequent legislation, most notably the Civil Rights Act of 1964. More ambitious than its predecessors, the 1964 act sought to banish the system of Jim Crow from American life by prohibiting discrimination in public schools, in federally funded institutions, and in most places of public accommodation. The law also created the Equal Employment Opportunity Commission (EEOC) to investigate reports of discrimination by employers and unions.[21]

Although the *Brown* decision, the results of the Montgomery bus boycott, and the changes in federal legislation all signified that the nation was entering a progressive new era in respect to civil rights for African Americans, the actions of protesters and lawmakers during this period were met with various hostile reactions by citizens who were unwilling to concede to the notion of social equality. Similar to the years that immediately followed Reconstruction, the period of the civil rights movement witnessed an increase in violent acts against African Americans. According to historians John Hope Franklin and Alfred A. Moss, Jr., "in 1957 and 1958 Negroes were murdered with impunity in South Carolina, Alabama, Georgia, and other Southern states" (436). In Mississippi alone, three brutal deaths in 1955 suggested extreme resistance to social advances within the black community. George Lee, a minister from Belzoni, Mississippi, who was the first African American to register to vote in the county since Reconstruction, was shot to death in May. In a similar incident, a black man who had voted in the Mississippi Democratic primary in August was gunned down on the courthouse lawn in Brookhaven (Hampton 2). Perhaps no other event of the period generated as much outrage as the 1955 killing of Emmett Till, a fourteen-year-old from Chicago's South Side who, after allegedly whistling at and making inappropriate remarks to a white woman in Mississippi, was abducted and brutally murdered. Despite eyewitness testimony, an all-white jury found the two men suspected of killing the youth not guilty (Hampton 1–15).

While the killings in Mississippi reflected the extreme reaction of a few individuals to the civil rights movement, several incidents during this period suggested a more collective resistance to social advances within the African American community. Despite the Supreme Court's 1954 ruling in *Brown*, desegregated public schools, especially in the South, remained little more than a legal proposition. Even at the university level, African American students were often barred from state institutions. When Autherine Lucy, a black applicant to the University of Alabama, attempted to enroll for classes in 1956, white students and townspeople rioted on the Tuscaloosa campus. The university suspended the young woman during the violence, and when she accused school officials of conspiring to prevent the admittance of an African American, the board of regents expelled her (Brooks 128). On September 4, 1957, in a similar incident that drew international media attention, nine black students who were scheduled by a federal court to integrate Central High School in Little Rock, Arkansas, were barred admission by the Arkansas National Guard. Governor Orville Faubus, whose political agenda consistently resisted integration, claimed that he deployed the units "to prevent violence and death in the disorders that became imminent" (Hampton 41). Reacting to Faubus's apparent disregard for national authority, President Eisenhower, despite his continued refusal to endorse *Brown*, nevertheless ordered one thousand troops to protect the nine African American students, who entered the school on September 24, 1957 (Nieman 160).

The integration of Central High School was indeed an important victory for the civil rights movement, but as the decade of the 1950s came to a close, it was more apparent than ever that the nation was still moving painfully slowly in granting fair treatment to African Americans. By 1961, only a small fraction of the biracial school districts in the Southern states had been integrated, and public accommodations—such as lunch counters, libraries, beaches, and hotels—often prevented black patrons from enjoying those services granted to whites (Franklin 439–43). The new decade, however, saw no decrease in the activities of those people determined to continue the struggle for civil rights. In an act of nonviolent protest similar to that which sparked the Montgomery bus boycott, students in Greensboro, North Carolina, after being refused service at a Woolworth's lunch counter in 1960, precipitated the sit-ins that in the following months would confront the Jim Crow system in many Southern cities. According to the civil rights historian Thomas R. Brooks, "the Greensboro sit-in set off a wave of nonviolent actions that toppled segregation in public accommodations" (147).

The sit-in movement was only the beginning of the nonviolent and direct action protests for civil rights that would culminate with the 1963 "March on Washington for Jobs and Freedom," the occasion on which thousands of blacks and whites peacefully demonstrated and on which Martin Luther King, Jr., delivered his famous "I Have a Dream" speech. Dissatisfied with the Kennedy administration's pace in responding to the immediate problems that African Americans still faced on a daily basis, in 1961 direct action groups such as the Congress of Racial Equality, the Southern Christian Leadership Conference, and the Student Nonviolent Coordinating Committee staged "freedom rides" in which black and white participants tested the degree to which Southern states were complying with legislation that prohibited segregation on interstate buses, trains, and terminals. Responding to the Freedom Riders and to pressure from Attorney General Robert Kennedy, in late September 1961, the Interstate Commerce Commission issued a regulation that banned the seating of interstate travelers with regard to race (Franklin 442–43). Like the examples of nonviolent and direct action protest that had precipitated social change throughout the 1940s and 1950s, the actions of the Freedom Riders resulted in another significant advance in civil rights for African Americans.

Although racism and prejudice continue to plague this country even as we near the twenty-first century, the period in American history roughly beginning with A. Philip Randolph's defiant actions in 1941 and ending with the monumental March on Washington in 1963 witnessed some of the most profound changes in the status of African Americans since emancipation. The defiance, protest, and direct action that characterized these years are indeed testimony to the enduring spirit of democracy, and to the dynamic nature of a democratic nation. It was during this period, and in the midst of this rapidly changing, exciting, and often frustrating sociopolitical milieu, that

Langston Hughes offered a unique journalistic voice to the country when he agreed in 1942 to write a weekly column for the *Chicago Defender.*

. . .

In an essay celebrating its fiftieth anniversary, Hughes termed the *Chicago Defender* "the journalistic voice of a largely voiceless people."[22] Founded in 1905 by Robert S. Abbott, a Hampton Institute graduate influenced by the journalistic and oratorical successes of Frederick Douglass, Ida B. Wells, and Booker T. Washington, the *Defender* boldly encroached on a relatively crowded market: the *Broad Ax,* the *Illinois Idea,* and the *Conservator* were, at the time, already established as representatives of the Chicago black press. Two influential outside newspapers, the Indianapolis *Freeman* and the New York *Age,* further limited Abbott's chances of financial success in publishing.[23] Nevertheless, the balance Abbott struck between reports of progress within the African American community on one hand, and sensational headlines documenting lynchings and other crimes against black people on the other, resulted in the *Defender's* gradual prominence both locally and nationally. Its banner proudly boasted "World's Greatest Weekly," and Abbott's paper soon established itself as an influential voice for African Americans in the Midwest, the West, and the Deep South.

The *Defender's* greatest moment of prominence came with Abbott's "The Great Northern Drive" campaign, in which he urged African Americans living in the Southern states to " 'Come North, where there is more humanity, some justice and fairness!' " (Ottley 160) Although biographer Roi Ottley claims that "single-handed, Abbott had set the great migration of the Mississippi Valley in motion" (160), many factors contributed to the mass exodus of blacks to the North. Between the years 1914 and 1917, low wages, floods, and increasing racial violence in the South stimulated dissatisfaction within the African American community, while labor shortages and the promise of more equitable treatment in the Northern states provided ample incentives to relocate (Franklin 472). Historian Lee Finkle writes: "If the *Defender* did not create the great migration, it nevertheless did all it could to encourage it. Its greatest achievement was certainly in easing the transition for those coming from the rural South to an unknown urban North by publishing news of job opportunities, train schedules, and available living quarters."[24]

The *Defender* had a great impact on Hughes long before he joined such distinguished writers as Walter White and S. I. Hayakawa as a regular columnist. Remembering the importance of the weekly to his formative years, Hughes writes: "As a child in Kansas I grew up on the *Chicago Defender* and it awakened me in my youth to the problems which I and my race had to face in America. Its flaming headlines and indignant editorials did a great deal to make me the 'race man' which I later became, as expressed in my own attitudes and in my writing. Thousands and thousands of other young Negroes were, I am sure, also affected the same way by this militant and stirringly edited Chicago weekly."[25] It was with great satisfaction, then, that Hughes agreed to write for the "World's Greatest Weekly." When Metz P. T. Lochard, editor-in-chief of the *Defender,* asked Hughes in 1942 to write a weekly column for the paper, the "Dean of Black Letters" had already established himself as a household name in the African American community. Despite numerous publications and a Broadway play to his credit, however, Hughes was, at age forty, still battling chronic poverty. Radio and the movies, major sources of money for white writers, generally barred talented African American writers from enjoying similar financial success. Hughes's eager acceptance of Lochard's offer thus served a dual purpose: on one hand he would reach a wider African American audience with his writings, and on the other hand he could look forward to a consistent paycheck.[26]

With its initial appearance in the *Defender* on November 21, 1942, "Here To Yonder," the first title assigned to Hughes's weekly column, would continue nearly without interruption into the turbulent years of the early 1960s. In the hundreds of essays that resulted from this long relationship to the *Defender,* Hughes explored topics of significance not only to the African American community but to the broader citizenship of the United States as well. It was also in the *Defender* columns that Hughes introduced his most well known fictional character, Jesse B. Semple. First appearing on February 13, 1943, "my simple minded friend," as Hughes referred to him, became a fixture in the pages of the *Defender* for the duration of the column. Collected by Hughes in such volumes as *Simple Speaks His Mind, Simple Takes A Wife,* and *Simple Stakes A Claim,* these columns came to represent Hughes's longest engagement with a common group of fictional characters. Biographer Arnold Rampersad writes:

> A migrant from the South, black in color (*light* black, he insists desperately, and of Indian ancestry), Simple is a sport of his youth in rural Virginia (to which he might gladly return but for Jim Crow) and his modern, Harlem destiny. Surrounding him eventually is an inspired supporting cast, almost all women, who dominate his life: Isabel, his difficult wife, from whom he dearly wishes to be finally divorced; Joyce, his attractive, likable, but too proper lady friend and later wife, who is determined to "improve" him; Zarita, his after-hours girlfriend, loud, flashy, and disreputable; his tyrannical landlady, almost always with a sharp word for "Third Floor Rear," as she prefers to call him; his importuning cousin Minnie; and others. (2, 64)

For Hughes, Simple became a voice—sometimes happy, sometimes disgusted, always irreverently humorous—through which he could comment on international race relations and current events to a wide audience. It was also through Simple that Hughes's desire to bring the concerns of the black working class to the forefront of African American consciousness was most successfully manifested. In his *Defender* article, "'Simple' Would Call Langston Hughes 'A Writin' Fool,'" reporter Bob Hunter writes: "Hughes insists he 'met' Simple in person in a wartime Harlem gin mill. On that occasion the author says he interrupted Simple's conversation with a friend to ask what kind of cranks he made in a New Jersey war plant he was boasting about—airplane cranks, machines? And Simple snorted: 'Just cranks. I don't know what them cranks crank. You know that white folks don't tell us Negroes what cranks crank.'"[27] Whether Simple was based on a true Harlemite or not, he came to represent Hughes's own close identification with the worries, fears, and frustrations of the working-class black community. Through the voice of Simple, Hughes could convey the peculiar experience of being black in America while retaining the emotional distance that fiction allows, a distance perhaps necessary to alleviate some of the pain he felt in his own life. The "Simple columns" also provided a degree of comic relief from the serious tone that was often characteristic of Hughes's nonfictional columns, the most important of which are included in the nine parts of this volume.

· · ·

Part 1, "The See-Saw of Race," contains essays that broadly address race relations in the United States. The humiliation and anger generated by racial prejudice and discrimination were themes that Hughes explored perhaps more often than any other in the pages of the *Defender*. In nearly every aspect of life, Hughes witnessed an American democracy that sought to do anything in its power to keep the African American community from enjoying the rights and privileges that it deserved. From the 1943 banning of zoot suits—worn mainly by poor Mexican and African Americans—in Los Angeles to the acquittal of thirty-one white men by an all-white jury in connection with the 1947 lynching of Willie Earl in Greenville, South Carolina, Hughes recorded in the *Defender* the violence and inequities of a nation that appeared to be moving backward in its treatment of nonwhite citizens.

In these opening essays, readers will note a balance of sarcasm and irony, anger and sadness, and defiance and hope, but the humorous edge that can be found in much of Hughes's writing is largely absent here. The blues imperative of "laughing to keep from crying," so prevalent in Hughes's body of creative work, appears to be overshadowed by the very serious nature of the topics included in this section: civil and social rights and freedoms, friction between various minority groups, the ironies of government spending, desegregation, and the ever-present fear throughout the United States of miscegenation.

Especially offensive to Hughes during the period in which he wrote for the *Defender* was the legalized segregation of nonwhite people taking place throughout the world, and most blatantly in the American South. Parts 2 and 3—"Jim Crow's Epitaph" and "Fair Play in Dixie"—contain ironic and often humorous indictments of Jim Crow, the former on an international scale and the latter limited to the South. In a 1948 column, Hughes lamented this glaring fault of the Southern states, and the connection he draws between that region and the rest of the world reflects the broadly conceived critiques of racial injustice present throughout his writings:

> That, for me, is what takes the sunshine out of the sunny South. Jim Crow puts a cloud over all the land, all the people. Evil begets evil—and an evil mist is rising out of the Jim Crow South, seeping across the nation, seeping across the world of democratic relations, seeping into the halls of Congress, into the Department of State, into the rooms where treaties are written and diplomacies are planned, making the papers stick together and the ink blur.[28]

While Hughes reacted against Jim Crow with anger, defiance, and sometimes bitterness, he nevertheless evidences throughout these sections an ability to satirically and often comically distance himself from the emotional weariness that such segregation created. Attempting to understand the motives that compelled Southern whites to cling to their antiquated supremacist doctrines, Hughes drew the following conclusions about the region: "It is the land of the great evasion. The land of the positive negative. The land of doing things backward. A Punch and Judy land, a tragi-comedy place where human beings block their own doorways."[29] While he was well aware of the negative effects such traits had on the African American community in the South, Hughes also conveyed in these columns the shrewd political results that could be gained by the region's backward ways. On the occasion of the death of Senator Theodore G. Bilbo, the Mississippi extremist who consistently denounced legislation assisting African Americans and other minority groups, Hughes pointed out that the politician "was by in-direction one of our greatest allies in our fight for political freedom in the United States." For all of Bilbo's rantings against African Americans, whether they concerned the right to vote or his desire that blacks be sent back to Africa, Hughes pointed out the paradoxical results: black people in the South became more determined than ever to get out their votes and to remain in the region they considered home.[30]

Despite the Jim Crow laws of the region, the South was certainly not the sole bastion of racial injustice and unrest in the United States during the period Hughes wrote for the *Defender.* Part 4, "Nerve of Some White Folks," contains essays that explore the odd, infuriating, and often humorous circumstances that Hughes found when one group of people in American society attempted to subjugate another purely on racial grounds. One violent effect of such subjugation was the Harlem riot on August 1, 1943, instigated after an African American soldier was wounded by a white police officer. In a series of articles aimed at white shopkeepers, Hughes struck a tone at once conciliatory and unwavering in its conviction and proceeded to make step by step suggestions on how future riots might be avoided. Chief among these were white participation in black community affairs, better employment opportunities for African Americans in white-owned businesses, and fair price ceilings on commodities sold by white store owners in black neighborhoods.

Also evident in these essays is Hughes's delight in the subtle ways African Americans were able to subvert the white community's racial prejudices and discriminations toward positive ends. The separation of "white" and "Negro" blood by the American Red Cross blood banks was an act that at once infuriated Hughes and caused him to chuckle. It was thus with great pleasure and a bittersweet appreciation of the ironies of life that Hughes reported a glitch in the Red Cross's blood machine:

> But an even better joke on our white folks than that of colored soldiers in white units, is what is happening to the Red Cross blood banks in some of the Eastern cities. Many light and, to the eye, quite near-white Negroes have of late—so I have been told—given their blood most generously to the Red Cross. In the process they did not mention the colored race, so naturally, their blood has gone into the white blood banks. Thus, by now, white plasma and colored plasma must be hopelessly scrambled together, and it amuses me to wonder how the Red Cross will ever get it straightened out.[31]

While Hughes could find some humor in the separatist practices of the American Red Cross, the war years brought disheartening evidence to the African American community, and to the United States as a whole, that the ugly seed of racism was spreading around the world. Part 5, "Brazenness of Empire," and part 6, "Segregation-Fatigue," address the African American experience during World War II, the former containing essays that draw connections between black Americans and oppressed people throughout the world and the latter including essays that focus on segregation in the American armed forces. Readers will note especially in part 5 the sense of hope that permeates Hughes's writing, most evident during the early years of the war. Perhaps overly idealistic at times, Hughes envisioned after the war an America and a world free of color prejudice, a world where the subjugation of certain groups of people was merely a bitter memory. Radio reports of Hitler's suicide in 1945 seemed to bring these dreams closer to reality, and Hughes seized on the event in the *Defender:*

Hitler, the man who wrote in *Mein Kampf* that you had just as well try to educate an ape as to educate a Negro! Hitler, the man who lynched thousands of Jews! Hitler, the man who supported Mussolini in his invasion of Ethiopia! Hitler, the man who put forth the unscientific theory of the superiority of Nordic blood for which the American Red Cross fell! Hitler, who yelled like Rankin and believed in Jim Crow for all the world! Hitler has committed suicide in the face of the approaching Red Armies![32]

Much less hopeful than the fall of Hitler was the segregation openly taking place in the United States armed forces, a situation that Hughes reacted to in the *Defender* with impatience and a good deal of searing irony. During a war that was supposedly being fought in the name of democracy, African American soldiers, both overseas and in United States training camps, found themselves treated with the same humiliating disrespect as their fellow black civilians. Jim Crow had infiltrated America's celebrated armies, and the black soldiers who were fighting and dying for the freedom of people, black and white, back home were paying dearly for the intrusion: separate and less desirable living and eating quarters, little opportunity for advancement, and even segregated latrines—all made life for the African American soldier quite unbearable. Documenting the shell shock, or segregation-fatigue, of one unfortunate soldier who managed to make it back to the United States alive, Hughes wrote: "He came through the dangers of the South Pacific all right, but here in our own Dixieland, Jim Crow got the best of him. He went off the beam, so the story runs, struck a white officer, and is now in a military prison."[33]

While Hughes saw in the United States armed forces only further evidence that America was moving backward in regard to race relations, the Soviet Union and its Red Army seemed to him to offer a glimmer of hope that people of different nationalities and colors could exist and work together peaceably. A little more than a decade after his visit to the Soviet Union, Hughes wrote a series of articles for the *Defender* that addressed his experiences there. Part 7, "Are You A Communist?" presents that series in its entirety, and also includes essays that concern the Red Army and the American witch hunts for Communists. Hughes was not completely unrealistic or idealistic about the Soviet Union and was quick to point out that it was not a paradise. He recognized the meagerness of resources to be a serious problem and found that the Soviet people did not enjoy the freedom of speech that was largely taken for granted in the United States. Despite its faults, however, Hughes saw in the Soviet Union a degree of hope that seemed sadly absent in America. While the African American community was still suffering the same violence and oppression it had endured for years, followers of the Soviet doctrines seemed decidedly better off.

Hughes's praise for the Soviet Union and his support of groups that followed Communist doctrines in the United States did not go unnoticed by reactionary politicians. In a column reacting to pressures from the Ku Klux Klan and Gerald L. K. Smith, leader of the far right America First party, that he retire from the lecture circuit, Hughes struck a tone at once bitter and defiant: "The voices who cry 'red' the loudest have never been known to be raised against segregation or color lines. In each case the persons or organizations who have opposed most strenuously my programs of poems in various communities from Akron to Los Angeles, are the very persons or organizations known to be the most anti-Negro, anti-Jewish and anti-labor in the community. In California they have opposed the relocation of Japanese-Americans."[34] While Hughes took very seriously the attacks aimed at him by reactionary individuals and organizations, he also recognized that the witch hunts were not without comic appeal. In a parody of proceedings by the House Committee on Un-American Activities, Old Ghost, a fictional character in the tradition of Jesse B. Semple, responds humorously to Chairman Georgia's "Boy, why are you here? We have no Negras on the agenda today. You was not subpoenaed." "'I am here to insult you,' said Old Ghost. 'I can see that my black presence is not amenable to your comfort. And the fact that I wear a hat, not a bandanna, irks you. Therefore, I am pleased! I will not take off my hat except in the presence of ladies.'"[35]

Where Old Ghost was able to expose the more ludicrous and laughable side of the American paranoia of Communists, Hughes found very little humor in the United States entertainment industry's classification of African American artists and performers as second-class citizens. The prejudices and discriminations addressed in part 8, "Beating Out the Blues," particularly infuriated Hughes, for it was in the areas of art and entertainment that African Americans had made some of the most visible and influential contributions to American culture. While many of the essays included here strike a celebratory tone, particularly those concerning individual artists such as Josephine Baker, Pearl Primus, and various jazz musicians, readers will note the sense of sadness behind Hughes's words as he draws connections between the African American presence in American entertainment and the state of race relations in general.

Also included in this section are essays that reinforce the artistic goals and ideals that Hughes established for himself as a young man during the Harlem Renaissance. Nearly twenty years after the publication of "The Negro Artist and the Racial Mountain," the essay that became a manifesto for many young black artists in the 1920s, Hughes conveyed similar ideas about art in the pages of the *Defender*. Although Senator Joseph McCarthy's "red scare"—and the serious implications it posed to radical artists, writers, and performers—lay waiting in the shadows of American history, Hughes again stressed the need for truth and integrity in art: "Unfortunately for the peace of mind of the artist, art has a political value, that is why, in times of stress, the politicians set up various open or covert censorships to try for their own ends to control art. In order to play safe, the bad artist often conforms to the political needs of the moment and creates a saleable tissue of conscious lies in order to keep his cupboard full."[36]

Hughes's deep convictions about art, and indeed about life, resulted in a professional writing career rich with experience and indebted to the inexhaustible resource of the human spirit. While the essays gathered here are informed by Hughes's own experiences during this long career, part 9, "Here to Yonder," contains those essays that are most consciously autobiographical. From the exotic foods he encountered as a correspondent during the Spanish Civil War to the contents of a typical day, and night, in his life as a writer living in Harlem, these essays allow the reader a glimpse into Hughes's own personal world. Evident in this section, too, is Hughes's profound sense of universal relationships and of the need for worldwide recognition and appreciation of the plights of all people:

> For the last 20 years, half writer and half vagabond, I have traveled from here to yonder around the world and back again, up and down the African coast, through Russia, through Asia, back and forth across America and, in general, from pillar to post. One thing I learned is that Alabama and Africa have the same problems. Stalingrad and Chicago fight the same gangsters. Two 14-year-old boys are lynched at Shubuta Bridge and Harlem shudders—also Chungking.[37]

For readers unfamiliar with Hughes's many volumes of poems, short stories, plays, nonfictional writings, and his two novels, this collection provides an excellent introduction to the man referred to as both the "poet low-rate of Harlem" and the "Dean of Black Letters." The essays gathered here point to Hughes's achievements in every literary genre and provide evidence of his substantial skill as a popular columnist. Readers familiar with his previously collected works will be rewarded by the insights these essays provide into the sources for Hughes's poems and works of fiction. The literary vision that he sustained from the Harlem Renaissance through the Black Arts Movement of the 1960s, and all the turbulent years that came between, was informed by the themes explored in these essays.

While the effects of Jim Crow and other forms of racial prejudice and discrimination did not die out during his lifetime, and indeed continue to violate the promise of a democratic country at the end of the twentieth century, the endurance of Hughes's popularity is testimony to the vision he sought all his life to sustain. Hughes believed in a coming freedom for all people, and in his writing this belief was expressed through a careful balance of celebration and hope, defiance and anger. Amiri Baraka, a leading proponent of the Black Arts Movement, recognized and acknowledged the importance of this balance to African American literature and culture. Baraka's words are indeed a fitting tribute to the clarity of vision that distinguished Langston Hughes's prolific career, a vision that can be seen and felt throughout the writings collected here: "There is a deep pride, a strength in blackness, a cry of independence from not only whites but also blacks—in the true manner of the petit bourgeois rebel, rebelling against *everything*."[38]

Part 1

The See-Saw of Race

No Half-Freedoms

January 16, 1943

Patrick Henry said: "Give me liberty or give me death." And his words have become one of America's great clarion calls down through the years. Suppose Patrick Henry had said, "Give me half-liberty and let me live half-dead." Nobody would have paid him any mind, nor would we remember his name today.

During the recent Spanish Civil War, Passionaria, the great woman leader and supporter of the Republican government, said: "It is better to die on your feet than to live on your knees." Suppose Passionaria had said, "It is better to exist on your knees than to die for liberty and freedom." Her words would have meant nothing then, nor would they have been a flame to the human spirit.

Christ drove the money changers from the temple. He didn't drive them to the vestibule and say, "You may sit here, half in and half out, and conduct your nefarious business."

The distinguished escaped slave, Frederick Douglass, in his speech at Faneuil Hall in Boston preceding the Civil War, said, "I shall always aim to be courteous and mild in my deportment towards all with whom I come in contact, at the same time firmly and constantly endeavoring to assert my equal rights as a man and a brother." Suppose Frederick Douglass had said instead, "weakly and occasionally endeavoring to half assert my half equal half rights as a half man and a half brother." Would his speech then have been remembered? Would it have acted as a spur to the anti-slavery movement?

Instead of "government of the people, by the people, and for the people," suppose Abraham Lincoln had said, "government of some of the people, by some of the people, for just some of the people." Who would have agreed with him, or paid any mind to his words except the exploiters and oppressors of the people?

Brown and Dabney

Warren Brown, Negro director of Race Relations of the Council for Democracy, writing in the *Saturday Review of Literature* (republished in the *Reader's Digest* for January), and Virginius Dabney, distinguished white Southerner writing in the *Atlantic Monthly* for January, both would seek to soften and quiet down the Negro press in its demands for freedom and equality for the Negro people in America.[1] I take it Mr. Dabney would also include such liberal white publications as *PM, The Nation, The New Republic,* and *Common Ground* for he says, ". . . if the disturbing elements on both sides of the color line can somehow be muzzled for the duration, and if the slow but certain processes of evolutionary progress can function, then better interracial relations and accelerated Negro advancement will go hand in hand— and we shall be able to get on with the war."

Mr. Dabney's article as a whole implies that Negroes, segregated, jim-crowed, and lynched as we are, should still not seek to disturb too much the status quo of racial oppression in America, and particularly in the South. He implies that we should not ask or expect freedom as such, or equality as such, or democracy as such. I gather that we are then to pay no attention to the proclamations of our national war aims as outlined in the speeches of Roosevelt, Wallace, and Welles.[2] I gather that the Four Freedoms for us—as Mr. Dabney believes we should be willing to have them—would be but Four Half Freedoms, or Quarter Freedoms, if that. And they would not include freedom of speech. I must confess that Mr. Dabney's article puzzled me exceedingly. What does he expect us to aim at, or believe in? Being Americans, does he not wish us to believe in the American dream, too—or is that dream just for white folks?

An American America

The Negro people of America today are not threatening to fight and kill white Americans in order to get their rights. It was Mark Ethridge who said that all the armies of Hitler and the democracies together could not make the South change.[3] We did not speak of armies. We did not mention violence. The most Negroes have threatened to do is stage a peaceful march on Washington to petition legal redress of grievances.[4] The most we are doing is writing and speaking about—and working for—freedom and democracy as a reality—not as a shadow. The most dire thought we are holding in our deep hearts is a dream of a real AMERICAN America. To shackle and muzzle this expression of that dream from Negro pulpits, Negro platforms, and from the pages of the Negro press would be to shackle the heart and to deny it hope.

Shall those of us who are colored in America ask for half-democracy? And shall we compromise with the poll-tax, with the segregation, with the Jim Crow car, with the Southern senators who are not elected by the people's vote, with the politicians who speak of liberty for the whole world and forget us, with the cheatery of the sharecropping system of the South, with the cheatery of the unequal distribution of public monies and the poor schools, poor parks, poor public services that we get? Shall we pipe down on dishonesty, cruelty, stupidity, and insults? Shall we dilute the Four Freedoms to the strength of near-beer? Shall we, who are the Negro people of America, have no great dreams? Shall we ask only for the half-freedoms that move nobody to action for the great freedoms that this war is supposed to be about?

Or shall we, with all other Americans of foresight and good will, seek to create a world where even Alabama will respect human decency?

Key Chains with No Keys

June 19, 1943

Sure, beat the reat pleat! Shoot the zoot suit! Rough up the tight cuff! Trim the wide brim! We got enough of him!

So the West Coast newspapers screamed last week. The solid citizens of Los Angeles agreed. Soldiers and sailors swept into the poorest of Negro and Mexican neighborhoods and started their illegal clean-up.[5]

Mobs always start with the poorest and weakest people. Nobody cared much about the zoot-suit boys, anyhow. Maybe their mothers cared, or their girl-friends. Or a few social workers. But nobody of weight or importance really cared. Even the better class of Negroes and Mexicans considered their neighborhood zoot-suiters "a disgrace to the race." And let it go at that. So the soldiers and sailors in California began tearing their clothes off.

But the soldiers and sailors—who were not Negro or Mexican—also began tearing the clothes off of Negro and Mexican war workers, and even off of intellectuals—like one of our 20-year-old students of aviation at the University of California. So you see, nice colored people, it would have been worth your while to start caring about the zoot-suiters a long time ago—before the mob starts tearing off your clothes, too.

No Logic in Mobs

Mobs are strangely illogical—just as race prejudice is illogical. When the government started evacuating Japanese to concentration camps, they didn't evacuate just Japanese enemy-aliens, but American citizens of Japanese descent as well.[6] Why the government left in peace the Italians and Germans—

naturalized and unnaturalized—I will never know, since we are at war with Italy and Germany, too. But then when you drop logic altogether and deny one group of citizens equal protection of the law, you are really making a hole in the dyke through which the most dangerous of waters can rush.

From the saffron-skinned Japanese-American citizens of Los Angeles to brown-skinned Mexican-American citizens is only a step. Of course, the Mexican government is our ally—but unfortunately, the Mexicans are an Indian-brown people. From the brown Mexicans to the vari-colored Negroes is only a step, too. Of course, we Negroes are pure Americans, here several generations, but still the wrong color.

Logically speaking, color has nothing to do with citizenship or democracy. But prejudice and the mob-spirit pay logic no mind. The zoot-suits on a handful of kids are a nice excuse for reactionaries—egged on, no doubt, by the undercover agents of Hitler—to start a campaign of big headlines in the Los Angeles press against the Negro and the Mexican people.

As for the zoot-suiters themselves, if their clothes are not already torn off, they might as well take them off. The City of Los Angeles has declared zoot-suits illegal. And the government of the United States, through the War Production Board, has issued an order ending all wide trousers, as well as tucks, bellows, gussets, and yokes on men's and boys' clothing. The zoot-suit is gone.

Depression's Kids

How did it come to be, in the first place? Dr. Joseph Catton, noted psychiatrist, is quoted as saying that the zoot-suit is the result of "an overwhelming inferiority complex." The wearer wants to show off.

Dr. Catton might be right. I am not a psychiatrist. But this I know, and it may have some weight, too. The zoot-suiters were depression's kids, growing up in a period when, in spite of the WPA and the NYA, they and their parents had too little.[7] (Relief standards in Los Angeles were lower for Mexicans, by the way, than for any other group. Out there, they're shoved around like Negroes.) Naturally, when these children of depression were able to buy a suit, having been penny-pinched so long, they got a coat that was much too lengthy, pants that had much too much cloth in them, and hats whose brims were like umbrellas—plenty of brim!

It made them feel good to go to extremes. In the light of the poverty of their past, too much becomes JUST ENOUGH for them. A key chain six times too long is just long enough to hold NO keys.

No keys. In California and the Southwest, you see, to Mexican and Negro boys so many doors are locked—and they do not have the keys. For yellow, and brown, and black men the world around, you see, so many doors are locked. We do not have the keys.

It's up to you, democracy, to give us a key. It's up to you, Los Angeles, to open the doors of industry and opportunity for all. It's up to you, Texas, to get rid of those white primaries.[8] It's up to you, America, to do much more than you've been doing about those doors closed in the face of your racial minorities. Letting mobs come into our ghettos to beat us is no solution.

Get Together, Minorities

July 17, 1943

On the streetcar the other day a "pure American" overheard a man of foreign background speaking in a language the "pure American" did not understand. Since I was paying no attention before the excitement began, I did not hear what language was being spoken. But, from the looks of the man, it might have been Spanish, Italian, or possibly Yiddish.

Anyhow, the "pure American" butted in and said in a loud voice, "Why don't you speak English? Why don't you speak the language of the country you make your money in? Huh?"

The man looked startled, but answered, "I do speak English. But I also have a right to speak my own language, too."

"If Hitler was over here you wouldn't have. You'd learn English, and pretty quick—if you got sense enough."

"I got enough sense not to bother other people when they're talking," said the man.

"You ought to be over there with Hitler," yelled the other fellow. "We want pure Americans over here!"

"Like you?" said the other man.

"Sure, you can be damned sure I'm a pure American." With that, he got off the trolley. Half the people in the car immediately began talking in foreign languages: Spanish, Yiddish, Italian, German—for we were riding through 125th street in New York.

Who Are the Pure Americans?

Certainly, in a free world, one has a right to speak any language one knows and can speak. As a Negro, I started wondering why that "pure American" had attacked another American—because the other man, when he spoke English, spoke as well as the "pure American," so he probably was a citizen, possibly American born of foreign parents. Anyhow, they were both white— and the "pure American" lit in on the other one.

News of the end of the investigation of the zoot-suit riots in California still found space on the back pages of the papers, when this happened. I think maybe these riots against Mexicans was what put in the "pure American's" head the idea to start bawling a strange man out about his language in a street car.

As the street car jogged along, I started wondering just who IS pure American. Almost nobody much that I ever knew. Thinking about my own friends, of those who are not colored, almost all are not much more than second- or third-generation Americans at best—except maybe Chester Arthur who runs way back, even past his grandpa, the former President Arthur. (So American, indeed, is that family, that they have Negro relatives, including Angelo Herndon, for whom Chester Arthur once gave a party when he discovered they were distant cousins.)[9]

But PURE, PURE Americans (other than the Indians and the descendants of the Mayflower and the Negroes who date back three hundred years) seem pretty scarce, at least around New York. I guess they have them in Texas though, as Martin Dies comes from there and he claims to be a pure American. I believe Bilbo and Rankin are, too.[10] And maybe the ladies of the DAR, also, although they're rather bad examples.[11] And perhaps "The Great Mother," the Red Cross—with her cans of Jim Crow blood—is "pure American."[12]

Minority vs. Minority

Then I got to thinking, well, anyhow, I am pure American, though colored. I date way back. But that other "pure American," I'll bet, would readily Jim Crow me on the New York street cars if he could.

Then a more evil thought crept into my mind. I started wondering if the man who spoke the foreign language would help me out if the "pure American" wanted to Jim Crow me? And I felt kind of doubtful, because often foreign-born Americans have Jim Crowed me, too, in theaters and elsewhere. Greeks have refused to sell me hamburgers, Polish Jews have directed me up back alleys to the "colored" entrance to see a movie, and Forno's, a Mexican restaurant off Broadway at one time would not serve Negroes.

And I got to thinking as the street car curved up Amsterdam avenue how nice it would be if not only the "pure Americans" but the foreign-born and the second-generation Americans, would all drop their stupid prejudices against each other, Catholic Poles hating Jewish Poles, Germans hating Italians, and all of them falling right in, by and large, with the American pattern of Jim Crowing Negroes. Anyhow, I thought, with the "pure Americans" getting so tough about things, for our own protection, it would be good if the foreign-born, the Jews, the Mexicans, and the Negroes all formed some sort of protective unity—before we get our collective heads beat for not being "pure American."

In other words, what I mean is, if you belong to a minority group, stop discriminating against any other minority group, and thus helping carry out fascist patterns—because those patterns will most certainly boomerang right back at you—and knock you dead out yourself.

The Jewish theater manager who Jim Crows Negroes, or the Greek lunch-wagon owner who refuses to sell me a hamburger, or the Polish bartender who says, "I won't serve you," are not going to be any more respected than me when the "pure Americans" start on the rampage.

The See-Saw of Race

April 20, 1946

Since I travel about the country a great deal, people are always asking me if I notice any improvement in race relations, if things are better or worse. To tell the truth, I really do not know if they have improved or not. Race relations look like a see-saw to me—up on one end and down on the other, up here and down there, up and down. If one community reports better race relations than before the war, another reports worse.

Certainly in some parts of our country there was little color prejudice shown in public places such as restaurants and theaters, until Army Camp commanders requested that local authorities Jim Crow Negro troops. Negro residents in many far Western states tell me that never were they refused a meal in a restaurant until the Army moved in.

On the other hand, in industry the war broke a number of color barriers, and the late President Roosevelt's famous Executive Order 8802 brought for the first time more than a million Negro workers into contact with machinery.[13] Since heretofore we have been largely barred from manufacturing plants and limited mostly to menial work, the entry of Negroes into industry is a distinct gain.

But on the other end of the see-saw, causing its right end to drag the ground, are those reactionary Congressmen who oppose all such legislation as the FEPC, the anti–poll tax bill, and Federal funds for education. Such lawmakers are a drag to race relations in America.

Better Jobs for Women

A distinct gain during the war years has been the releasing of thousands of Negro women from the underpaid servitude of white kitchens and laundries. At least for a while they have made better money, enjoyed shorter hours, and have had more freedom. But, according to one authority on Southern race feeling, this liberation of Negro women has made Southern white women so mad that increasing racial tensions have developed.

The Navy and Army have dropped some of their traditional color bars. But very few Negroes are able to get beyond the lower officer grades. In a really democratic Army, Negroes should have as much right to officer whites as whites have to command Negroes.

The wasteful, uncivilized, inconvenient and stupid Jim Crow travel system of the South still prevails. The Jim Crow car is a disgrace to America, and is an open and unashamed symbol of all the other Nazi-like inequalities to which Negroes are subjected. Great inequalities in the use of public funds are also still in evidence. Until these antiquated handicaps are removed, one end of the see-saw of American race relations will never rise off the ground weighted down as it is by the asses of white supremacy. Even an ass should be able to see that keeping one group of people down does the other group harm.

Some Advanced Far

On the cultural side, however, some Negroes have gone way up on the see-saw of race relations. In *Othello* Paul Robeson played at slapping a white lady on the public stage nightly for many nights, then choked her at the final curtain. Marian Anderson and Dorothy Maynor are drawing larger audiences than ever. Richard Wright has had his second Book-of-the-Month. Hazel Scott has married a congressman. And Walter White has flown in Army bombers from the ETO to the Pacific. Practically every Negro writer who can write has a book contract. And practically every Negro actor who does not stutter is in a play. Dr. Du Bois' "talented tenth" has done well.[14]

But the other end of even the cultural see-saw is weighted down by that old color line. No Negro writer has made a $100,000 sale to Hollywood. No Negro actress has had a leading role in a motion picture. No Negro singer is singing at the Metropolitan. No Negro band has a sponsored program on the air. Statesman that he is, Walter White has not been sent by our Government as an ambassador to a major power—or even as consul to any little old colored country.

Prejudice in the arts, the intellectual fields, and high cultural circles in America is just as effective in its refinement as is prejudice in the Southern Railway Station in New Orleans where there is not even a decent place for a Negro traveler to wash his hands. America does not yet permit Negro artists and intellectuals to wash their hands in the waters of cultural freedom. America gives us just a little bit of such water now and then, into which the ladies of the DAR occasionally spit.

Sorry Spring

May 31, 1947

It is a sorry springtime and a sad and sorry May. The animals and birds and trees must wonder what makes men act this way. Four Hundred Million Dollars for "democracy" in Greece and Turkey while the 31 lynchers of Greenville, South Carolina, go free.[15]

Four Hundred Million Dollars from our government to build up resistance to Russia in Greece and Turkey, but what to build up resistance to mob-rule in Dixie? What to build schools and resistance to ignorance for all the people, black and white, in South Carolina and Georgia and Mississippi where schools are needed most? What to build up respect for law and order all across the South?

"The United States is preparing to embark upon a long and costly program of protecting the smaller nations of the world from aggression," says the radio today. "The Four Hundred Million Dollar aid to Greece and Turkey is only the beginning." But how, we Negroes wonder, can our country save whole nations from aggression when it cannot save one man, Willie Earle, in South Carolina, and when none of his lynchers, NOT ONE, is punished?

The President signs the Four Hundred Million Dollar Aid Bill to Greece and Turkey this morning, and tonight the radio announces that another lynching of a Negro has taken place in the South. Weeks of senatorial discussion and Four Hundred Million Dollars of our money to help far off Greece and Turkey, but when the Anti-Lynching Bill comes up—choked, filibustered to death, killed.[16] And not a penny to help the decent people of the South to protect themselves and their faith in democracy from the Greenville lynchers.

Millions to Build "Democracy"

Four Hundred Million Dollars to the anti-democratic governments of Greece and Turkey to help them build "democracy" when poor white folks who can't pay their poll tax and poor Negroes who can't pass for white are denied the vote in large portions of our own country.

Four Hundred Million Dollars to build up the Grecian and Turkish armies as a bulwark for "democracy" when in our own armies colored Americans are segregated and humiliated and denied enlistment rights and officers' promotions and march in dark ranks alone and apart from the pure white representatives of our democracy.

Four Hundred Million Dollars for Greece and Turkey when the University of Texas sadly needs some of that money in order to learn the difference between a shanty and a first-class law school.

Four Hundred Million Dollars for Greece and Turkey when Tennessee sorely needs some of those millions to teach its white doctors and nurses that it is not humane to turn away gravely injured students rushed to their doors from an auto collision, simply because those students are colored, as happened in the recent death of a Clark College athletic star carried up and down the road in an ambulance, refused by two white hospitals on our democratic soil, and finally dying by the time a black hospital was found.

Four Hundred Million Dollars to Greece and Turkey while the lynchers of Greenville, South Carolina, walk the streets free to lynch again, and the lynchers of Monroe, Georgia, have never been worried at all about the two men and their wives whom they killed.

No Money to Fight Mobs

Four Hundred Million Dollars to help monarchist Greece and feudal Turkey get ready to fight Russia, but not one cent to help the decent white people and the decent Negroes of the South to fight the mob that threatened all decency, white or colored.

Greece—South Carolina. Turkey—Georgia. Far off strangers—blood brothers of our Commonwealth. Where does charity begin? *At home,* so the saying goes. *But the Four Hundred Million Dollars goes to Greece and Turkey.* The Greeks and the Turks must be laughing up their sleeves as they take that Four Hundred Million Dollars. The taxicab drivers of Greenville, South Carolina, must be laughing, too. And there must be laughter in the white hospitals along that Tennessee road where the blood of a black student ebbed away as his ambulance frantically sought a democratic door.

U.S. Likes Nazis and Franco Better Than Its Own Negroes

November 6, 1948

The Negro neighborhoods are, too often, the neighborhoods of the poor. That is why hunger, prostitution, and crime are so frequently blamed on color rather than on poverty. That is why, too, neither of the major political parties, no matter what their promises of Civil Rights, can really solve our problems. Our basic problems are not color, but poverty. If all of us were to turn white overnight, 90% of us would be poor whites. And poor whites, even with the vote, are still poor, and more bedraggled looking than ourselves. Color is at least a protection against drabness.

The late Jelly Roll Morton is reputed to have said, "It takes ten Negroes to make one police dog, but it takes ten Indians to make one Negro."[17] Which reminds me that Indians can't vote at all, nor buy a drink in many Western states—which is a hard fate indeed—and they were the first Americans.

A few weeks ago I read about an Indian girl who started East to college, got Jim Crowed on a bus in Texas, so she turned around and went back to her reservation. One seldom hears of any Negroes turning around and going back home on account of Jim Crow. Is it that Negroes have more gumption—or less pride? Is it that we take the back seat to get where we are going in spite of all—or that we just take the back seat?

A lot of people and papers apologized profusely to the Indian girl for what happened to her in Texas. But I have yet to hear all those people apologizing to Negroes—who are Jim Crowed in one way or another every day all over the U.S.A. Of course, if our white folks apologized to us every time they should, they wouldn't have time to do anything else. Right now, it is incumbent upon them to teach the rest of the world democracy—so we shouldn't be so rude as to expect them to bother much with democracy at home—at least not in relation to poor folks, Indians, and Negroes. The Germans and the Greeks come first. "Then, after you, my dear Gaston."

But don't worry. Those Europeans need democracy worse than we Negroes. They are white, with all the breaks, and still don't know how to behave themselves as nations toward each other. The only catch is, can they learn from folks with Dixie-like manners? I mean, can they learn to be democratic from gentlemen who practice only confederate democracy?

The rebel spirit of slavery dies hard. Eighty-five years, and it is not dead yet. A Negro is still sub-human to many white Southerners, therefore "human rights" do not apply to us. The United Nations Commission is going to have a harder time getting America to recognize Negro rights than they would have in persuading us to recognize Nazi rights or Franco rights. A much, much harder time! Even during the war, in that very Texas that Jim Crows Negroes and Indians, Nazi prisoners ate in station dining rooms where colored American soldiers and officers were not permitted to set foot. Even the Nazis were a bit surprised at how much better we were at maintaining color lines than Hitler, especially with our Red Cross following the Nordic blood bank policy.

I'm sitting here thinking that for the sake of democracy, we must wipe out such policies. But for the sake of truly happy children and wholesome healthy adults, poverty must go, too. Bellies are basic. In fact, bellies are the first line of defense for the soul. A desperately hungry man out of self-preservation will steal, thus putting a blot on his moral soul. A woman without clothes or money or work may sell her body in prostitution, thus entering into what folks call sin. Poverty-stricken children fall much easier than others into petty crime and wrong doing that puts a mark upon their physical and spiritual characters.

Bellies are basic—because a hungry belly can twist a person's or a community's soul all up. Poverty is anti-Christian because it sorely tries God's children. Poverty and Jim Crow are sisters under the skin. To make a decent, happy America, both must go. The sooner the better.

A Sentimental Journey to Cairo, Illinois

May 15, 1954

I have always been a blues fan.

Last year in its series of Americans, Audio Archives brought out a fascinating long-playing record of some of the compositions of W. C. Handy.[18] With the "Father of the Blues" himself acting as narrator, playing both guitar and cornet, and singing parts of the songs, this record is a valuable addition to the history of American music, as well as being both informative and entertaining.

In telling how he became interested in Negro folk music, Mr. Handy says that when he was a little boy in a rock quarry in the Deep South, he used to hear the workmen singing a song that went something like this:

> Hey-ooo-oo-o! Heyooooo
> I wouldn't live in Cairo!

And this song made him wonder what was wrong with Cairo. Was it too far up North to be down South—or too far down South to be up North?

Years later when Handy wrote his greatest blues, he mentioned Cairo in that song. I first heard its name in "The St. Louis Blues" which the Negroes in Kansas City were singing when I was a little boy.

Cairo is a levee town three hundred and sixty miles south of Chicago, on the Mississippi, at the extreme southern tip of Illinois. Several months ago it was in the news a great deal when the legal battle to integrate the schools there was at its height. Then it was reported that mob violence was feared. When I told a friend of mine that I intended to visit Cairo, he told me a joke about a Negro who once got off a train in a strange Southern city. No sooner had the train departed than a group of white men walked up to him. One of them said, "Say, Negro, don't you know we don't allow no colored folks to light here?"

The Negro replied, "No, sir, I didn't know."

"The last Negro that lit in this town, we hung him," the white man said. "But since you declare that you didn't know that we don't allow Negroes here, we will give you a chance—providing you catch the next train out of town."

The Negro said, "Since you'll give me a chance, boss, I won't wait for the next train. I'll catch the one that's just gone!"

Of course, nothing like that happened to me in Cairo. In fact, nothing untoward at all—until I was about to leave town. I had a very pleasant afternoon and evening there, and satisfied my curiosity about the place. Everyone I met kept asking me how come I had stopped over in Cairo. So I kept explaining that I was making a sentimental journey to a town I had always wanted to see ever since I first heard that line in "The St. Louis Blues" which goes, "If I get to Cairo, make St. Louis by myself."

On the train to Cairo was a Negro student from the university who introduced himself and, when we got to his home town, he took me to the high school to meet his former teachers and the principal.

I also met the principals and some of the teachers from the other colored schools—which are no longer segregated schools, since colored pupils may now, thanks to the NAACP, go to any school in the neighborhoods in which they live. Some of the teachers drove me about the city, another invited me to dinner with her family and saw that I got my train that night.

Just before catching the Panama Limited south, I was driven past the house of the white lawyer for the NAACP to see that now famous neon sign pictured in *Life* and *Jet* which his neighbor to the rear has put atop his garage, to flash off and on at night pointing to the home of the man who had the nerve to aid Negroes in breaking down the school barriers.

I had thought the sign was gone by the time of my visit. But, no, it was still there, pointing its red arrow of bigotry at this man's house. As we drove by, another car pulled up just behind us and slowed down. We continued to the corner where we turned to come back. The other car went by us picking up speed.

As we again passed the house, a white man ran out straight toward our car, in his shirt sleeves, one hand in his pocket and an angry look on his face. We stopped. Fortunately, he recognized the Negroes in the car as teachers whom he knew, and they recognized him as the lawyer who lived there. We were startled, naturally, at the wrath in his face, until he told us that someone had just thrown a rock through his front window—evidently an occupant of the car that had slowed down behind us.

This lawyer said that almost every week people drove by at night and threw rocks at his windows. But he said, "No one will drive me out of town!"

Meanwhile, as we talked, the beautiful red sign flashed off and on, off and on, atop his neighbor's garage, its arrow pointing to him. It was there in the dark street a moment after a stone crashed through his window, that I met David Lansden, a courageous white man in Southern Illinois who believes in democracy, equality, and racial decency. It was my privilege to tell him how much I admire his courage and his integrity. Having seen Cairo, I can now never forget it—nor the stones that are still being thrown there at democracy.

The Dilemma of the Negro Teacher Facing Desegregation

October 1, 1955

From Booker T. Washington to Mary McLeod Bethune, James Weldon Johnson to Countee Cullen in the writing field, Jessie Fauset, Sterling Brown and Margaret Walker, some of the greatest names in American Negro life have been teachers.[19]

Ralph Bunche was a teacher before his fame as a social scientist brought him to his present high position in the United Nations.[20]

Thousands and thousands of honorable men and women of color, less famous but nevertheless highly respected in their communities, have been teachers.

The Negro teacher has occupied a most important place in the life of our race and of our country. Will they occupy a less important place as formerly all-Negro schools become desegregated?

This should not be permitted to happen. In the first place, on the lower educational levels of the grammar school, the junior school, and even the high school, Negro teachers are on the whole scholastically and socially better prepared for their jobs than are most white teachers.

Value Differs

Teaching among whites has not been as highly esteemed on the lower educational levels, nor has it carried with it as much social prestige or community value as it has among Negroes. A white grammar school teacher is just another teacher.

A Negro teacher has community standing and influence beyond that enjoyed by most whites. This, I think, should, and will, continue to be true for a long time to come under integration.

However, the problem will be to see that Negro teachers are integrated—just as it is expected, or at least hoped, that Negro pupils will be. Negroes are citizens.

As citizens, they should have the right to teach in ANY school, just as our children now have Supreme Court approval to enter any school.

If the same rights as pupils have are not accorded colored teachers, then we will just have to go to the Supreme Court again and again until such rights are accorded.

And when granted, and Negroes teaching anywhere is no longer exceptional, as in most cases now, I am sure Negro teachers will acquit themselves excellently in mixed schools.

The problems of an integrated school could be no more difficult, if as difficult, as problems most Negro teachers have already faced.

On the college level, the newspapers are beginning to report the possible closing of certain institutions of higher learning that have until the present been all-Negro in faculty and student body.

Why this should be so, I do not understand. These until now Negro institutions should be opened to any citizen.

There are not enough educational institutions in the United States, as it is. To close any of them would be to cut down on facilities of which we already have a shortage.

What are now all-Negro colleges, therefore, should prepare themselves at once to begin soon to be all-American colleges.

And those teachers who are good teachers should remain in their positions, teaching any and all students who desire to learn.

The Negro college has long occupied a unique position in American life. Perhaps ways might be devised to keep that position unique, and to incorporate as an integral part of the curricula of such colleges courses not readily found elsewhere.

For example, with the emergence of Africa on the stage of world politics, why should not our now predominantly Negro campuses institute special courses in African history, politics, and the problems of transition from colonialism to independence?

Also, since the American race problem will hardly be solved simply by integrating education, why should not the now all-Negro colleges become centers of educational material for all interested in seeking ways to completely solve our racial problems in America?

As, for example, Harvard is noted for its School of Business, or Carnegie Tech for its Department of Drama, why should not Fisk and Howard and Langston and Southern and Lincoln become centers of interracial culture and social engineering designed toward the building of a better America, with particular emphasis on race relations?

Then young white students and Negroes as well would have study centers specializing in the problems which all Americans have to face and seek to solve.

Who could better help in vitalizing such studies than Negro teachers themselves?

In the transition from segregation to desegregation, just as in any other vast social change, there are bound to be certain temporary maladjustments.

But such a change in our American schools should not be permitted to bring about major or widespread dislocations and difficulties for the thousands of citizens of color whose profession is teaching.

Ways and means of preventing this cultural disaster should be set in motion at once.

There is too much good in the Negro teaching profession for any of it to be even temporarily lost in this already educationally deficient America of ours.

How to Integrate without Danger of Intermarriage

November 26, 1955

One of the things about integration that seems to most worry some white American citizens is intermarriage. They seem to think that if colored and white children attend the same schools when young, they will intermarry when old. There is one sure way to prevent this. Let us take for example a little dark boy and little blond girl sitting across the aisle from each other in the third grade in Jackson, Mississippi. Suppose the little brown boy says to the little blond girl, "When I grow up I would like to marry you. Will you marry me?" How can such a marriage be prevented? That's the question.

Let us take another example from a field other than education, that of housing. Suppose Negroes and whites live in neighboring apartments in a federal, state, or municipal housing project. And suppose a Negro family and a white family develop a speaking acquaintance as neighbors. Suppose a little farther—there is a teenage girl in the Negro family, and there is a teenage boy in the white family. Suppose the white boy asks the colored girl for her hand in marriage. How can this be stopped? I know, and will tell you.

Again, let us take a case that might develop from the Fair Employment Practice, should such a practice become really national. Suppose a white man and a colored woman in Memphis are working side by side in a factory at the same machines opposite each other. And suppose they find they have interests in common, such as raising chickens, or listening to bop music. Suppose one fine day the white man asked the colored woman to marry him. How can consummation of his request for matrimony be prevented? I will tell you in a word in a moment.

But first let us consider another area of possible integration, the area of Civil Rights. Suppose all the hotels all over America admitted Negro guests, all the trains dropped their Jim Crow cars, all the street cars and buses in the South discarded their COLORED and WHITE signs separating the races, and all public facilities everywhere were open fairly and equally to everybody, black or white. Let us imagine then a colored youth in Atlanta spotting a white maiden on a street car and wishing in his heart so desperately to take her to himself as a bride that he writes her a note proposing, "Will you be mine?" How could such a proposal be successfully thwarted? It is really no problem.

One more area should be considered before an answer is given, that of the purely social. Let us imagine that all clubs, fraternities, sororities, festivals, parties, socials, and dances from coast to coast all over the U.S.A. were open to colored participants as well as white. And a colored boy and girl found themselves dancing together in Birmingham so smoothly that they liked it. But the boy liked it so much that the urge to dance through life with the girl caused him to gather up enough courage to ask her, "Will you marry me?" What should that girl do? How could she stop him from marrying her? How could such legal miscegenation be prevented?

These are questions troubling the minds of many white people in the South today as the word "integration" invades the news and the national consciousness more and more. In some white minds "integration" and "intermarriage" are almost synonymous. They don't want the former much—but the latter they don't want at all.

They seem to think, too, that intermarriage would present a mass problem, a broad social challenge, and a general catastrophe with which the whole white race could hardly cope. I see the problem, on the other hand, as being of no such enormous proportions. I do not see where it would call for the participation of millions to solve it all. Marriage really involves only two people. And consent to marry actually concerns but one—the woman who must first give her consent. So the answer to the problem to me seems extremely simple. The way to integrate without intermarriage is for the girl to decline to get married. If a man, white or colored, says to a woman, colored or white, "Will you marry me?" all the woman has to do to prevent marrying the man, is say, "No."

Why anything so simple should cause so much discussion, I cannot for the life of me understand. Can you?

A Brickbat for Education—A Kiss for the Bedroom in Dixie

March 24, 1956

If Miss Lucy wanted to go to bed with a white man instead of to college with one, nobody at the University of Alabama would throw stones at her, nor defy the Supreme Court.[21] It is common knowledge in Dixie that some of the Southern politicians who are loudest in defiance of integration keep Negro mistresses, and some have fathered colored families whom they are men enough to support. The millions of mulattoes in the South today are living proof of integration from a long time ago right up to the present.

The "Southern way of life" seems to be a brickbat for education and a kiss for the bedroom—when it comes to whites aiming at Negroes. Miscegenation is an old, old story south of the Mason-Dixon line. If it were not, all of the Negroes down there would be quite dark, African dark, instead of brown, light brown, coffee-and-cream, tan, ivory and white.

Complexions are related to racial heritage, and lots of Negroes in the South are related to white people. Sometimes, as the distinguished Southern author Lillian Smith attests, a man will have a white family and a colored family in the same town—and everybody knows it.[22]

For long standing proof of integration in the deep South, I need go no further than myself. If there were no white blood in my veins, I would not be in color half way between African and Caucasian. On both sides of my family, my white slavery-time great grandparents are clearly remembered.

In my great-uncle's book, *From The Virginia Plantation to the National Capitol* by John Mercer Langston, the white ancestry on my mother's side is recorded in print for anyone to read.[23] Once I was speaking on a Northern campus where all the students were white. One of them was introduced to me as having the family name Langston. I asked the young man where he was from. He answered: "Louisa County, Virginia."

I said, "Why, that's where my great-grandparents were from, too. Perhaps we are related."

The young white man blushed a deep red and, not inclined to pursue the subject further, disappeared. But I'll bet he was a distant cousin of mine.

On my father's side, everyone in the family knows that one of the great-grandfathers who generated my generation was a white slave trader in Kentucky who became enamored of one of my great-grandmothers. Instead of selling her down the river for profit, he kept her himself—for love. Result, among others, me! I am not proud of this bastard white blood in my veins. I had just as leave I did not have it.

But my ancestry is no fault of mine, nor of my African grandparents living under the ruthless conditions of slavery. I myself, however, am living proof of integration long before the Supreme Court ruled upon the subject. Current Southern hypocrisy in the matter of integration, therefore, makes me laugh. But the bricks thrown at Miss Lucy make me cry.

Southern white men in slavery time were not the only integrators, however. Some Southern white women went to bed with their male slaves and loved it, so history records. And a number of white women married Negroes long before the Civil War was fought. There were both male and female integrators of the white race way back yonder! Integration is nothing new. Why the white South should raise such a hue and cry over it today is beyond me. Either white Southerners have lost their minds, or else they are just Great Pretenders. I don't know which. Quiet as it is kept, I think they are Pretenders.

Southern gentlemen merely act like they are mad when they throw bricks at Miss Lucy. The truth of the matter is, they had rather throw kisses. And, I expect that that alleged woman in Mississippi over whom the alleged Emmett Till was allegedly killed might really have wished Emmett had been just a little older and, instead of allegedly whistling, he had actually come a little closer to her.[24]

I have known several Southern white women who have followed Negroes out of the South to live with them in wedlock or in sin in Chicago or Detroit or New York. Integration is a four-way street—white, black, male, female, vice versa—and has long been a pretty busy thoroughfare in the USA. A few brickbats will hardly make much difference now.

The Man of the Year for 1958

June 14, 1958

The man of the year for 1958 is a 16-year-old boy. He is Ernest Green, the first Negro to graduate from Central High School in Little Rock, Arkansas.

Just being the first Negro to do something does not necessarily make a person great, or even famous. But there are still so many "first things" that colored people have not yet been permitted to do in the United States, that just the achieving of any one of them usually has about it some extraordinary merit requiring more than ordinary grit, ability, or stick-to-it-tiveness.

In some parts of our country just average day-to-day living needs from Negroes more courage and determination than it does from whites. When something a little out of the ordinary is done, it may call for heroics.

In my book 16-year-old Ernest Green is a hero. In his hands a high school diploma becomes a banner of singular glory, and something of which all the Negroes in the world can be proud.

Teenager Ernest Green took his life in his hands to get that diploma. He walked through mobs, endured spit and curses, braved brickbats, and passed lines of soldiers with unsure bayonets to get that diploma.

Without the protection of the police or the powers of the Governor of his state, he went to school to get that diploma. In the classroom he suffered whispered threats from unfriendly students, and in the halls intentional pushing and ugly jeering, but he got his diploma. To graduate was his determination. He did—and so becomes THE MAN OF THE YEAR for 1958.

And in that diploma of Ernest Green are the hopes and dreams of millions of Negroes long dead who never got an education. The dim wonder of "book learning" in the minds of countless slaves who dared not touch a book for fear of flogging lies in that diploma.

The blood of young black men and women beaten by overseers until their backs were raw for daring to study in secret is soaked into the paper of that diploma. The tears of slave mothers who desperately wanted their children to learn moisten all the letters on Ernest Green's diploma.

His diploma is no ordinary diploma. No! It is the diploma of all the people who remember grandfathers and grandmothers who did not know how to read and write because they never had a chance to learn, for whom the barriers to learning were too high, or the terrors in the way too great.

When, after the Civil War, the Knights of the White Circle and the Ku Klux Klan burned schools and killed teachers who sought to educate Negroes, the pain of those deprived of learning did not die. It lived in the air to fall gently as the evening dew over that stadium in Little Rock where, on the evening of May 27, 1958, Ernest Green received his diploma.

And the dew of ancient pain moistened his diploma, and the tears of all the generations of enforced ignorance fell upon his hand as he reached out to accept the token of graduation, his diploma!

The cold sweat of fear and the hot sweat of work, the sweat of all those early teachers, Negro and white, who braved physical danger and did physical labor laying bricks and sawing logs to build schools, all this sweat, too, is rolled into Ernest Green's diploma. The sweat of Booker T. Washington, of General Armstrong, of Lucy Laney, of Ida B. Wells.[25]

And if there is a ribbon about the diploma which Ernest Green received at Little Rock, it is the ribbon of prayer, the prayers of thousands of little Negro churches whose pennies and nickels and dimes and dollars for so long a time were a major part of the support of Negro education in the South.

And if there is a golden seal on Ernest Green's diploma, it is the seal of song, that song in the hearts of black congregations as they raised the offerings for education, that song in the hearts of the first Fisk Jubilee Singers as they sang up the money to build their college, that song of many an unknown Negro washerwoman who toiled all day over the tubs to send her children to school.[26]

Ernest Green's diploma is stamped with song and tied with a prayer. Now, thank God, he has his diploma—which is, in a sense, our diploma, too, hard won on our part and on his. But had it not been for Ernest Green's courage and determination, no dark hand would have received a diploma from Little Rock's Central High School.

Out of so many years of struggle, this 16-year-old graduate becomes 1958's MAN OF THE YEAR.

loses sight of original goal of black art. (handwritten)

Sit Tight—and Don't Squirm

September 16, 1961

It is not pleasant to see anyone faced at last with his sins—which are usually pleasurable enough in the doing, but unpleasant in retribution. That is the trouble with sins—so happy in the happening, often so vengeful in the aftermath. Little did I think I would live to see the white man squirming on his own mercy seat. He is already beginning to squirm.

When I was a child there was a lynching almost every week—one of my people, a Negro, strung up or burned to death, or shot down like a dog. But not just shot—usually instead, to use a phrase common in the press, he was "riddled with bullets." Sometimes the mob was reported in the papers as "dancing and shouting with glee." Photographs were shown of the whites around the often mutilated body. Identification of mobsters was easy, but no one was ever punished. Protests to local, state, or federal officials went unheeded. From 1906, Atlanta, to 1943, Detroit, there were race riots North, South, East and West—big scale lynchings with black property going up in smoke. Do you think any whites were even arrested as a rule? Nobody.

All over the Middle West where I lived, if you were colored, forty years ago, no ice cream soda at any downtown fountain on a hot day, not even for a little child who had no notion yet of the sharpness of the color line. If you were colored, no admittance at all to the movies, or just a row at the very back reserved for Negroes. If the picture was a popular one and those rows were filled, no getting in that night for anybody not white. Chinese, Japanese, and Indian Americans usually suffered a similar fate. And do not try to get a meal in a public restaurant.

"We don't serve you here." There might even be a FOR WHITE ONLY sign up outside in the North. In the South, no sign was needed to let a black man know he would not be welcome.

If a Negro went to get a job—porter, maid, ditch digger, groom, cook, shoe shine boy—no advancement. Unions against you as well as employers. Education? Half the United States had separate "colored" schools, inferior in every way to the white schools. Educate yourself? Try the public libraries? In New Orleans up until World War II, the colored branch library got the old torn up books from the white libraries. You want to see a lion? Oh, no! Not in the public zoo which your tax money helps support. Why should a darkie in the South want to see a lion?

Now, in this year of our Lord, 1961, much has changed and is changing. And there is a megaton bomb sitting way off across the ocean somewhere waiting to change things even more—just by its presence, if it is never discharged. And there is China bigger than ever just over the horizon remembering, no doubt, the Oriental Exclusion Act. And Japan remembering Hiroshima. And Africa—"old black funny-looking Africa"—remembering the slave ships.

But nobody mentions memories. It would hardly be polite. It might even sound vindictive, bullying, not at all diplomatic, *comme il faut,* or according to the United Nations Charter. But memories have very little to do with diplomacy. Even when suppressed and subconscious, memories burst out in spite of Freud, the Sorbonne, NATO, or whatever summit is in the offing. The summit is the top of somebody's head kicked in the head so hard last year his hind-brain got jarred loose.

Not his fault! But some old hard-kicking sinner did kick. Brain got jarred. "The sins of the fathers, etc., etc., etc., even unto the third and fourth, etc., etc." Too bad! Nobody likes to see guilt by association running backwards to catch a ghost. But why, one must keep asking why, did the descendants of ghosts let things come to such a pretty pass? I was lynched sometimes at the rate of one a week or more. Why did the nice white descendants of white ghosts, not protest—except a handful of radicals, liberals, suffragettes? Why nobody sent to jail—except Negroes left alive after the mobs got through? Why no weeping and wailing and beating of breast then to half the extent tears flow and wails arise and breasts are bared for Hungary, Cuba, Berlin now? Why? Why? Why? (Those white Cubans who bathe on Florida beaches where black Americans cannot go!) Why? No need to point the moral. Start testing your bombs again. Sit tight—and don't squirm.

Part 2

Jim Crow's Epitaph

Are You Spanish?

September 18, 1943

The South-bound train from New York crossed the Potomac at Washington and headed through Virginia in the early morning. In New York the night before a colored woman had gotten on the train, gone to her Pullman compartment and gone to sleep. Awaking as the train left Washington, she got up, dressed, and went into the diner to have breakfast.

It was a crack limited train and the diner had beautiful white linen on the tables and gleaming bright silver. The colored woman was a handsome well-groomed woman. It was still early and the diner was not yet crowded so she took a seat at an empty table, one of the small tables for two. The colored waiters looked at her with interest and admiration, but none came to serve her. She studied the menu, made her selection, and waited.

Finally the white dining car steward approached her with the order slips, but he did not hand her a slip, or say good morning. Instead he asked rather abruptly, "Are you Spanish?"

Amazed, the woman said, "No, I'm not. I'm an American."

"Then I can't serve you," said the steward.

"I beg your pardon?" said the woman.

"You are colored?" asked the steward.

"Of course," said the woman. "An American Negro."

"You'll have to come back after the third sitting," said the steward. "Or else I'll send your breakfast to your car."

Why We're at War

From the window of the diner the dome of the Capitol was still visible in the distance and the woman did not believe it was the Capitol of Spain. Surely the train had not crossed the ocean in the night.

"Why do you ask am I Spanish?" said the colored woman.

"Because it is against the law to serve Negroes," said the steward.

Until then the woman had not realized she was in Virginia. She had not been South for many years, having lived in New York and Paris, and she had forgotten about its silly system that Jim Crows American citizens of color. But suddenly she remembered that legally such laws did not and could not apply to interstate passengers on railroads. So she simply said, "I boarded this train at the Pennsylvania Station in New York with a first class ticket. I am an interstate passenger, so I do not intend to wait until after the third sitting, nor do I intend to be served in my car. I wish a half grapefruit, two soft boiled eggs, dry toast, and coffee, please."

The steward flushed a darker red. "You will not be served," he said, and started to walk away as the diner began to fill with white passengers. But suddenly he stopped in his tracks as the colored woman's voice rang through the car.

"Come here!" she called. "How dare you refuse to serve me? How dare you ask me if I am Spanish? Spaniards may be served in this diner, may they? But not an American citizen buying war bonds and paying taxes and sending relatives to fight in Europe for democracy!"

"Madam, do not cause any excitement, please!" said the steward.

"I will cause excitement," said the woman. "I must be Spanish to get a cup of coffee on this train in my own country? I will cause excitement! Furthermore, I think you ought to know what Americans are fighting for, and why we're at war. Just stand here and I will tell you."

"Good for You"

But the steward did not stand there. He did not wish his car thrown into an uproar by a New York colored woman demanding her democratic and legal rights. He walked away. In a few moments a waiter appeared grinning with a half grapefruit. The woman was served.

"Good for you," the waiter whispered in her ear.

More and more such stories of colored travelers throughout the South demanding the travel rights for which they have paid come to me these days. I say, more power to you, pioneers on the wild frontiers of local fascism! I hope more and more Negro citizens will stand up for their due rights as travelers. After all, our tickets cost as much as the next person's.

All colored students going South this fall to college, be sure to go into the diners and have your meals. You will be helping to educate the dining car stewards and the Southern traveling public to the fact that you have as much right to eat in a diner as any one else.

If you have to raise sand to eat there, then raise sand. Be firm and logical about it. Don't use bad language. Don't threaten. Simply say you are an American. Your relatives and friends are in the war, too. You pay taxes and buy War Bonds, too. Then say that you do not intend to wait for a fourth sitting exclusively for Negroes or sit behind a curtain or have your food on a tray in another coach because, in the light of the Four Freedoms such fourth class service doesn't make sense. And sense and decency and courtesy are needed at home for everybody. So let me see the menu, please.

Doc, Wait! I Can't Sublimate!

March 4, 1944

I once heard a Negro in Cleveland explaining why he had left the South where he was born and lived for some thirty years. It seems that one day a white man tried to put him in his place. Many times before white men had put him in his place but, according to the Negro, "It looked like this time something just snapped in me. I couldn't stand it no longer. I hauled off and beat him real good." Then, of course, he got out of town—but quick. He came North and stayed.

Some folks are able to adjust themselves permanently to the worst forms of Jim Crow. Others apparently adjust, then some day, some little thing happens, all self-control deserts them, and they go off the beam. The last straw that broke the camel's back was probably just a little old straw, but the camel "couldn't stand it no longer."

The late great psychoanalyst, Sigmund Freud, said that the hysteric symptom has its roots in an individual's historic past. In other words, a hysterical, perhaps violent, outburst may be the result of a slow piling on of straw after straw after straw. Such a slow heaping up on black backs of the Jim Crow logs, scantlings, splinters, and straws of discrimination produced the Harlem riots of last August.[1] When that white policeman shot the colored soldier, that was the last straw. The camel's back broke down.

There's a Limit

A camel's back can bear just so much. A human being's mental and emotional system can stand just so much. There is a limit to all things. Intelligent and progressive white Americans know that Negro Americans can stand just so much—and that that so much is already too much—so they are trying to do something about the situation. Other white Americans who are both stupid and reactionary, are seeking to make us bear not only the old logs of Jim Crowism, but are trying to add new logs, scantlings, and straws thereunto—like the comparatively recent segregated blood bank of the Red Cross which is purely Hitlerian in theory and practice.

We are fighting the Germans, but German blood is not segregated. We are fighting the Italians, but Italian blood is not segregated. We are fighting the Japanese, but Japanese blood goes in the blood bank. Just American Negro blood is put into separate cans and marked with a Jim Crow label. That is a hard straw to bear from our fellow countrymen.

Some kind and well-meaning white Americans advise the Negro to sublimate his resentments, to be better, in other words, than his oppressors, to rise spiritually above the battle. Well, those white friends do not have to ride in Jim Crow cars. If they are women, they do not have to read signs saying JOIN THE WAVES and be turned down because they are colored women. They do not have to desire to vote in Texas and run into the "white primaries" which bar them. They are not lifted up by the Four Freedoms only to be pulled down by Jim Crow.

Psychoanalysis for All

The human soul, like rubber, won't stretch but so far. Pull it too taut and something is bound to happen. That is why I think the public health services all over the country should set up psychiatric clinics for the treatment of Jim Crow shock, segregation-neuroses, and discrimination-fatigue. Likewise, prejudiced whites should be treated for what ails them. Until we correct the racial defects in our current social system, psychoanalysis might make a study, with a view toward correcting, the symptoms of pre-riotitis. Nobody likes riots, but when an over-zealous white Jim Crower collides with a too-much Jim Crowed Negro, hysteric sparks might fly capable of lighting dangerous emotional fires.

If psychoanalysis can treat battle-fatigue on the war fronts, it should be able to help segregation-fatigue on the civilian front. It should also be able to ameliorate the Nordicized superiority complexes of some unfortunate white people. Some persons, in fact many persons, may be able to sublimate their difficulties as Richard Wright sublimated his Jim Crow shocks into a mighty novel, *Native Son,* or as Roland Hayes sublimated his Georgia head-beating into song.[2] But there are others who just can't sublimate. All they can do is keep quiet. Or explode. To those liable to explode, I suggest psychiatric treatment. A stitch in time saves nine.

Down South, if a colored man protests too strongly against Jim Crow, his white townsfolks are almost certain to say, "That Negro is crazy!" Perhaps they come nearer truth than poetry. At any rate, he should not be lynched. Nor should the sheriff be called. Send for a psychoanalyst—for all of them.

Theaters, Clubs, and Negroes

September 23, 1944

The other day I went to buy two seats to Broadway's newest smash hit with an all-Negro cast, *Anna Lucasta*. Just ahead of me at the box-office was a well-groomed, pleasant-looking white woman. As the ticket-seller handed her her seats, she said, "I hope I won't be sitting between Negroes."

"What a shame you feel that way," I said right out loud.

She had not noticed me standing behind her, but when she did as I spoke, she turned, became quite red, and said, "Oh, I didn't mean it the way you think I did."

"If you feel that way," I said, "not wanting to sit beside Negroes, I do not see why you would want to see a Negro show."

"I have put my foot in it," she said, "and I'm sorry."

"I am sorry, too, for the way you feel," I said.

The woman went away with her tickets. Then I turned to the box-office man, who had tossed off her hope that she wouldn't be sitting between Negroes, with a breezy, "Oh, no!" I asked him how he could assure anybody that they would not be sitting beside colored people.

The box-office man said, "I can't. But we occasionally run into those kinds of questions, so we tell them anything. But colored people can buy seats anywhere in this theater."

I told him that I had always found that to be true in New York playhouses. In twenty years of play-going on Broadway, I have never, so far as I know, been segregated in any dramatic theater. I have often seen colored people in the most expensive orchestra seats at Broadway openings.

I remember once at a downtown movie house where the Negro film *Hallelujah* was being shown, they seated the Negro patrons all around the outer edges of the orchestra like a band of mourning. But that did not last very long.

Club Zanzibar Mourns

That is the way the famous Zanzibar Club, where Cab Calloway is currently appearing, mourns about the Negro problem—by seating its Negro patrons all around the edges.[3] It is so crowded with Negro patrons, however, that it soon is going to have to get some more edges around which to seat them. Colored folks seem to love the place, especially out-of-towners, and flock there in large numbers.

The show is one of the best night club shows on Broadway, with a beautiful lot o' chorus girls, top stars, staged by Clarence Robinson. Negro customers are usually led straight to the raised platform running around three sides. They are never put on the center-side facing the stage until the side-sides are full, then maybe a few dark folks spill over onto the main level.

The last time I was down there, the head waiter led me and the girl I was with as far back in the corner behind the band as he could. So I said, "Listen, man, I am not in the show! I came to see the show!" So he led me back down the side a ways, but still on the "colored" level. They put a few whites up there, too, so you can't swear it's segregation—but it is. And colored Harlem has been complaining about it ever since the Zanzibar opened. But they still go, so I reckon the man thinks we like it.

Each time I go there, I swear I am not going back any more. But then the very next week somebody from Chicago, or Detroit, or somewhere turns up who "just must see the Zanzibar." And I say, "You will be segregated there and put on the side sure. Let's go to Cafe Society, or the Downbeat and hear Billie Holiday, or someplace like that where they don't Jim Crow you."[4] And they will say, "Well, we'll decide the night we get ready to go."

The night we get ready to go, I say, "Where shall we go?" And they say, "Wherever you suggest, but let's stop by the Zanzibar on the way." So up those steps again I go, to the Zanzibar. Most politely the head-waiter guy receives you, and leads you dead straight across the place to the farthest side, and starts toward the back behind the band, unless you stop him on the way, and say, "Why go so far?"

Only Four Sides

Now, an ordinary room has only four sides. The Zanzibar has only three for tables, as the band-stand and stage take up one whole end. Of these three sides, one runs across the center, facing the stage with a good view of the show, so they put mostly white people there, leaving only two sides for colored. These two sides, each time I have been, overflow with Negroes. If many more colored people patronize the Zanzibar, they are going to have to build more sides. But I do not see where they can build more sides to a four-sided room that has only three sides already.

Since white and colored people dance all over the same dance-floor there, and jitterbug and bump all up against each other, and nobody seems to mind it in the least, the sensible thing, it would seem to me, for the management of the Zanzibar to do, would be to let people of any color sit anywhere, and stop putting that chocolate band of humanity all around the walls.

Adventures in Dining

June 2, 1945

Eating in dining cars south of the Mason-Dixon line these days is, for Negroes, often quite an adventure. Until recently, for some strange reason, Southern white people evidently did not think that colored travelers ever got hungry while traveling, or if they did get hungry they were not expected to eat. Until the war came along, and the Mitchell Case was won, most Southern trains made no arrangements at all for Negroes to eat in the diners.

But now some Southern trains do arrange for Negroes to eat at times by having one or two tables curtained off in the dining car, and serving colored travelers behind the curtain. But not all trains do this. Some expect Negro passengers to eat early, others expect them to eat late, and others still expect them not to eat at all, but just go hungry until they get where they are going.

I have just come out of the South, having been during this lecture season from the Carolinas to Texas. On some trains heading southward from Washington through Virginia, I have been served without difficulty at any table in the diner, with white passengers eating with me. Further South, I have encountered the curtain, behind which I had to sit in order to eat, often being served with the colored Pullman porters and brakemen. On other trains there has been no curtain and no intention for Negroes to eat.

Chattanooga Incident

Coming out of Chattanooga on such a train, I went into the diner on the first call for dinner because sometimes these days if you wait for the second call everything will be gone. As I entered the diner, I said to the white steward, "One, please." He looked at me in amazement and walked off toward the other end of the car. The diner was filling rapidly, but there were still a couple of empty tables in the center of the car, so I went ahead and sat down.

Three whites soon joined me, then all the seats in the dining car were taken. The steward came and gave the three whites menus, but ignored me. Every time he passed, though, he would look at me and frown. Finally he leaned over and whispered in my ear.

"Say, fellow, are you Puerto Rican?"

"No," I said, "I'm American."

"Not American Negro, are you?" he demanded.

"I'm just hungry," I said loudly.

He gave me a menu! The colored waiters grinned. They served me with great courtesy, a quality which I have always found our dining car waiters to possess.

A few days later, in the great state of Alabama, I was riding in a Pullman that was half sleeping-car and half diner. There were only six tables in the dining portion of the car so, when the Filipino steward announced luncheon, I got up and went forward. I took a seat at one of the middle tables. Two white Navy men and a WAVE occupied the table with me. The Filipino steward looked very perturbed.

He walked up and down the aisle and gave a menu to everybody but me. Then he gave order checks to everybody but me. Then he disappeared in the kitchen. Finally he came out and addressed me nervously in broken English.

"Chef want to see you in kitchen," he mumbled.

I said, "What?"

He repeated, "Chef want to see you in kitchen."

"I have nothing to do with the kitchen!" I said. "Tell the chef to come here."

He disappeared again. Finally he came back and gave me a menu. Since he was both waiter and steward, he served me himself. Nothing more was said.

Negro Stewards in Texas

On some dining cars in Texas, I found that they have colored stewards, although they do not term them stewards, but "waiters-in-charge." It happened that I knew one "waiter-in-charge," an intelligent and progressive young Negro, who invited me to be his personal guest at dinner. He told me that he seated colored passengers right along with the others. Certainly there is great variation in railroad dining for the race these days in the South. Just exactly what to expect still remains a mystery for Negroes—but it has the aura of adventure.

I would advise Negro travelers in the South to use the diners more. In fact, I wish we would use the diners in droves—so that whites may get used to seeing us in diners. It has been legally established that Negro passengers have a lawful right to eat while traveling. If we are refused service or ejected on grounds of color, we can sue. Several cases have been won and damages assessed recently. So, folks, when you go South by train, be sure to eat in the diner. Even if you are not hungry, eat anyhow—to help establish that right. Besides, it will be fun to see how you will be received.

Encounter at the Counter

March 30, 1946

Flying West to the Coast this winter, I broke my trip for a day at Kansas City, the town where Cab Calloway recently got his head beat by a prejudiced white cop. I kept forgetting how prejudiced the Middle West is toward Negroes so after leaving the airport, I went into the Fred Harvey Restaurant in the Kansas City Union Station for an early breakfast before taking the train to Lawrence. I thought the hostess was just being courteous when she beckoned me to follow her to a table.

"I had rather sit at the counter," I said, "because I am in a hurry and must catch a train."

"I have a table for you," she said.

She led me into the dining room at the back, straight on through the dining room—which was not crowded—past many empty tables, and right on back into the farthest corner to the last table beside the kitchen door. But she did not stop there. She went around the last table and pulled out the last chair away back in the corner.

I said, "I have no intention of sitting here in this corner. I prefer to sit at the counter, anyway."

I turned and walked back to the counter with her trailing along behind me. There were many empty seats at the counter, so I sat in the middle. The hostess tapped me on the shoulder.

"Would you mind letting me seat you?" she said.

"Certainly you may," I said, "but here at the counter."

A Seat in the Corner

I got up and followed her again. She led me to the very end of the counter, again passing many empty seats, and put me at the end in a corner against a pillar.

I said, "I am not going to sit at the end of this counter in a corner. My relatives fought and died in this war the same as yours, and colored people are tired of being put in corners."

Again I turned and left her and took a seat at the middle of the counter. Flushing very red, she followed me and gave me a menu. A waitress who had watched all this smiled as she came to wait on me. She served me most courteously, as though to prove that not all white people wish to be rude to Negroes.

Friends of mine in Kansas City told me that this Union Station restaurant has often in the past been uncivil to Negro travelers. It seems they prefer that colored persons eat standing up at the little sandwich counter across the station. So I suggest that ALL Negro travelers going through Kansas City make it a point to eat in the big Harvey House Restaurant and sit dead in the middle and get those provincial folks accustomed to seeing colored people in that dining room. President Truman's home state really should be more cordial to American travelers of Negro descent.

In fact, for many years, I have been puzzled as to where and how America expects Negro travelers to eat. Many communities have no Negro-owned or operated restaurants. And even when there are colored restaurants, how is a complete stranger to know where the Negro places are located? Colored travelers do not usually have time to walk all over town looking for a place to eat.

"Sorry, No Can Serve"

At least a hundred times (making a conservative estimate) I have been refused service in public restaurants in strange cities. Once, driving East from Los Angeles, we reached Yuma, Arizona, about ten at night. Not a restaurant on the main street would serve us a sandwich. At one Greek cafe, the Greek looked at us and said, "Why, you boys ought to know better than to come in here."

Near the bus station in Flint, Michigan, last year I went into a Chinese chop suey place. The Chinese proprietor said to me, "If I serve you, my white folks all go! Sorry, no can serve!"

I said, "Thousands of Negro servicemen fought to help China against Japan." He said, "Sorry! No can serve."

Greeks, Chinese, Italians, Mexicans, anybody can say to us Negro Americans, "Sorry, no can serve!" And all over this American country we are expected to take it—and like it—and go hungry. American democracy has a long way to go in learning human kindness and decency.

Our newspapers, in cities whose restaurants will not serve Negroes even a toothpick, have the nerve these days to blast away at Russia for "suppressing personal liberties and individual freedom." For a whole year, as a journalist, I traveled all over the Soviet Union from Moscow to Siberia, and not one single restaurant refused me service. The same was true in France, in Japan, in Italy, in Loyalist Spain. Not until I come home to the U.S.A. does anybody say, "Sorry, no can serve."

Freight

May 10, 1947

It is true that, against our will, the first Negro slaves were brought to this country as freight chained in the holds of slave ships. There is no good reason, however, why, three hundred years later a leading Washington hotel should insist that Negroes visiting the Democratic National Committee should use the FREIGHT ELEVATOR. The party to which the President of the United States belongs should see to it that the hotel housing its offices in our national capital be brought up to date on the facts. American Negroes are no longer freight.

That not all white people are alike, though, is attested by the recent action of the Actors' Equity Association to which all the great stars of our Broadway stage belong, and the major portion of all the actors of America. This Association has given the National Theater in Washington, which does not admit Negroes, until May, 1948, to change its ways, or else no stage shows having Equity casts will play there—which means virtually *all* stage shows.

We are too prone, in speaking of the Jim Crowisms of which we suffer, to say, "white folks this" and "white folks that." By implication blaming the entire white group. *All* American white people have never been against us. Even in slavery times there were those who wrote, spoke, and fought for our freedom. Today there are many who do not believe we are freight, who do not believe in Jim Crow. So when we speak of democracy's enemies in relation to Negro rights, we should say "some white folks," *not* just "white folks."

"White folks do not mind letting a Negro die," said one of the Clark College students in Atlanta last week when news came of the auto wreck in which the star of Clark's track team lost his life.

It seems there were no hospitals up or down the road on which the wreck occurred that would admit an injured Negro, even for first aid treatment. So in the night on a lonely Tennessee road, three injured athletes in ambulances were carried first this way miles from the wreck to a white hospital. Refused! Then back down the road sped the ambulances past the wreckage many miles to another hospital, white. Refused! Finally, fifty miles away at a Negro hospital in Fayetteville, they were admitted for treatment. From exposure and loss of blood, Jeffrey Jennings of Houston died a few minutes after the ambulances arrived at the colored hospital.

The beloved Juliette Derricotte of the YWCA died that way, too, 15 years ago. Injured in a wreck on a Southern road, that cultured woman was denied hospital treatment at the nearest white hospital. By the time a Negro hospital was found miles away, she was dead.

The Tragedy of Death

Bessie Smith, greatest of the blues singers, died in that fashion also. Perhaps the most moving and beautiful page in the Mezrow book, *Really the Blues,* is devoted to the tragedy of her death, with Jim Crow guarding the doors of the hospitals of the white South. None would take America's greatest folk singer in although an auto crash had almost torn one arm from its socket.[5]

Such behavior seems hardly human, yet Southern white doctors and nurses who turn desperately injured Negroes away from their hospital doors, must be human. They talk like people and they look like people. They speak English. They say, "No!"

Perhaps they consider injured Negroes freight—freight too lacking in value, too cheap to live. Jeffrey Jennings, college student, freight! Juliette Derricotte, American YWCA executive, freight! Bessie Smith, deep-throated singer of American songs, freight! Black freight! Dying freight, denied opiates, comfort, treatment, healing, or even an easy death. On the Southern roads, injured Negroes are less than freight. Even inanimate perishable freight from an overturned truck might, in wind and storm, be given emergency shelter in a white hospital corridor or garage—but not bleeding, breathing men and women who happen to be black.

Liberty, Justice for All

The Oath of Allegiance all Americans, black and white, learn in school closes with the words, ". . . with liberty and justice for all." And medicine's great Hippocratic Oath says, ". . . The regimen I adopt shall be for the benefit of my patients according to my ability and judgment, and not for their hurt or for any wrong . . . Whatsoever house I enter, there will I go for the benefit of the sick, refraining from all wrong-doing or corruption . . ."

Has the noble Oath of Hippocrates been forgotten? Has the great Oath of Allegiance to our Flag been forgotten by those white doctors who turn away a Juliette Derricotte, a Bessie Smith, or a bruised and bleeding Jeffrey Jennings? Will not even pain, suffering, and the wings of death move them, when the pain and suffering is black? Is it true in the Southland, "White folks will let any Negro die?"

With the Crumbling of the Old Chain, Jim Crow Crumbles, Too

October 8, 1949

What is happening in China is important to Negroes, in fact, to people of color all around the world, because each time an old bastion of white supremacy crumbles its falling weakens the whole Jim Crow system everywhere. Under the Nationalist government in China with its white Western backers, there was a great deal of Jim Crow. I saw it with my own eyes in Shanghai and Nanking when I was there before the war. Being colored, I felt it, too. I do not like Jim Crow in either Chicago or China. The majority of Chinese people did not like Jim Crow either. But the Chinese Uncle Toms liked Jim Crow because they grew rich from it. Chiang Kai-Shek was a Chinese Uncle Tom.[6]

Emerging slowly from feudalism with large sections of the country dominated by war-lords, China has long had slavery—child-slavery, woman-slavery, "white-slavery." From this ancient slavery white Westerners have long profited along with the rich Chinese. Factories in which children purchased from their parents at an early age worked twelve and fifteen hours a day under guards brought huge profits to foreign and Chinese investors alike. Child prostitution and the dope rackets profited people in far off London and Paris. Our own United States, with large investments in China, supported the Chiang Kai-Shek regime that permitted these antiquated and inhuman exploitations to exist.

I am not speaking of what I have read. I am speaking of what I saw myself in China. With American Y.W.C.A. workers I visited factories in Shanghai where children of eight to twelve worked from dawn to dusk under overseers who carried bamboo canes to throttle them if they became idle. I saw the miserable dormitories where these purchased children slept in virtual imprisonment. And I was told that wealthy and respectable stock-holders in far off Tokyo and London and New York and Paris lived on the dividends produced by the frail hands of these children.

In Shanghai's International Settlement where the great powers of the world had their consulates and their laws and their police, I saw in the amusement centers children with guardians, not there to enjoy themselves, but rather offered in prostitution to any wishing to pay the fee asked by their "nurses." American newspaper men explained to me that often very poor parents sold their offspring into this horrible business rather than see them starve.

Quite openly in Shanghai before the war one might see a white foreigner curse or even strike a rickshaw driver—the rickshaws being the human taxis of the East pulled by a man running, running, running all the time. No policeman would arrest a white foreigner for striking a rickshaw man—just as no policeman would arrest a white man for striking a Negro in parts of Mississippi or Georgia today.

In Shanghai when I was there, there was a big Y.M.C.A. building for whites and a kind of "Harlem Branch," separate and elsewhere, for Chinese and other colored peoples. There were, right in China's greatest city, many hotels and restaurants for EUROPEANS ONLY, which meant WHITE ONLY. Such was the nerve of the Western powers in the Far East before the Japanese invaded the mainland of Asia! The Japanese swept the color-line out of existence. But the Japanese did not sweep away exploitation and child-labor. That is why the revolutionary armies now sweeping over China are doing a better job. They are not only against color-lines and Jim Crow. They are also against child-labor, child-prostitution, dope-rackets with headquarters in Europe, and dividend collectors who grow rich in far away lands from the dawn to dusk hours of Chinese workers.

MacArthur Lives in the Waldorf-Astoria; Gilbert Lives in Jail

June 2, 1951

The papers say that General Douglas MacArthur paid no mind to certain orders of his Commander in Chief of the Armed Forces, President Truman. But he came home in style to take up lodgings in the Waldorf-Astoria. Lt. Gilbert failed to carry out an order from a much lesser officer, but Gilbert went to prison for twenty years. MacArthur is rich and white. Gilbert is poor and colored.

Senate crime investigators have alleged that certain known and highly publicized personalities have grown wealthy on illegal activities and have sent other men to death via Murder, Inc., and the gangster ride. Yet these shady characters are free. They live in fine New York apartments or Miami Beach mansions and fly back and forth across the country at will. Willie McGee was alleged, on much lesser authority (the unsubstantiated charge of a white wife who said she was raped in the dark and didn't even see the man) to have attacked a woman. Willie McGee stayed in jail for years. He died the other day in the electric chair. The men named by the Senate Crime Committees are illegally rich but legally white. Willie McGee was legally poor and legally colored.

But some colored people are rich, too. Nevertheless, traveling on the same plane with white fellow passengers, when a Negro gets to a Southern airport he is never sure he can ride into town without waiting hours until a colored conveyance is called to transport him. If a plane is grounded, a colored passenger in the South is never sure of food and shelter, unless he wants to eat from his own lap outside the dining room of the airport, and unless there is a colored hotel in the place where the plane is stalled.

So, the words RICH and POOR could be left out of this article in so far as Negroes are concerned, money not making much difference. Color should not make any difference, either, but we all know that it does.

"Anyway, why bring it up?" some readers say. "The Negro press is full of nothing but Jim Crow all the time!"

Well, Jim Crow and color inequities are one of the big problems of all America, and one of its urgent problems. Certainly, this problem won't let US rest. So why should we let it rest? It is a problem which ALL Americans of good will wish to solve—and soon. One way of helping solve it is to talk about it, write about it, and continually bring its various facets to the attention of every citizen who can be reached, in hope that action will be taken toward a prompt solution.

Some people think because they live well, everybody else does, too. Then again some people just don't think at all. Maybe the written word will help them to think. Some Negroes believe that since they have, through wealth, educational or geographical location, managed to avoid the rigors of Jim Crow living, everybody else should have been fortunate enough or clever enough to have devised such means of escape, too. Well everybody is not fortunate, or clever or born in New England. And some folks want to live happily right where they are, whether it be Mississippi or Boston. Some folks even want the WHOLE U.S.A. to be a decent place racially speaking. And some people are really ashamed of our America wherever it has nooks and corners marked FOR WHITE ONLY or RESTRICTED or MEXICANS NOT SERVED.

Of course, if you're colored, you are not only ashamed of your homeland for being prejudiced and provincial-minded, you are also inconvenienced, chagrined, stymied, frustrated, put out, and frequently mad. Nobody likes to be Jim Crowed, not even an Uncle Tom. White folks definitely would not like it if Negroes were to Jim Crow them. Therefore, why not write about the stupidities of Jim Crow each and every day in each and every issue of each and every Negro paper?

From Rampart Street to Harlem I Follow the Trial of the Blues

December 6, 1952

About a month ago I heard it on a juke box in New Orleans. The other day I found it in a shop in Harlem, and ever since it has been whirling around on my record player: Little Caesar singing "Goodbye, Baby" to music by Que Martyn on a Hollywood label, which bids fair to be classed among my favorite records. It is a little two-minute drama in blues with a cast of two, a guy and a doll. The guy catches his girlfriend waiting for another man. She thinks he is the other man when he knocks. Then the explaining begins while Little Caesar caterwauls his blues.

The explanations do not take. At the end he shoots her: BANG! BANG! Then moans, "I can't stay here by myself." And he is gone, too. BANG! Folks who liked Pearl Bailey and Jackie Mabley's recording of "Saturday Night Fish Fry" will like this one.[7]

Years ago I spent the better part of a summer on Rampart Street, so I have a fondness in my heart for that long old roughneck thoroughfare and the songs it loves. I followed the Mississippi River down from Memphis, stopping in Vicksburg and Natchez and Baton Rouge that summer.

I arrived in New Orleans in a Jim Crow car and roomed with a lady on Rampart Street who ran Saturday night fish fries. I got a job on a banana boat and made a trip to Havana and other Cuban ports and back, where I lived in the French Quarter for a time, but soon gravitated back to Rampart where there are more colored people. Toward the end of the summer I left in a Jim Crow car for Mobile.

This time when I left New Orleans I departed in a private room on the deluxe Panama Limited. I was given the private room because I am colored. Formerly Negroes could not ride on this all-Pullman train at all, but the recent Supreme Court decisions have changed that for the better.

Now they will give a Negro passenger traveling between Southern stations on this train a roomette, drawing room, or bedroom without extra charge rather than seat him in the club or parlor cars when his ticket calls for a seat. There is sometimes some advantage in being colored—when the accommodations given are separate but better than whites receive for the same money.

In my experience, this only happens in Pullman travel, however. Before the recent Court rulings, it was the Southern railway custom to give a Negro "Lower 13" which meant a drawing room, rather than have him in the body of the Pullman car, providing the drawing room was not already sold.

This happened to me a few weeks ago traveling on the Gulf, Mobile and Ohio's fine little train, The Rebel, which runs between New Orleans and Jackson, Tennessee. I was going to speak at Lane College in Tennessee. My ticket called for a lower berth.

Although there were only two other persons, both white, in the Pullman car, the conductor gave me the bedroom, where I had complete privacy, even to my own washroom and toilet. This would have cost more than twice as much as my ticket, had I paid for it. But it was given to me free! Anything to keep Negroes segregated! Our white folks strike me as being real simple.

When the writer, Melvin Tolson, and I left the Literary Festival at Jackson College, Mississippi, the ticket seller took a very long time and held considerable consultation with others in the office before selling us seats on the Southbound Panama Limited.[8]

Finally he gave us two seats in the Club Car, numbers 4 and 5. But when we went to board the train just as it was pulling out of the Jackson station, rather than seat us in the Club Car, the conductor held up the train for more than two minutes while he went from car to car until he found a coach that had an unsold drawing room in it where we would be separate from other passengers. In the rich privacy which our color gained us, we left Mississippi, vastly amused at the lengths to which Southerners go to preserve Jim Crow. A crack train held up that two Negroes might suffer segregation by being given its finest accommodations rather than permitted the democracy of the open coaches!

The many lawsuits brought by Negro travelers in recent years against Southern railroads, and the NAACP's legal battles were demonstrated to me in an amusing fashion on my recent trip when I went alone into a diner in Mississippi to eat.

The former curtain screening the "Negro" table was gone. I was seated with great courtesy, but at an end table, nevertheless. I have always found dining car waiters all over the country most polite. This time, however, the white steward and the Negro waiters seemed to be giving me unusually attentive service.

The steward stopped twice at my table to ask me if everything was to my liking, and if I was enjoying my meal. Two waiters attended my every need. At the end of the meal, one of the waiters said to me, "We are delighted to have you on this train, Mr. Marshall."

"Mr. Marshall?" I asked. "Which Mr. Marshall?"

"Thurgood Marshall," said the waiter.

It turned out they thought I was the NAACP lawyer![9] I was sorry to have to say that I was not. Someday somebody is going to write a wonderful satirical Southern railroad blues about how it feels to be a Negro traveling in the South, even in these days of transition from the old Jim Crow to the new.

When you get off the Panama Limited in New Orleans and leave your fine free deluxe drawing room, being colored, you have to use the Jim Crow part of the Union Station—which is on Rampart Street, that old street of the blues. In the Jim Crow waiting room there is no news stand, no shoe shine stand, no clock, none of the refreshments to be found in the big main waiting room. No mirror or sink in the Men's Room, which is as dirty a toilet as I've ever seen. All of which is enough to give a colored traveler the blues.

In Racial Matters in St. Louis "De Sun Do Move"

May 1, 1954

The Reverend John Jasper, born in slavery, was almost a hundred years old when he died in 1901.[10] He had been preaching for over 50 years and those who heard his sermons never forgot them.

As pastor of the Sixth Mount Zion church in Richmond, Virginia, his congregations overflowed into the street every Sunday. One of his great sermons was called "De Sun Do Move."

I thought about this sermon when I was in St. Louis the other day.

My first memory of St. Louis is as a little boy. My mother and my grandmother were taking me to Mexico City to visit my father. We rode in a coach with other people, white and colored, as far as St. Louis.

But when we changed trains there to go into Arkansas and Texas, we were put into a car with only colored people—my first segregated car, and from that time on, in my mind, St. Louis and Jim Crow were connected.

Once, years later, as a teenager, coming up from Mexico and getting off the train at St. Louis on a very hot summer day, I went up to the soft-drink stand in the center of the station.

I asked for a malted-milk. The clerk looked at me and said, "Are you colored or Mexican?" I said, "I'm colored." He said, "Then I can't serve you."

Again St. Louis and Jim Crow.

Many more years passed. I became a writer with two or three books published. I was invited to give a talk in St. Louis. On that trip I remember a little cubby of a lunch counter hidden away at the far end of the station which was the only place there where Negro travelers might eat.

And the Negro hotels—rather bad ones in those days—were the only public places where one might sleep. But this Spring of our Lord, 1954, when I was invited to speak at the Pine Street Branch YMCA Forum, and I wrote ahead asking the committee to arrange lodgings for me, I was informed that I might make a reservation at any of the downtown hotels.

I made a reservation at the Statler. When I got off "The Spirit of St. Louis" from New York and went to the Statler, I was never more courteously received nor more politely served at any hotel where I've stopped anywhere in the world. All I could say to myself was, "De sun do move!"

At the Statler I found a message from Miss Edith Wilson, the charming Aunt Jemima of the Quaker Oats radio and TV shows, asking me to call her at the Sheraton Hotel, another formerly all-white hostelry nearby. I learned that Miss Eartha Kitt of *New Faces* was also stopping there.[11]

When I went out into the streets, I saw Negro conductors on the street cars, and learned that there were about to be Negro bus drivers. And later on a tour about the city, I saw lovely Negro homes in what had formerly been all white sections of the town.

And before I left, just to see if it were true, I asked for a malted-milk at the station soda fountain, and was served without question. So I departed from St. Louis still saying, "De sun do move!"

St. Louis! The town where Scott Joplin and Tom Turpin used to play ragtime. The town that W. C. Handy made famous in his great song, "The St. Louis Blues." The town where Josephine Baker started out as a $15.00 a week waitress, and ended up in Paris as one of the most glamorous stars of the international theater.[12]

St. Louis, the town that gave a laugh-hungry world the joy of E. Simms Campbell and his rib-tickling cartoons of *Esquire* and King Features fame.

The town where the river boats used to run from New Orleans with Louis Armstrong's horn blasting the night away.[13]

St. Louis, where T. S. Eliot and Marianne Moore came from—and another century sported its money away on Targee Street—whose shades and shadows gave birth to Arna Bontemps's beautiful little novel, *God Sends Sunday* which in turn became the Bontemps-Cullen Broadway musical, *St. Louis Woman* that is now about to become a Hollywood movie.[14]

St. Louis, that old city of river boats and ragtime, jockeys and blues, diamond rings and glamorous women, Josephine Baker and T. S. Eliot, Old Man River and old Jim Crow, and a sun that "do move."

I swear it do!

Old Customs Die Hard

September 29, 1962

I had thought that the custom on the part of whites of automatically equating Negroes with servants had died out in New York. Therefore, I was surprised to read recently in the public prints that the very charming Dr. Jane Wright of the cancer research staff at New York University Medical Center, when paying a social call, had been directed by the doorman of a fashionable apartment house to use the service elevator.

Dr. Wright is not only distinguished in her field, but beautiful as well and always handsomely gowned. Why any doorman would take her for a domestic is beyond me. But old customs die hard. She is brownskin. There was a time in Manhattan when many downtown apartment houses and hotels directed all Negroes to the service entrances.

Are You Delivering Something?

I remember not too many years ago, togged in my best blue suit, I went to an ASCAP meeting at a big Times Square hotel. As a lyric writer, I have been a member of the American Society of Authors and Composers for many years. When I walked up to the elevators and asked the young woman starter where the ASCAP meeting was, she looked at me and inquired rather tartly, "Are you delivering something?" When I replied that I was not delivering anything, she told me where the meeting was and I went up without further incident.

But once upstairs, it occurred to me that since ASCAP has many members of color and some of them (like some of the white song writers) are of the rather tough and profane school of hard boiled old-time show business, such personalities might be inclined to make a scene were they asked brusquely, "Are you delivering something?"

For the sake of racial amity, I thought it wise to go back downstairs, find the manager's office, and report what had happened to me. I did. The manager was most courteous, but evasive, and offered no apology for his employee in charge of elevators. Instead, the manager informed me that they often had pimps, prostitutes, and other undesirable individuals to contend with, and that his staff could, if its members felt the need, inquire as to a person's business in the hotel.

I had already informed the manager that I was associated with ASCAP and by profession a writer. He proceeded to ask me if I had ever read Richard Wright's *Native Son,* and when I said, "Yes," he stated that he thought it a disgraceful book.

"You see the kind of people Richard Wright writes about," he said.

I replied that it seemed to me it was not the kind of people Wright wrote about, but how he wrote about them, that made his novel important. "But," I continued, "so far as I know, there are no Bigger Thomases in ASCAP. Even if there were, it would not be wise of your elevator starter to ask them on the afternoon of a meeting, 'Are you delivering something?'" I informed him that one of our Negro song writers once wrote a song called, "There'll Be Some Changes Made." With that I departed. I have since been in the same hotel many times. No such discourtesies occurred again.

Call to Hostess

Some years ago, before the Supreme Court decision affecting the public schools (I don't believe the court has as yet taken up the question of elevators) my aunt went to visit friends in a West End Avenue apartment house. The doorman informed her, "Servants use the service elevator." My aunt replied, "I don't doubt it," and walked into the lobby to enter the lift. The operator refused to take her up. She then asked him to get the manager. The manager came, but backed up his employee, again directing her (since she is colored) to the servant's car around the corner through the delivery entrance. My aunt had gone to the nearest telephone and called her hostess— who then came down to the lobby to meet her—before she could get upstairs. Her hostess was, of course, most apologetic for the ways of white folks.

At restaurants in New York and other cities about the country, I have noticed lately a subtle form of discrimination-with-a-smile that occurs too often to be coincidental. It is the custom on the part of polite and very gracious headwaiters or dining room hostesses to lead a Negro customer to the least desirable table.

I had occasion a few weeks ago to spend a couple of days in a charming New England inn. Each time I went into the dining room the same thing happened. A smiling young woman led me the first evening at dinner to a table right next to the bus boy's stand in an obscure corner.

In the Kansas City Union Station I was shown past dozens of empty tables to one hard by the kitchen. It even happened in Puerto Rico at a restaurant frequented by white vacationists. The table by the kitchen door. When I asked the headwaiter, who was as brown-skin as I am, if he could not do any better, he grinned and said, "I know what you are thinking. I used to live in New York."

I said, "Then you've had tables in the rear, too, when others are empty." He said, "Yes, I have. Come on, move up." This time he put me at the very front of the restaurant. After he took my order, he discussed the race problem. We decided it is hard to behave like Rev. Martin Luther King.

Jim Crow's Epitaph

December 1, 1962

Now, you take old Jim Crow. I have known him all my life. I met him first when I was just a little small child. Every time I turn a corner, I have met him since.

I have met him down home and I have met him up North, out West, and back East, from New Orleans to New York, Portsmouth to Portland. He don't have to get around, because he is already there, everywhere I go. I do not like Jim Crow.

Jim Crow is a low dog.
Jim Crow is a skunk.
Jim Crow is a buzzard.
Jim Crow is a snake in the grass of democracy.
Jim Crow is a wolf in Uncle Sam's clothing.
He looks like a man but he ain't nothing but a varmint.
Jim Crow is a disgrace to the family, but they won't disown him. (He's
    still white, ain't he?)
I do not like Jim Crow.

In Too Many Doors

He stands in too many doors and says, "You can't come in here!"

He is the principal of too many schools and states, "You cannot send your children here!"

He is the pastor of too many churches that say, "Nay! Here Negroes do not pray!"

He sells too many bus tickets at too many Jim-Crow windows.

He puts me in too many back seats and ushers me into too many balconies at the show.

He is on too many registration boards, daring me to vote.

On Draft Boards

He is on too many draft boards, sending our boys to labor battalions.

He has done throwed too many rocks through my windows, and put too many bombs under my front porches when I moved into a house too near to him.

He writ a letter to Hitler during the war and said, "You are all right with me because you do not like Negroes, either."

Jim Crow is sick in the head. I hear tell he is also ailing in body, as well as in mind. Them peoples in Asia has got him worried almost as much as I got him worried. In a little while the Mau Mau is going to worry him some more.[15] The United Nations bugs him. The Russians is done long ago made him mad.

Wish Him Dead

He is on the verge of nervous prostitution. I wish he would break down and die.

If Jim Crow was to die—Amen!—I would preach his funeral. For that funeral they would not need to hire Reverend Monroe, neither Adam Powell, neither Fosdick nor Billy Graham, Bodie nor Brother Joe Mays. I would take charge.

I would holler louder than Channing Tobias and bellow like Mordecai Johnson.[16] With old Jim Crow laying in his casket, and me standing over him, I would rise and take a deep breath, and say just a few simple words. But them words would be enough.

"Go to Hell"

From standing in the pulpit where I would be standing, I would look dead inside his face, and I would say:

> Jim Crow! Jim Crow! Oh, Jim Crow!
> The Lord has taken you away!
> Jim Crow! Jim Crow!
> You will never again drink
> From no WHITE water fountain
> Whilst I go dry.
> Never again, Jim Crow,
> Will you set up in front of buses

From Washington to New Orleans
Whilst I ride in the back over the wheels.
Never again will you, Jim Crow,
Laying here dead,
Rise up and call me out of my name.
I got you in my power now,
You dirty dog.
And I will preach you to your grave!
Ah-hhh-hhh-hh-h-h! Jim Crow!
You did not know a Negro
Was going to preach your funeral, did you?
Well, I is! Me, just plain old me
Who was made in the image of God
From time eternal, yes, time eternal,
From the clay of the Infinite,
Into whom was breathed the breath of life,
Just to preach your funeral, Jim Crow!
And to consign you to the dust
Where you may rest in peace
Until the world stops spinning around in the universe,
Until this old earth comes to a halt.
So all-of-a-sudden hell-fired quick
That it will fling you, me and everybody
Through the A.M. and P.M. of Judgment
WHAM to the feet of the throne of God!
God will say, "Jim Crow! Get away!
Away! Hie yourself hence!
Make haste—and take your place in hell!"
I'm sorry, but that is what God will say, Jim Crow
So I might as well say it first. Therefore,
It gives me great pleasure, Jim Crow,
To close your funeral with these words—
As the top is shut on your casket,
And the hearse pulls up, outside the door,
As the Dixiecrats[17] wipe their weeping eyes,
The Klan blows its nose,
And every coach on the Southern Railroad
Is draped in mourning,
As South Africa cablegrams sympathies
Whilst the Confederate flag is at half-mast,
Barnett faints and Faubus shakes with grief,[18]
As the pallbearers step forward

And the D.A.R. swoons,[19]
As they prepare to wheel you down the aisle
And on to your eternal rest,
All I can say is, Jim Crow,
GO TO HELL!

Part 3

Fair Play in Dixie

Letter to the South

July 10, 1943

Dear Southern White Folks:

You are as much a problem to me as I am to you, I mean personally and figuratively speaking. For one thing, if it were not for you, I, Langston Hughes, might have a nice Hollywood job, like almost every other respectable American writer (who's white) has at one time or another. But you won't let Hollywood do anything decent with Negroes in pictures, so Hollywood won't hire Negro writers—not even to write about Negroes. They are afraid in Hollywood that we won't write the kind of scripts you like down South, so they won't hire us at all.

You, dear Southern white folks, are also a problem to me personally even way up here in New York. You come up here and start spreading the ugly old Jim Crowism you have down home all over Manhattan Island. You even try to get the Broadway theaters to segregate me where I have never been segregated before. You are not satisfied to keep segregation down South. Before the war, you even took it to Paris and Rome. Now, you take it abroad in the Army.

Another thing you do is bring your old prejudice about not wanting to work beside a Negro up to Jersey and Detroit and even Seattle, Washington. You start anti-Negro strikes and riots. You hold back liberal employers, and keep liberal unions from permitting me to have jobs that I might otherwise have. I have a hard enough time getting a job, without you gumming up the works from Hollywood to Hoboken.

I tell you, you are really a problem to me. Still being personal, I, as a writer, might have had many scripts performed on the radio if it were not for you. The radio stations look at a script about Negro life that I write and tell me, "Well, you see, our programs are heard down South, and the South might not like this." You keep big Negro stars like Ethel Waters and Duke Ellington off commercial programs, because the sponsors are afraid the South might not buy their products if Negro artists appear regularly on their series.[1]

Dumbest Congressmen

You are really a problem to me, dear Southern White Folks. You send the dumbest congressmen to Congress—congressmen who don't seem to realize the world is round, or that there are human beings on the other side, too, and that we have to get along with them after the war is over. But not to speak of the other side, your congressmen don't seem to realize either that we all have to get along here at home if we are to have a peaceful and happy America. Some of them red-bait and Negro-bait and labor-bait and Roosevelt-bait so much that I don't see how they have any time left to think about the state of the nation, or your welfare.

But what I am really concerned about is them in relation to me. They keep the anti-poll tax bill from being passed, and they kill every anti-lynching bill. I really do not want to be lynched. If a law would help keep me from so being, I would like to see that law passed. But you-all don't care anything about a Negro being lynched down South, do you?

Dear Southern White Folks, your Jim Crow cars I do not like at all. I do not like your Jim Crow waiting rooms in the stations where I have to stand patiently at the ticket window until all the white folks at the opposite window are served before I can even buy a ticket. I do not like having to sit next to the baggage car and not be able to go to the diner to eat when I get hungry. I do not like the white baggage-car men and the news butchers and the conductors and any other train employees sitting in whatever extra space there may be in my Jim Crow car, smoking, spitting, and cussing in front of colored ladies.

Post-War Problem

YES, I SAID LADIES! I know you say "colored women" down your way. And I know you never address a colored man as Mr.—which I think is stupid. And I know you take pride in being just as rude and ill-bred as you can be to Negroes in public places. But I do not care so much about your manners as I care about you. Dear Southern White Folks, you are cutting off your nose to spite your face.

All the bad things you do to Negroes, Latin America knows about in spite of the censorship. Asia knows, too. Do you think your allies who are colored trust you? They do not! And in the post-war world, you are going to need that trust. You are terribly simple-minded if you think you can live on this earth by yourself.

We may be problems to each other, but for your good and mine, from Beaumont to Detroit, we ought to get together and straighten our problems out. Certainly, I personally would be willing to talk sense with you and try to come to some solution because, God knows, YOU ARE A PROBLEM TO ME, dear Southern White Folks.

Hold Tight! They're Crazy-White!

March 11, 1944

Some white folks have gone crazy from being white. (Not all, but some.) They are under the delusion that they were born to run the world and everybody in it. This seems to be particularly true in Dixie, Hitler's Germany, and in South Africa. I am forced to the conclusion that they are mad, wrong in the head, abnormal, and need to be psychoanalyzed. Certainly, I know something is very definitely wrong with our own white folks down South.

Mr. Mark Ethridge in his now famous Birmingham statement, implied that not all the armies in the world could make Southern white people act right toward their Negro fellow-citizens. If that be true, it would seem to me that these strange white people reckon without regard for the forces of history, the dynamics of progress, God, the C.I.O., and Negroes themselves. But a people who are mad are inclined to be irrational, to ignore reality, and to talk out of their heads. Mr. John Temple Graves, Mr. David Cohn, and others who agree with Mr. Ethridge may be sane themselves, but they are acting as spokesmen for a group of people who obviously are not, and whose standard of racial conduct cannot be measured by any civilized norm.[2]

It does not make sense to deny Negroes the vote and then call Negroes bad citizens when they have no chance to be good ones. It does not make sense to deny Negroes equal educational facilities and then berate the Negroes as being ignorant. It does not make sense to intimidate, brutalize, and hinder the progress of a people, and then blame that people for not progressing more rapidly. It does not make sense to want to call all Negroes by their first names, but expect to be called Mr. yourself. It does not make sense to eat the food that Negroes cook, yet refuse to eat with Negroes.

Insanity in Action

E. Franklin Frazier, the distinguished sociologist, says in *The Pathology of Race Prejudice,* that, "We are forced to regard certain manifestations of race prejudice as abnormal behavior." He contends that in our Southland, "Race prejudice shows precisely the same characteristics as those ascribed to insanity." And that the Negro-complex on the part of prejudiced whites "has the same intense emotional tone that characterizes insane complexes."[3]

These statements I believe to be true, for I have on a number of occasions seen this insanity in action. Once a white man sat down at a table with me in a dining car in Texas. When he looked across the table and saw that I was colored, he jumped up as though he had sat down with a lion, and ran out of the car crying that I was a Negro.

Another time, there being no news-stand in the colored waiting room of the Savannah, Georgia, railroad station, I went into the white waiting room to buy a paper. When I started out a cop said to me, "Negroes can't come in and out that front door."

"How then can I get out?" I asked. "I just came in that way."

"You can't go out that way," he said. So I had to go all around by way of the train sheds and the railroad tracks to get out, which made no sense at all, so far as I could see, since I was already at the door when the cop came up.

This domination-complex which many Southern whites have toward Negroes seems definitely pathological. I wish some big foundation like the Carnegie fund or the Julius Rosenwald foundation would put up some money to psychoanalyze their heads, and help to straighten them out a bit because, as we know, they will not listen to reason on the subject of the Negro. I figure the reason they will not listen is because they have no reason to reason with. Their color-neuroses have got them down. They need help to get back to their right minds. Our various boards of public health ought to do something about them, because they are dangerous.

Maybe if they could just talk out their problems with someone, conversation would help, since a part of psychoanalysis is a kind of frank outpouring of one's inner fears. The Negro is continually talking and writing frankly about his problems. The Negro press acts as a great psychological safety valve for colored folks who thus get off racial steam. To suppress or censor Negro papers, as some whites wish to do, would be to drive colored folks crazier than they already are. Hitler and Hirohito would be tickled to death if we all went mad over here, both whites and blacks. The fascists would love to see America go up in a series of race-riots harmful to the war. Such riots would not make sense to me, but they would to the fascists—and, I guess, to some local white folks, too. It's awful to be crazy-white.

Nazi and Dixie Nordics

March 10, 1945

"I doubt if education will change them," said an American schoolman who speaks German and has traveled much in Germany. We were talking of the Hitlerites. "Nazi ideologies are too deeply engrained to change them with books."

"They are certainly fanatics," reports a soldier back from the European front, who has seen Nazi prisoners.

"They have killed and tortured my people," said a Jewish American of

German background. "How to get that cruelty out of them will be a problem after the war."

"The Germans are the victims of a mass psychosis," says an American sociologist. "It will take drastic measures to control them when peace comes."

These people were talking about Germans in Germany. To a Negro, they might just as well have been speaking of white Southerners in Dixie. Our local Nordics have a mass psychosis, too, when it comes to race. As the Hitlerites treat the Jews, so they treat the Negroes, in varying degrees of viciousness ranging from the denial of educational opportunities to the denial of employment, from buses that pass Negroes by to jailers who beat and torture Negro prisoners, from the denial of the ballot to the denial of the right to live.

What to Do with Dixie?

Just as the allied administrators of a conquered Germany will be puzzled as to what to do about the Nazi character, so American Negro citizens are puzzled as to what to do about the Dixie character. When a whole people are accustomed to kicking another group of people around—in Germany the Jews, in America the Negroes—education seems a very weak and long-range remedy indeed, although it must certainly be a part of any solution.

Unconditional surrender and armed intervention will go a long way in controlling German behavior toward what few Jews are left there. But nobody is confronting our Southerners with Unconditional Decency as regards their Negro neighbors.

How are we going to get rid of the stupidities of Jim Crow in the South? What are we going to do with a people who want all the best things for themselves, just because they are white—the best seats on the buses, the best coaches on the trains, the best schools, the best jobs—just because they are white?

What are we going to do with folks who wish to continue to deny Negroes the ballot—as the Germans denied it to the Jews in Europe? Who wish to continue to segregate Negroes as the Nazis ghettoized Jews in Poland? Who wish to continue to force our Red Cross to mark Negro blood AA—*Afro-American*—as things Jewish are labeled *Yude* in Germany? What are we going to do with people like that here in America?

Our Own Bigots

Such people certainly do not believe in Americanism. They do not believe in democracy. They do not believe in law. They do not believe in social decency. They do not even believe in courtesy.

What are we going to do with the millions of white Americans of the South who pay our United States Constitution not the least mind when it comes to democratic treatment of their Negro fellow-citizens?

I think our Congress had well take up that problem, along with the problem of what to do about Nazi Germany. The two problems have much in common—Berlin and Birmingham. The Jewish people and the Negro people both know the meaning of Nordic supremacy. We have both looked into the eyes of terror.

Klansmen and Storm Troopers are brothers under the skin. The Grand Kleagle of the Klan has already stated to the press that there will be 5,000,000 Ku Kluxers ready to reorganize their Klaverns after the war. That will be quite dangerous for Negroes—but it will be much more dangerous to America as a whole, especially labor, Jews, Catholics, and the foreign born. We had better consider that problem now. It is just as important as what to do about Germany.

Democracy, like charity, really begins at home. With a mote in one's own eye, it is hard to remove the beam from another's. A general eye-cleaning from Dortmund to Dixie wouldn't do any harm. The whole English-speaking Caucasian world, from white Australia to Jim Crow South Africa, needs its eyes opened. They are full of the dust of race prejudice. Our own American Southland is almost blind as a result.

Where can we find a specialist to treat eyes clouded by Nordic "superiority?" We intend to lead Germany, but it is not easy for the near-blind to lead the blind. We must do something about our own bigots, too, and soon!

Fair Play in Dixie

March 17, 1945

I regret to say it, but so far as I can see, the Southern majority in our country has no sense of fair play at all. For instance down in Dixie, Southern whites are constantly accusing Negroes of being ignorant, yet at the same time, they constantly oppose the Negro's having an equal share of public school funds so that he may learn. It is not fair to call a man ignorant when everything possible is done to keep him so by the ones who do the name-calling.

Southern whites say Negroes are uncultured. But if Southerners wanted Negroes to be cultured they would not close the state universities to them, nor the public libraries. They would not bar us out of all theaters in Washington. They would not try so hard to keep us from getting culture. To claim our lack of culture as a reason for treating us as low-caste, then to prevent us from having access to the avenues of culture, is hardly fair play.

The Klan Idea

The Ku Klux Klan idea probably had much to do with Dixie's current way of not playing fair with colored citizens. The Klan, as you know, rode in masked bands, hooded and sheeted so nobody would know them. Gangs of thirty, forty, fifty, would take an unarmed defenseless Negro out in the woods and beat, tar and feather, or lynch him. For so many men, masked at that, to jump on one Negro was hardly fair. The present Klan's chief says they are going to revive the Klan after the war. An enlightened prospect!

In little every-day matters such as civil decency and common courtesy, the Southern white majority is most uncivil to Negroes. For some strange reason, most Dixie whites think it is all right for them to be impolite to a colored person, yet they expect courtesy in return. For example, south of Washington, most whites will not call a colored man *Mr.* Or a colored woman *Mrs.* But they expect colored people to address them properly. In some sections of the South, whites still expect Negroes to step all the way off the sidewalk when they pass. In railway stations, they expect colored passengers to wait indefinitely at the Jim Crow ticket window until *all* the whites have been served on the opposite side. That is hardly fair. Certainly, it is a most provincial conception of courtesy, and slightly lopsided, to say the least.

It is most regrettable that this lopsided idea of undemocratic living has been permitted by our Federal government to spread all over America and the world by way of official Jim Crow in our Army, Navy and Red Cross. Of course, our government knows that it is in no sense fair play to take the same amount of taxes from a Negro citizen as from whites, then to limit that Negro citizen's son or brother largely to labor battalions in the armed services.

There is no democracy or fair play in General Almond's reputed statement to the effect that he never foresees the day when colored officers may command whites.[4] Yet, why not? Whose money supports the army and navy? *Ours*—as well as any one else's. Who pays the General's salary? We do. Why is it fair for him, *white,* to be always on top—and me, *black,* with never a foreseeable chance to share command with him? Where is the fair play there?

A National Problem

The South's narrow conception of race relations is a national problem. It affects every citizen from Dallas to Denver, from Washington to Seattle. The transit system in our national capitol, for instance, gives us an excuse for not hiring Negro motormen or conductors though most of their employees were born in the South. The implication is that the Southern conception of fair play is so limited that the South does not want to permit a Negro citizen to be a streetcar conductor *on a car that runs over streets for which Negroes also pay taxes.*

That is in our national capitol, the heart of this citadel of democracy. But when the South carries its Jim Crow ideas to London, Paris, Melbourne, Naples—sets up Jim Crow clubs and canteens for our soldiers of color in lands that never practiced such rude goings-on themselves—that is really Dixie's bad manners and lack of fair play too far afield for our national honor to countenance.

I swear, I am personally ashamed that our high military officials permit the rest of the world to get so provincial an idea of our democracy! This U.S.A. is my country, and I hate to see it represented in England and France and Italy by Americans who are not polite enough to be courteous to colored people, and who are so unscientifically educated as to insist on having dried blood plasma marked *black* or *white*—as if there was the least difference. Such goings-on in front of our allies embarrass me!

Dear Old Southland

February 15, 1947

Funny thing about the South, but in any country it is different. Andalusian Spain is quite unlike Northern Spain. Southern Spain is the land of the flamenco (which really means blues) and gypsies. It is the land of the Southern slur and drawl. Northern Spaniards all speak like Bostonians, and walk faster than the Southerners.

Provence in France and the Cote d'Azur are sections very different from the North. Even the food is different. The Soviet Union is like that, too. When you get way down South in Georgia on the Black Sea, you find folks more easy-going—even about Communism. Certainly there are nuances and qualities about our American South that immediately strike a visitor from the North as slightly different, to say the least. Birmingham and Boston certainly have opposite folkways. For instance, the South is:

South's Doorway Loungers

THE LAND OF LOUNGING DOORWAYS. As far as the eye can tell, more people lounge in doors down South than in any other part of the Union. You start to go into a store and you have to weave your way through several people standing in the doorway. You wish to enter or leave a shoe-shine stand and you have to say, "Pardon me, please," to somebody sitting on the door-sill and somebody else leaning against the jamb looking out in the street. As to cafes and bars, at least six people seem to be always standing right in the entrance. Down South both humans and dogs seem to love doorways. Also the South is:

THE LAND OF THE POSITIVE NEGATIVE. If you ask a clerk in a drug store if he has any soap, he is likely to say, "I *sure* don't." Ask a student if he has finished his class assignment and the answer is likely to be, "I *sure* haven't." Ask any one if he has seen the latest *March Of Time*. If not, the answer will be, "I *sure* didn't." Southerners are very positive about their negatives, which adds a quaint verbal charm to the language. Quaint, too, but not nearly so intriguing is the fact that the South is:

A Jumble of Opposites

THE LAND WHERE SOMETHING ALWAYS DOESN'T WORK about almost everything. Door-knobs have a habit of coming off in your hand when you go to open them. Toilets have a way of keeping on flushing and not stopping. Windows get up and won't come down, or get down and won't come up. Trains run later in the South and more off schedule than anywhere else in the U.S.A. There are also more party line telephones, and somebody else is almost always using the line. Slightly more serious, however, is the fact that the South is:

THE LAND OF BLACK AND WHITE AND THE CURTAIN BETWEEN. Sometimes but a hair divides. Again it is a curtain—and an iron curtain, at that. There are black seats on buses, black coaches on trains, black toilets, black schools, black water fountains, and even black booths in record shops for playing records—often designated not by a COLORED sign but by a picture of Marian Anderson!

Even the intellectuals and liberals who practice social equality are divided by the curtain. A group of Southern Negroes and Southern whites will take tea together and discuss the race problem on a very liberal and intellectual level—meaning every other word they say. But as soon as the whites leave the house, or campus, or wherever they are, the Negroes break down and say what they really think and feel. I imagine the whites do, too, when they get out in their car.

Land of the Great Evasion

THE SOUTH IS THE LAND OF WHAT IS ISN'T. It is the land of the great evasion. The land of the positive negative. The land of doing things backward. A Punch and Judy land, a tragi-comedy place where human beings block their own doorways.

I wish I were a Southerner so I could understand the South. To an outsider it is a fascinating place, full of contradictions, personal courtesies and mass rudeness, well-meaning kindnesses and general incompetences, good food and bad service, wide doors, not wide enough for both standees and passersby, colored folks and white folks and a whole lot of mulattoes between, an iron curtain and a hair-line fence, separate water fountains and relatives in common. The South is really a wonderful place where Alice-in-Wonderland walks upside down.

But then the South is like that everywhere—in Spain, in France, in the U.S.S.R. Even in China where the Cantonese have nothing in common with the folks from up North in Peking. There is something about the South all

over the world that makes what *isn't* is, and what *is* isn't. Why? Do I know?
I *sure* don't! *Do you?*

The Death of Bilbo

August 30, 1947

Senator Bilbo is gone. Within a few hours after the news of his death came
over the radio, I saw gaily colored streamers pasted across the mirrors of a
Harlem Italian-owned bar announcing in holiday mood: BILBO IS DEAD! I
gathered that at least two American minorities had teamed up to rejoice.

However, it is usually the custom to say something nice about the de-
ceased, once dead, no matter how bad the person might have been in life.
So instead of joining the Italian-Negro-Jewish-American jubilation that is
taking place, I will mourn the old fighter from Mississippi who has recently
departed this life. And I will say something good about him.

Bilbo was by in-direction one of our greatest allies in our fight for political freedom in the United States. By his being so determined that Negroes
should not vote in Mississippi, he simply made Negroes, not only in Mississippi but throughout the South, that much more *determined to vote.* By attacking us so crudely and rudely, he simply made us *fight back the harder.* By
attempting legislation to send us back to Africa, he simply made us bent,
bound, and determined *to stay here.* By attacking Italians and Jews, Bilbo
simply helped the Negro by giving us *other allies* against him and his political philosophy.

Made Them Fight Back

Future historians will probably conclude that Bilbo did the cause of democracy more good than harm for, by fighting so hard against democracy,
he made many hitherto apathetic and sleeping friends of democracy wake
up and fight back. By fighting so hard against the ballot for Negroes, Bilbo
made thousands of Negroes who had never given the ballot a thought suddenly have a great hankering and longing to vote. By insisting that the ballot should be only for white folks, Bilbo made the ballot seem like something greatly to be desired by colored folks. After Bilbo's recent fight against
the right to vote, more Negroes than ever before in history down South made
up their minds to *vote* just to spite Bilbo. Thus was made easier the hard work
of organizing Negro political clubs in the South.

There are those who called the late Mr. Bilbo a rat. Taken literally, there are
always millions of rats around. And it would be sensible to rid our world of

rats. But almost nobody pays any attention to rats as long as they stay in the alley and come out only at night. But when a rat comes in the house in broad daylight and jumps in the crib and bites a baby, then mama and papa get all heated up about rats and begin a campaign of extermination. Bilbo figuratively jumped up in the crib and bit the baby—and not just Mose, but Isadore and Giovanni, too. Given time, he might have started on Patrick. And he did not sneak around in the night to bite. Bilbo worked in broad daylight.

"Frank—and Loud"

Therein lay Bilbo's value to the democratic cause. He was frank—and loud. Some cartoonists pictured the late Mr. Bilbo as a snake. But at least he was a rattle snake. He gave warning of his intentions by making plenty of racket. He was not a silent snake in the grass striking your heel unawares. He gave you a chance to fight back by coming up hissing and shaking his own tail violently. He bared his fangs for all to see. Bilbo did not shout democracy out of one side of his mouth and spit Jim Crow out of the other. He stuck out his tongue for the world to observe how closely it resembled a swastika. He said he believed in white supremacy.

Mr. Bilbo did not say he loved Negroes and that all men are made in the image of God, then proceed to bar Negroes out of everything from church to cabaret. Mr. Bilbo quite frankly wanted us all out of the U.S.A. Mr. Bilbo did not give a paltry few thousands to Negro colleges while giving millions to white colleges. He did not give a few hand-picked Negroes "good" jobs while keeping the black masses all the way down the economic ladder. Bilbo did not give anything to Negro colleges and he did not believe in any Negroes having good jobs. He did not shadow-box. He tried his best to upper-cut in the clear.

That is what made Bilbo a good enemy—such a good enemy that he became an ally for democracy by furnishing such a broad target, such a violent rallying point, that he pulled together against him many sleepy forces that nobody else had as yet succeeded in awakening to battle for the protection of democracy. The "good" white folks of the South who for years have been patting Negroes on the head and saying, "Now, now, Dr. So-and-So, be patient, it isn't time yet for you Negras to vote. Here's a hundred dollar check for your Old Folks Home." Those "good" white folks lulled to sleep the democratic urge. That is why they hated Bilbo, too, because in his ferocity, in his very fight against democratic decency, Bilbo made millions of people, black and white, realize for the first time the value of the true American heritage.

The Sunny South

March 6, 1948

After snow, snow, snow in New York, then running into the heaviest sleet storm in a quarter of a century in North Carolina, it was sort of wonderful to have my Southern lecture tour end up in St. Petersburg, Florida, for a couple of days with the sun shining like mid-summer and the mercury at 85. What a Paradise Land the Sunny South—if only it were not for Jim Crow!

And what sweet and wonderful people, the colored people of the South! Living as they do under the pressure of constant bigotry and insult, the Negroes of the South have about them nevertheless an air of decency and dignity that I do not believe any similarly segregated group has anywhere else in the world. Teachers trained at Columbia and the University of Chicago teaching in crowded, ill-equipped schools, lighting up their classrooms with a sweetness and a warmth that could be an example of teacher-pupil relationships to pedagogs everywhere!

White and Colored

But maybe it is because I was born in the West and I have lived in the North most of my life that every time I have to go into a Jim Crow coach it rubs me the wrong way. And every time I see those Southern signs WHITE and COL-ORED—and find that the whites have the best go—the biggest and brightest and cleanest waiting rooms in stations, the white covered tables in terminal restaurants while we have barren counter if any place at all to eat—I get mad.

Certainly evil begets evil. When I went into the dining car in South Carolina and was directed to an end table and as soon as I sat down the white steward came up and rudely jerked a curtain between myself and the rest of the coach, I began to wish an atom bomb would suddenly wipe all the white people diners in that coach off the face of the earth.

A nice-looking old white lady—probably a Northern liberal—came into the dining car. Suddenly the train lurched and she almost fell, grabbing the Jim Crow curtain for support. I found myself against my will wishing that she would break her leg. Immediately I was ashamed of myself, but as Horace Cayton pointed out in his column recently, it is very hard to sublimate one's feelings in the face of open and expressed prejudice.[5]

As the waiters passed me serving fish to the white passengers in the coach, I kept thinking in spite of my Christian upbringing, "I hope they choke on the bones!"

No wonder race relations are in such a bad way in the South. No wonder hatred spreads like an evil mould beneath the sun. No wonder there is an uneasy peace down there between the whites and the Negroes. How could it be otherwise in a land where white Americans will pass without shame Negroes segregated behind a curtain in a dining car? A land where whites will occupy three or four clean air-conditioned coaches on a train with plenty of empty seats while ALL the Negroes on the train are segregated into one-half of a baggage car that is the Jim Crow coach.

The Jim Crow Car

I got on such a coach at midnight in Petersburg, Virginia. It was crowded to capacity, bags and baggage in the aisle. It was full of smoke, women and little babies coughing in the stale smoke-filled air. I asked the conductor if I could get a Pullman on into New York. He said I could, so having the money to afford it, I took my bag and went through the train to the Pullman cars. On the way I passed through three white day coaches. In the first coach there were exactly eight people, in the second thirteen, and in the third about the same number. All that empty space, many empty seats in the white cars—but ALL the Negro day-coach passengers crowded into less than a whole coach—the Jim Crow car! Many of them were inter-state passengers, too, going from the South to Baltimore, Philadelphia, and New York.

That, for me, is what takes the sunshine out of the sunny South. Jim Crow puts a cloud over all the land, all the people. Evil begets evil—and an evil mist is rising out of the Jim Crow South, seeping across the nation, seeping across the world of democratic relations, seeping into the halls of Congress, into the Department of State, into the rooms where treaties are written and diplomacies are planned, making the papers stick together and the ink blur.

So many of our government officials in Washington come out of the Jim Crow South, no wonder our Department of State, the Army, and the Department of Justice find it hard to cope with democracy!

Far from Living Up to Its Name, Dixie Has Neither Manners nor Shame

April 26, 1952

To say that, "It's the same old South," is not entirely true. During and since the War, racially speaking, in some ways the South has changed greatly for the better. In other very serious ways, it has not changed at all. On the daily level of ordinary living, insofar as race relations go, the South seems about the same to me as it was a quarter of a century ago. There is still the same old disregard of the Negro as a normal human being needing the same respect and self-respect as other people. Dixie must think we "ain't human."

Having twenty minutes between trains in Houston in the early morning, I asked the woman at the Information Desk where I might get a cup of coffee. Without batting an eye and with no shame whatsoever, she pointed at the brightly lighted modern cafe in the station and said, "You-all just walk right straight through the dining room and back into the kitchen. You will be served there."

When I said that I was not used to eating in the kitchen in public restaurants, she simply turned her head away. Had I been a citizen of Houston directing a stranger in a railroad station to the kitchen to eat, I would have been ashamed, but not this Southern white woman. She did not even blush.

I remember in another station asking where I could get a shine. Although there was a shoeshine stand in the white waiting room, I was told, "The nearest shine stand for colored is six blocks up the street." My informant was not in the least embarrassed to separate me from all other Americans in relation to such ordinary travel conveniences as a shine.

Therein, I think, lies the tragedy of the American South—that it is simply taken for granted Negroes neither expect nor deserve the simple courtesies or conveniences of ordinary everyday life. The shadiest park benches have signs on them WHITE ONLY, if indeed Negroes are permitted in the park at all. Ice water fountains in department stores are marked FOR WHITE. Booths in record shops are often for the use of WHITE ONLY—Negroes are expected to buy records without playing them. Taxi cabs in most Southern cities are WHITE and COLORED. Try to find a COLORED cab in the downtown business districts, and usually it is just about impossible. At a New Orleans railroad station this spring, I waited an hour for a COLORED cab. A half dozen WHITE cabs were parked at the taxi stand, but I could not ride in any of them. And the white taxi drivers did not care whether I reached my destination in the city on time or not.

From all I can gather in the South, the average white person does not give a tinker's damn whether Negroes have available to them the same public treatment as is given an alien enemy. Any white Nazi prisoner during the war could drink out of a WHITE fountain. But not me. I still can't—and I was born in Missouri. And the shame of it is that nobody is ashamed.

If white Southerners were ashamed of all the FOR WHITE signs dotting their landscape, they would tear them down. I saw such signs when I first went South in the 1920's. I see them still there today in 1952. And I haven't yet seen a white Southerner blush for their own sakes. They do not need to blush for me. The discourtesies, the inhumanity, and the civic backwardness of such signs are not mine. I didn't make them. I don't believe in them. I would consider myself anti-American, anti-Christian, and anti-human if I did. So the folks to blush are the ones who keep such signs on display.

FOR WHITE ONLY should be changed to FOR SHAME ONLY. A dog can sit on a WHITE bench in a WHITE park and, if his legs are long enough, lick water out of a WHITE fountain. I cannot. I will be put in jail. My color makes me less than a dog to those who run the South—from taxi cabs to governor's mansions. Whoever said or wrote that the South is the home of genteel culture, and that white Southerners are charming, gracious, well-mannered people, must be Southern. To me, Negro, with few exceptions they are the rudest, crudest, most ill-mannered people I have ever seen anywhere on the face of the earth—and I have been around the world.

The white South does not live up to its name as a land of grace and good breeding. It is callous and boorish to anyone who is not white. The kindest thing a Negro can say to Dixie is, "Shame on you—until you learn to be ashamed of yourself!"

The Quaint, Queer, Funny Old South Has Its Ways

April 24, 1954

The quaint, queer, funny old South is, racially speaking, still quaint, queer, and funny today.

On its railroads, even the whistle-stops where there's no station, only a platform, have a sign at one end, WHITE, and the other end, COLORED— although there is nothing there but boards and open air.

But white Americans and Negro Americans are not even supposed to stand together. Such quaint, queer, funny, antiquated ways amaze me. I swear they do! I never saw the like anywhere in the world, and I have been all around the world.

Changing trains in Flomaton, Florida, on a rainy night, Negro and white passengers were standing out of the rain beneath the main portico of the station waiting for the train which was due at any moment.

A white station official came out and told all the Negroes, including my-self, that we could not stand there. We would have to go around to the little COLORED waiting room at the far end of the station.

A Negro sailor and a white sailor apparently were traveling together, so together they went through the rain around to the side door of the COL-ORED waiting room. In a few minutes the white official appeared there and told the white sailor he could not stay in the COLORED waiting room.

He would have to go back to the white side. The sailor left his Negro buddy and went out into the rain again. Such irrational behavior I have never seen anywhere on earth except in the American South. Such strange people live down there!

When I got off the early morning train in Miami, there were no colored taxis at the station, and the regular cabs would not haul Negro passengers. I said to the white cab driver, "I thought I had heard Miami had become a liberal city of late. What's the matter?"

The taxi driver said, "I don't know, some kind of regulation, I can't haul you."

There were several colored travelers waiting for cabs, with a dozen white cabs standing idle. The redcaps were of no help. Finally I gave my redcap a dime and prevailed upon him to go inside and phone for a taxi for me.

At last a Negro cab came, pulling up away out in the street, rather than at the station platform. Such strange funny people in the South, I swear there are! I asked the Negro driver why he did not come up to the station entrance.

He said, "How did I know where I was to come? Somebody just phoned for a cab to come to the station. I'm at the station, ain't I?" which seemed to me a rather quaint idea of service.

He slammed my baggage in and pulled away as if he were mad having to come to the station at all. He made no effort to take any of the other colored passengers in his cab. For all I know, they may still be standing there, all those white taxis around. What's this I keep reading in the Northern papers about how Miami has changed?

The COLORED waiting room in the station I was in is a disgrace and a shame. And there was nobody at the COLORED ticket window for the longest time on the day when I went to get my seat reservation to come North. (I have always marveled at the patience of Negro travelers at those COLORED ticket windows, where a ticket-seller might show up when he has nothing better to do.)

On the train leaving Miami for New York, every last living Negro coach traveler had been assigned to the front car, the COLORED car, although most of us were interstate passengers. I walked all through the other cars and did not see a colored soul.

Apparently neither the law nor the Supreme Court mean a thing to the railroads leaving Miami. But the radios down there are blaring with high flown proclamations about democracy and the Free World, etc., etc., etc., all day every day. Funny, funny South!

Such things go on down South every day right now in 1954 without the least shame, while our statesmen are telling the rest of the world how to behave democratically.

Not long ago, when I asked in the railroad station in Houston, Texas, where I might get something to eat, the white lady Information Clerk said, "Walk right through the main dining room and back in the kitchen and you can get something to eat." She did not even blush as she said it.

When I said, "I am not accustomed to eating in the kitchen in public places," she just shrugged and turned away.

The shameless old, funny old, quaint, queer, bad-mannered, old South. I really think when Secretary Dulles gets through flying around the world teaching democracy to foreigners, he ought to make a little speaking trip through the South, and start teaching our white folks there how to be democratic, too—or at least good-mannered, and sensible.[6] They seem so foolish now.

Concerning a Great Mississippi Writer and the Southern Negro

May 26, 1956

I wonder what will happen to Mr. William Faulkner, the famous, white writer from Mississippi, the next time he goes to get a passport to travel abroad, now that he has allegedly said in the public prints that he would take up arms against his own government in case worse came to worse down South.[7] Will Mr. Faulkner get a passport? Paul Robeson had his passport taken away from him for allegedly saying something not nearly so "subversified," so Mr. Robeson now cannot leave the U.S.A. to sing abroad.[8] In the case of Mr. Faulkner, I am not suggesting, nor do I wish that the government take away his passport. As far as I am concerned, Mr. Faulkner can go to the moon, Mars or Venus if he wants to travel. In fact, the farther away he goes the better—so that he might get away from us Negroes who upset him so badly. The last thing I ever like to do myself is upset anyone.

So distinguished a man and so great a writer as William Faulkner, I hate to disturb under any circumstances. Personally, I respect genius, and I respect sincerity. I believe Mr. Faulkner is an excellent writer and a sincere citizen. He is not a political demagogue talking for votes. So when he says what he says, he really means what he says. But WHY he says what he says is not clear.

Doesn't he want me to go to school ever in life with the rest of the Americans in Mississippi? Am I a varmint or something that he wants me, colored, to wait and wait outside the gate to the good life, while everybody else white, Mexican, Oriental, native and foreign born, Jew or Gentile, go to the University of Mississippi if they want to but me? Does Mr. Faulkner think I'm simple? If so, why does he want to keep me that way? He can write some noble words sometimes. He got the Nobel Prize. I thought he loved humanity. But I thought humanity included me. I still think that, even if Mr. Faulkner marks me out. I refuse to leave the human race, neither will I leave Mississippi, nor the U.S.A. just because Mr. Faulkner says me Nay!

I think, regrettably for American literature, he has blowed his top. But if he thinks I am going to blow my top in return, then I know his wig is gone! Which is not a very dignified way of saying that he must be a little disturbed, a little off his psyche. I am really sorry! Mr. Faulkner ought to be colored for just a week in his home state, Mississippi, and then see what would happen. If he gets that upset over being white, what would happen to him if he were black—especially after making such statements? I know what would happen. He would be in jail, else investigated by Senator Eastland's committee, surveyed by the FBI, and called all the names in the book by the patriotic editorial writers who damned Josephine Baker to hell and gone for exaggerating a little about lynchings shortly before the white gentry of Mr. Faulkner's state dropped little Emmett Till in the river with an iron wheel tied to his feet.[9] Suppose Mr. Faulkner was Emmett Till's mother? Do you reckon he'd choose sides so gallantly against the Supreme Court's moving racial decency up to a snail's pace? "All deliberate speed" is hardly rushing matters, is it? It's been almost 100 years since slavery and Mississippi hasn't gotten very far yet, racially speaking.

In my opinion the people who are not ready for democracy are the Southern whites, not the Negroes. Without wishing to boast, I can't help but believe that the Negroes are twice as intelligent as they are, twice as clean, twice as moral, and twice almost everything else—except as simple.

The Same Old Fight All Over Again in Dixie

July 13, 1957

Once more the South prepares to fight against the Negro. With the Civil Rights Bill facing the Senate, the daily press reports Senator Richard B. Russell, Democrat of Georgia, as saying on the floor of Congress, "There are not enough jails to hold the people of the South who will today oppose the use of raw Federal power to forcibly commingle white and Negro children in the same schools and places of public entertainment."[10]

Such behavior has been going on for a long time, this Southern blocking of Negro progress. It began in slavery days when any Negro attempts at freedom were met with the whip and the gun and the Bible.

But slavery times are almost a hundred years gone, and freedom in theory is almost a century old. Why do so many Southern white people still behave in the same old-fashioned way, still talk and act as if social philosophies, Negro achievements, and world aspirations had not advanced beyond the 18th Century? Is Senator Russell of Georgia an uneducated moron, a vicious monster, or merely a wily politician? Logic and kindness both impel me to incline toward the latter view. Surely the Senator has been to school and is not a moron. Surely the United States Senate would not permit a vicious monster to occupy a seat in its August body. So the gentleman from Georgia must be playing politics and aiming for the support of the wood hat vote.

Now, that is all very well for the gentleman from Georgia. But there is a question of morality involved. Are the votes that send a man to the Senate worth the betrayal of one's own morality? Surely Senator Russell does not think it right that children be deprived of decent schooling simply because they are not white. And surely the solon from Dixie does not wish to continue to harm the United States in the eyes of the civilized world by appealing publicly to the most antiquated of race prejudices, in defiance of decent thinking everywhere. I know nothing of Senator Russell's background or financial status. But could it be that he so badly needs his Senate job in order to live and eat, that he must stoop to seeking to warp the lives of colored children in order to continue to draw his senatorial salary? I can think of no other reason for a man of his standing saying the things the newspapers report him as saying. Unless he is disturbed.

The word "disturbed" is used to cover a multitude of sins these days. A child who shoots his mama, papa, and all his brothers and sisters is described as "disturbed." A teenage girl who elopes with a middle-aged man is said to be "disturbed." A young married man with a nice wife and family who goes around strangling and raping school girls is defended in court by a plea of being mentally "disturbed." And I would agree that perhaps all such people are "disturbed." Folks in their right minds usually do not behave so strangely. Neither do most folks I have met in my lifetime talk and act as does Senator Russell of Georgia. Most people I have known believe in living and let live, and allowing children to go to school wherever there are schools.

There is no record stating that when the first Negroes were landed at Jamestown, Virginia, in 1619, anybody was very much disturbed at having them as slaves. But as soon as history began to record that Negroes did not enjoy being forced to work for nothing, the records indicate that white folks began to be disturbed. And when Negro slaves started to run away, and Denmark Vesey with Gabriel Prosser and Nat Turner fomented their great slave revolts, a widespread disturbance swept all across the South.[11] Southern nerves have not been the same since. Maybe this disturbance has come down in the white Southern bloodstream, even unto Senator Russell. I would be jittery, too, if I were white and had mistreated Negroes all my days, even back into the third and fourth generation. I expect that I had rather defy human decency myself before I would be willing to let a colored child go to school and learn the woeful history of the South in relation to the Negro people. To tell the truth, if I was white, I would be scared.

Part 4

Nerve of Some White Folks

Jokes on Our White Folks

December 12, 1942

Our white folks (I mean our reactionary white folks, not the decent ones) must all have rocks in their beds these days. At the moment they are howling so loud and so Hitler-like—witness Bilbo, Rankin, Dixon, et al—that they can't be sleeping in comfort.[1]

Personally, I hope all their pillows are full of lumps. To me—colored as I am—they have been very lousy. And, like Hitler, they have to be taken seriously. Sometimes, however, their antics are not without humor. And, occasionally, we colored folks have our little jokes on them, too—purely at their expense.

What the legal federal definition of "Negro" is I do not know. I shall probably someday write the Selective Service bureau and find out since, in reference to the draft, I am curious. When I registered, the lady simply looked up at me and checked "Negro" on my draft card. ~~labeled strictly by appearance~~

But suppose she had looked up at Walter White—who is as white as Henry Ford—how would she have known? In fact, I have heard of several cases in which registrars have not known, and have marked down light colored men as white. And some of them have gone on in the army, into non-segregated units, and are marching and mingling with the white troops right now.

Passing for White

Into a Harlem bar the other day where I was sitting eating barbecue, came a young soldier, pale olive in complexion. Several fellows immediately recognized him as a neighborhood boy home on his first furlough.

To their delight, he told how the army officials had taken him for white, and how he was serving in an all-white company—having fun aplenty—in the very middle of the South. Having registered from a small up-state town where he was working, the clerk put him down white in the beginning so he simply carried the joke through.

Like this lad, there are probably hundreds of Negroes "passing" for white in the army—knowledge of which should put plenty rocks in the beds of the High Command that so far refuses to allow even one single experimental mixed colored and white brigade—so intent are they on preserving racial separatism.

But an even better joke on our white folks than that of colored soldiers in white units, is what is happening to the Red Cross blood bank in some of the Eastern cities. Many light and, to the eye, quite near-white Negroes have of late—so I have been told—given their blood most generously to the Red Cross.

In the process they did not mention the colored race, so naturally, their blood has gone into the white blood banks. Thus, by now, white plasma and colored plasma must be hopelessly scrambled together, and it amuses me to wonder how the Red Cross will ever get it straightened out. Even the charming mulatto ladies of Jim Crow Washington, so Eastern gossip has it, have gleefully added to this confusion, putting on their light makeup and baring their lovely arms to the needle for the sake of a patriotic and harmless little joke on unscientific Nordics.

Some Practical Good

Seriously, however, these colored pranks in regard to the blood bank might accidentally do some practical good.

Suppose, for instance, Washington were bombed by our enemies, and Senator Bilbo were hit by a bit of shrapnel. Suppose this white and distinguished Southerner were then rushed to the hospital, and a blood transfusion required. Suppose further that the doctor called for a can of white blood, but that the can that really arrived—innocently labeled WHITE—would be only colored blood "passing" for white. Suppose this colored blood were then mistakenly injected into the veins of Senator Bilbo, thus saving his life but making him black—for one drop of black blood makes a man black in the South.

Might it not then be that when the Senator recovered his health and strength, and the anti-poll tax bill came up again for consideration, these drops of black blood coursing through his veins might change his whole attitude toward the bill and cause him to vote for it?

Just for Fun

There are, as we all know, a great many colored people passing for white in the United States. Personally, I have known well a dozen or more who, frustrated by the color-line, have simply stopped being colored and started being white. Some sociologists have tried to estimate the number who go over into the white race each year. It is thought that they run well into the thousands.

Most Negroes light enough to pass do so, of course, for practical reasons. Usually to get a better job, or to attend a college from which they would otherwise be barred.

In Washington where no colored people can go to any downtown theaters, light colored folks who wish to see Katharine Cornell in the flesh, or a Theater Guild play, or attend a concert in Constitution Hall, or something dramatic or cultural like that, frequently put on their white powder and go ahead.[2]

So for jobs or culture, passing has long been in vogue. Not until recently, however, have I heard of people passing just for fun, just to have a gay and harmless little joke on our white folks—like mixing the Red Cross blood plasma all up with colored blood—which is an amusing way of putting rocks in reactionary beds.

Letter to White Shopkeepers

August 14, 1943

Dear White Shopkeepers Who Own Stores In Negro Neighborhoods:

Today in Harlem many of your plate glass windows are broken. Many of your shops have been looted. On some of your shelves nothing is left—goods stolen, scattered in the street, destroyed.[3]

Eight years ago, during the riots of 1935, the same thing happened. Only a few weeks ago it happened on Hastings street in Detroit. It could be Baltimore, Pittsburgh, Chicago next.

You, as merchants, are puzzled, chagrined, angry. Why should it happen to you? I feel that I as a Negro owe you, as best I can give it, an explanation. Here it is:

The damage to your stores is primarily a protest against the whole rotten system of Jim Crow ghettoes, Jim Crow cars, and Jim Crow treatment of Negro soldiers. But, you say, you are not responsible for those Jim Crow conditions. Why should your windows be broken? They shouldn't. I am sorry they are. But I can tell you WHY they are broken.

One phase of the history of the Negro people in America since slavery has been their long struggle to gain decent employment. The community which you serve is 99 per cent colored. That community remembers when you would not, if you could help it, employ a single Negro clerk. When, in recent years, the militant picketing of Negro protest organizations in the larger cities forced you to employ some colored people in your places of business, why did you employ just one, or the very minimum necessary to be able to say to your customers that you had Negro help? Why is it that the single colored person you employ is often hired as a kind of combination clerk and janitor?

Recently, I went into a drugstore in the early morning to make a purchase. The colored girl employed there was out in front sweeping off the sidewalk. The white male clerk was sitting on a stool smoking a cigarette. That makes us mad.

Big Bags of Money

Another sore point, and one which makes Negro communities a fertile field for fascist-type of anti-foreign, anti-semitic propaganda, is the fact that many businesses in colored communities are owned by foreigners who often have not been in this country many years but, since they are white, they can much more easily buy property, get credit and insurance than can Negro citizens of several generations. More power to them. I personally am glad America is a land of opportunity for somebody.

But since the war and the fascist persecution in Europe, many such foreign-born business men have brought their relatives from Europe and, scarcely have these relatives stepped off the boat (often speaking not a word of English) than they have immediately been put to work in colored communities.

Even in the worst days of the depression, the Negroes living right next door to your shop have not been able to get a job with you. If so, it was only as errand boy. When a newly arrived employee from Europe comes in and starts ringing up the cash register before he can even count in English, that makes us mad.

At the branch banks in Harlem—whose tellers are all white—when colored people go to cash their small weekly checks, they wait in line a long time as white merchants with whole sacks of money make deposits and go away lugging huge bags of change, often with armed guards accompanying them.

Your prices are always a few cents more than in any other part of the city, and colored people know that with these extra profits from OUR buying power you often open bigger and finer shops downtown where we can NEVER work, sometimes cannot even trade. And we know you live in nice neighborhoods with trees and lawns, where we cannot live. And we see you at the bank with these big bags of our hard-earned money—so that makes us mad.

Born of Frustration

The New York papers after the riots quote you as saying you do not understand why this should happen to you, a decent white business man, your windows broken and your shops looted. I am sorry it did happen. I do not condone it. I do not believe in mob violence as a solution for social problems.

But I do understand what it is that makes many young people in Negro neighborhoods an easy prey to that desperate desire born of frustration—to which you contribute—to hurl a brick through a window.

Suppose, up in shady White Plains where you live, or down on broad and beautiful West End avenue where the garbage is collected regularly, all the neighborhood shops there were owned by Negroes WHO WOULDN'T GIVE A WHITE PERSON ANY WORK, except as a janitor-clerk permitted to wait on customers after the scrubbing is done.

Would YOU like it? Well, we don't like it, either. *another form of slavery*

Suggestions to White Shopkeepers

August 21, 1943

Since you who are white shopkeepers in Negro districts usually do not live in our neighborhoods, but make your income from our neighborhoods, I would suggest that you take a greater interest in the problems of the colored people who are your customers.

As things stand now, you seldom take part in our efforts to better our community. You do not serve on our citizens committees trying to wrestle with the problems of delinquency, poverty, and high rents. Often you collect the rents, but you do not live with us. You live in less ghetto-like sections of the city where the garbage is taken up every day and there are parks and playgrounds for your children.

I am glad you do not have to live where we do, but I suggest that nevertheless you take an interest in our problems. I suggest that you join the Urban League and the National Association for the Advancement of Colored People, both of which accept white members and whose programs are based on cooperation with white people. These are national organizations having local branches, so I would suggest further that you join the purely local neighborhood groups or committees seeking to deal with specific problems in the very block where your shops are.

I would suggest also that you form a Neighborhood Chamber of Commerce with colored shopkeepers as full members. In other words, I suggest that you become a part of the community where you do business, even though you may not live there.

Colored Trades People

I would suggest that EVERY employee in your shop be colored, from the manager on down. You will say, perhaps, that trained colored tradespeople are hard to find. I would suggest then that YOU train them—since your profits derive from them. The downtown shops will not train Negroes in clerkships or any of the higher positions involved in merchandising. Certainly it is the duty of shops in colored neighborhoods to do so, otherwise where will we ever learn?

I would suggest that all of you advertise in the Negro press. Many of you ignore it entirely, and spend practically no money at all in the neighborhoods where you sell. I would suggest that you seek to cultivate the good will of your customers, not merely the good will of the cops in your precinct— because in Harlem and Detroit you see how helpless cops really are when people start throwing stones at your plate glass windows.

If you are Jewish or foreign-born, and if your own people abroad have known the evils of Hitlerism, that would seem to me all the more reason why you should be interested in the problems of your colored customers in America who have long known the evils of local fascist practices—although in the past we have not called Jim Crow by a fascist name. If your relatives come from abroad and work in your shops in Negro communities, tell them to please be careful not to adopt Jim Crow along with the English language.

Price Ceilings

Try to comply with the ceiling prices on commodities. And do not over-charge. Colored people have such large rents to pay out of their small salaries that even a little over-charging on food or clothing eats into their income too heavily for them always to grin and bear it. Colored people have relatives to take care of, too, and children to educate. And just as those of you who are of foreign blood may have folks you would still like to get out of Europe as soon as you can, so many of us have folks we would like to get out of Alabama—for in the South they treat us like Hitler treats you in the Third Reich.

Please don't feel that I am mad at you personally. Please don't feel that I would throw a brick through your window, or encourage anyone else to do so. I am merely trying to explain to you why some people who are perhaps more emotional than I am, and more weary of being Jim Crowed, and more susceptible to mass hysteria occasionally break out with a violent desire to throw a brick through your window. And do throw it. They feel that you don't care very much about them, so why shouldn't they? They know that you called the police when they picketed your shop for jobs a few years ago. They feel that neither you nor the police care much whether colored people live or die.

If you would show your customers in actions rather than in words that you care about them, that you will hire them when you need clerks, that you are interested in their problems, that you are trying your best to get decent garbage collection for their neighborhood, playgrounds for their kids, the anti-lynching and the anti-poll tax bills through Congress, and that you are also against Jim Crow in the armed forces and police brutality toward soldiers and civilians of color, and that you are not interested in simply making money from Negroes, then I think that even the hoodlums would know about your reputation and help protect your property against mobs. Certainly those of us who are not hoodlums would like for you to be a little more friendly in a community way. Why not? If our world explodes, yours does, too.

The Snake in the House

October 16, 1943

This is a column to be clipped and sent to any nice white people you may know, or for whom you work, because we need their decency to save America. They must be made to realize that a poisonous snake in the house is just as dangerous as a wolf outdoors. This simple truth many Americans of good-will do not yet know.

The ugly snake of race hatred right here in America can do as much to wreck national unity, impede the war effort and destroy the decency of the peace of America—and the world—as Hitler is doing in Europe.

The logic of fighting Hitlerian ideas abroad and letting them lie coiled and dangerous in one's own front room just doesn't make sense. Besides, the snake of fascism that bites me, colored, is just as likely to whirl around and bite you, white. The same Hitler that began by killing and humiliating the Jews ended up by killing and humiliating the French, the Norwegians, the Greeks, and various other Gentile and lily-white nationalities. He would have humbled the Russians, too, but fortunately they had the Red Army.

The same America that for generations has mistreated the Negro, lynched him, Jim Crowed him physically, humiliated him spiritually, packed up all its West Coast Japanese citizens (I didn't say aliens—I said citizens) and put them in concentration camps. Lately, Los Angeles has started in a big way on the Mexicans. Anti-Semitism is growing. The racist idea spreads. Snakes like to bite, and it is hard to teach them to bite only certain people. Fascism is a snake, even when its local name is Jim Crowism, or Ku Klux Klanism, or Native Sons of the Golden West-ism, or hotel advertisements: RESTRICTED CLIENTELE.

Tough Traveling

Negro travelers and Jewish travelers have to eat and sleep, too. As regards Negroes, being one myself, I know how that works. Several times I have driven from coast to coast. From New York to California, starting at Newark, I am never sure even when I may buy a hamburger and sit down and eat it. In most towns, I can't eat a meal unless I search for a Negro restaurant—and many places haven't any. I do not expect any white person to invite me to dinner. I merely want to buy it and pay for it.

As for sleeping, I guess Negro travelers are not expected to sleep. Hotels and tourist camps almost uniformly refuse colored guests. Mind you, I am not asking to sleep with any white man's daughter. I merely want to SLEEP—and be on my way.

Until the war came along and hands were needed badly, I found it hard as Hades to get a job. Advertisements: WHITE ONLY. When the peace comes along, will it be the same way again? It will be, if the many Americans of good-will do not come to realize how terribly alive and viciously dangerous our own fascist-marked snake of race prejudice is, and how, when they permit discrimination against me, it spreads to include Mexicans, Japanese, Jews, Italians, Poles, Catholics, workers who belong to unions, intellectuals who tell the truth, scientists who prove Jim Crow blood banks unscientific, and by and by anybody who isn't also a snake.

Test of Tomorrow

Americans of good-will, the nice decent church people, the well-meaning liberals, the good-hearted souls who themselves wouldn't lynch anyone, must begin to realize that they have to be more than passively good-hearted, more than church-goingly Christian, and much more than word-of-mouth in their liberalism, if they want to save America from turning into the kind of Hitler-land we are sending millions of young men to rescue from the quagmire abroad.

What happens now to me, a Negro, in Beaumont, Camp Stewart, or Detroit, is the test of what happens to America tomorrow. If the real Americans want to let the Klan-minded keep on as they are going, growing stronger and stronger, more and more evil, spreading their hate and terror from me to Japanese-Americans, to Mexican-Americans, to Jewish-Americans and, once well-started, on and on until NO American who isn't armed with viciousness like a Chicago gangster will be safe, then God knows we are in for a dark age sure enough. And it won't be just dark people who will suffer.

Are only Jews suffering in Hitler's Europe? It was easy for many good citizens here to merely sigh and do nothing when Hitler started with the Jews. They didn't realize that that was just a start. It was equally easy to simply shrug their shoulders when Germany and Italy invaded Spain and backed up the Fascist Franco. It is still easy in America to not mind too much when the fascist-marked snake bites the little colored boy who lives across the railroad track—while you are white and live in the pretty part of town, and do not realize what it is to grow up Jim Crowed, to be seated in the last row on the left in the movies, barred out of the track meets in high school, offered a janitor's job when you graduate, lynched down South if you act too much like you don't care for our very ugly snake.

Wake up, nice people, in the pretty part of town, before that snake bites you!

Nerve of Some White Folks

August 4, 1945

Some white folks, both Protestant and Catholic, Jewish and Gentile, Christian and non-Christian, English and American, Nazi or Republican, foreign-born or native, have an amazing amount of nerve. I swear they do!

Here in America, they have the nerve to run night clubs with all Negro bands and entertainers—like the Zanzibar in New York—and then Jim Crow Negro patrons.

They have the nerve to run Young Men's Christian associations with CHRISTIAN real big in the title, and not let a Negro in the door. No shame about it, either!

They have the nerve to turn out motion picture after motion picture in Hollywood, purporting to represent American life, with not a Negro in the cast, except maybe sometimes servants. Yet Negroes are mailmen, bus drivers, doctors, lawyers, nurses, motormen, just like anybody else, a part of American life—one out of every ten—but not a part of their movies.

[handwritten margin note: contra- dictory]

They have the nerve to accept our money, like the Metropolitan Life Insurance company, thousands of dollars every week, but not hire a one of us in their offices.

They have the nerve to draft us into the army without having a single Negro on the Draft board in many parts of the country, and to command Negro troops with white officers without ever letting Negro officers command white troops.

No Negroes Allowed

I swear they are an amazing people! They will own real estate in Negro neighborhoods and rent it out at high rentals, but live themselves where restricted covenants won't let a Negro light. Peace, it's truly wonderful!

They will open up a restaurant for the public on a street where we pay taxes—but if we come in, it suddenly becomes FOR WHITE ONLY. They'll hire us to cook the food in the kitchen but won't let us eat it in the dining room.

They'll let us nurse white babies, but if we sit down beside those same babies when they are grown, they holler "social equality." No lie, they do!

They drain a country of all its wealth, like India, then when the Indians come to the Mother Country, England, they are treated like a step-child, in spite of the fact that India is "the brightest jewel in the Empire's crown."

They stake off Africa and make it a land for *their* bombing bases and airports, but if the Africans want a little self-government and decent wages, they holler, "No!" and act like Africa belongs to the white races rather than the black. That's the truth!

They set up in dusky Asia lily-white churches, clubs, and schools where an Asiatic dare not enter. Thousands of miles away from home, they draw a color line in somebody else's country. Even in Panama and Trinidad, FOR WHITE ONLY—and everybody around them dark. They have all that nerve!

They offer a Good Neighbor Policy to Latin America, and then start Jim Crowing brownskin Latins at the Miami Airport before they hardly set a visiting foot on American soil. Jim Crow hospitality! Por dios! Carramba!

They Think White—Not Right

They will sell a Negro a phonograph record down South but won't let him play it before buying; sell a colored woman a hat but won't let her try it on; sell a brownskin kid a coke in Kansas but won't let him drink it inside the store; sell a black man a hamburger in Delaware—but in a sack to eat outside. Yet this is America! Yes, it is, too!

Of course, not *all* white people are that way, but so many of them are that it isn't funny, particularly of Anglo-Saxon origin. All around the world they Jim Crow, from Chicago to China, from London, England, to Lincoln, Nebraska. They set up separate segregated Red Cross clubs all over the United Nations—except in the Soviet Union. (I reckon they would have them there if it wasn't against Russian laws.) They have an enormous nerve, some white folks! Oh, but they do!

Where do they get all this nerve, and how? Well, I guess it's because they have been getting away with it for so long, it has become a kind of second nature. Now, they are surprised that we want a decent table at the Zanzibar, or that we wish a Christian Y.M.C.A. to be really Christian, or that we are puzzled at *never* seeing a colored school teacher in a Hollywood picture, but always a maid.

They are surprised that some colored boys get psychiatrically upset at being drafted into a Jim Crow army by a Jim Crow draft board in a Jim Crow state where colored men cannot vote because of Jim Crow. Or that some Indians do not want to fight for Britain, or that some Africans have no desire to kill Greeks for the Empire. They are surprised that Negroes would like to lead armies, too, since armies must be led. They are amazed that we even dream of wanting to command white soldiers. But why not? White soldiers command us.

I am afraid the nerve of some white folks has gone to their heads and affected their brains so that they can't think right—only white—which is too bad, because this is *our* world, too, so they had better get over that.

Our White Folks: Shame!

March 20, 1948

Our white folks want to be liked and admired in the world. And they want us colored folks to respect them. But the way our white folks behave, we are forced to wonder sometimes how they can expect to be respected, liked or admired. Racially speaking, God knows, for some of the things they do, they OUGHT to be ashamed of themselves.

For instance, take Jim Crow all over America. If I were a white Southern tax collector, I would be ashamed to take a Negro's taxes when he can't even sit on a bench in the Court House yard, let alone be a tax collector himself— because in the South there are no black tax collectors.

If I were white I would be ashamed to crowd into the buses down South and take ALL the good seats and let my Negro servants and friends—whom the Southerners LOVE and UNDERSTAND so deeply—sit over the wheels in the back. I would also be ashamed, if I were white North or South, when the bus stops for a rest period to go into the bus station restaurant and get myself a nice hot cup of coffee and piece of pie, while my colored fellow citizens have to remain in the bus eating out of a bag, if at all, because the restaurant counter will not serve colored people. I would be ashamed if I were white.

I would also be ashamed, practically all over America outside the large Northern cities, if I were white to sit downstairs at the movies while all my Negro friends are segregated into the last rows of the top gallery, if admitted to the movies at all. And I would be ashamed in many cities to have the right to use the public library while black citizens cannot come inside to look at a book or a magazine. I would also be ashamed to dive into a municipal swimming pool paid for with public funds while my colored neighbor whose taxes helped to build the pool is barred out. I really would be ashamed.

But are our white folks ashamed? Not at all! If they are, they surely do not show it. They flock to the movies and sit all nice and smug and white together and let me climb to the gallery. They draw books out of the public library and read and read and do not improve their minds enough to concern themselves that I cannot use that library. They cool off in city swimming pools and do not give a good gosh darn if my children swelter in the August heat with no place to swim. Our white folks enjoy themselves all over this American nation and get mad at us if we act like we want to enjoy ourselves, too. They race-hate and red-bait and say, "The Communists are inciting our Negroes," if we have the nerve to want to dive into a city pool FOR WHITES ONLY.

Puzzling Mentality

There is something puzzling about the mentality of our white folks. I have been acquainted with them for forty years now and I do not understand them yet. They sing and pray on Sundays, they talk democracy on the air and in their papers. But just ask them—if you are colored—for a little Christian brotherhood and a little real democracy and they yell to high heaven nowadays not only, "Negro!" (spelled with an i and two g's) but also they scream, "Red!"

Race-hating and red-baiting have a lot in common. Those who do the least for Negroes are the greatest red-baiters. From Ku Klux Klan Georgia to Gerald L. K. Smith's Middle West, the Negro-haters are the loudest red-baiters.[4] Now they have combined the two activities. Witness the long list of highly respectable and socially conscious Negroes published in the reactionary white newspapers last year as reds. Witness Peoria where Paul Robeson could not sing, and Springfield where I could not speak.

"If I Were White"

If I were white I would not have the nerve to loudly proclaim myself 100% American and a noble champion of democracy in a town where a Negro child cannot use a public swimming pool on a hot day or eat a dish of ice cream in a downtown confectionery. I would not red-bait a great Negro singer, and at the same time race-hate a small black boy or girl. I would be ashamed to do that, if I were white. I certainly would be ashamed.

But then I would be ashamed to be a great Secretary of State in Washington defending the right to vote three thousand miles away in the Balkans but not saying a word about the right to vote for thousands of black citizens in his own home state. Maybe it is because our BIG white folks set such strange examples, that our little white folks in Georgia and Illinois act so badly. Anyhow, I would be ashamed.

Our White Folks: So?

March 27, 1948

It is time now to say, *So?* to our white folks. Meaning, *So what?* Meaning, *Just what are you going to do?* Because they have talked enough.

All during the war our white folks talked loud and long, day and night, in public and on the radio, about democracy, freedom, the democratic rights of free people, liberty, the right of the ballot, the right to govern oneself, the democratic way. And we colored folks have practically none of it yet right here in our U.S.A.

Hundreds of books and thousands of editorials have been written about democracy in the last ten years, and how good it is. And on our problem—the Race Problem—thousands of surveys have been finished and completed. Millions of resolutions have been passed by this body and that church, this convention and that union. Reports have been drawn up. Words have flowed on paper, on the air, and out of speakers' mouths. Even the President has delivered a Civil Rights message to Congress. And still I can't get a coca cola at the corner drug store because I am colored.

To all these speeches, printed and verbal, it is about time somebody said, *So? So what? What are you going to do?* Freedom of speech is a wonderful thing, but there has to be some action sometime if the talk is to mean anything. We can keep armies in Germany and Japan, and vote billions of dollars to protect the Turks and the Greeks—but to protect black men and women from lynching and segregation down South, how much has votes? So?

Nice Resolution

Various of our white church groups have voted nice resolutions about improving race relations in recent years, and the power and glory of our churches spread all over this American country, but Jim Crow still flaps his wings high over their steeples everywhere. Take the Jim Crow car, for instance. If church groups really wish to abolish the Jim Crow car, all Christians would have to do is to ride in it. If every white Christian in the South would use the COLORED coaches when traveling there would soon be no Jim Crow cars—because the white folks would crowd the colored out and back into the nice air-cooled coaches that they have been enjoying alone for so long.

Another thing Christians could do to help break down segregation is move to the back of buses in the South and sit with the Negroes as Christ would do if He were alive today. "Oh, but that is against the law!" I hear them say. But it is not against the moral law, it is not against the law of God.

Also, since so many nice resolutions have been passed, the church groups could open up their church schools all over the country to Negro students, and let us study book learning and religion and Christ on campuses now closed to us—although Christian. But groups other than the church have duties to perform, too. The churches are not alone in wonderful talk and little action.

Need Negro Radio Men

Consider the radio—that marvelous instrument sending words of freedom to the ends of the earth. Radio, broadcasting the President's message on Civil Rights. Fine! But at the same time, Mister Radio, that you are putting such shining and splendid words on the air about equal rights, employ some Negroes in your studios. There are all too few Negroes in radio, and those few are mostly actors of very specialized parts in New York or Hollywood. Almost all the radio offices or control rooms I have ever been in are lily-white.

Radio of the fine words, do some fine deeds, too. Let Negro men and women have a chance to learn to be radio engineers, technicians, script writers, program directors, and announcers, too. You are a billion dollar industry, but you employ only a handful of Negroes. Just talking on the air about freedom does not do black people very much practical good.

I heard you broadcast to the whole world last week about democracy. But right here at home, radio, what do you do? Sit tight and stay white? Or try to practice that democracy you are always talking about? I want to know? So? Heh? So.

Our White Folks: Boo!

April 3, 1948

Somebody has snuck up behind our white folks and hollered *Boo!* real loud and scared them to death. It must have been Russia. All you can hear on the radio these days is Russia this, and Russia that, and the Communist did, and the Communist won't, and the Reds Oh! they are black in their hearts!

Set up a WPA in Europe to fight the Reds. Federal Relief in Italy to fight the Reds. Money to China to fight the Reds. A hundred thousand planes to fight the Reds. Arms to Greece to fight the Reds. Woof! Woof! Woof! Bark at the Reds. And we had better stop Russia now!

For Russia, our late ally in arms, our white folks have now not a single kind word. For the Russian people who stopped Hitler at Stalingrad, who drove Hitler all the way back to Berlin, who lost in the war millions of men, millions of acres of crops destroyed, hundreds of cities bombed into ruins, for the blood and sweat and tears of the Soviet people mixed with those of the Allies to win the war, not a kind word now. Snarl, bark, growl, hiss, hump your back and spit at Russia. Bare your teeth and show your claws. Rear back on your hind legs. Did Russia holler, *Boo!* or what?

Been Doing It for Years

Of course, the thing that puzzles us colored folks about our white folks is that all the things they now accuse Russia of doing, our white folks themselves have been doing to us for years. They accuse Russia of denying a free ballot to Poland, Hungary, the Russian folks themselves, and now Prague.

Our white folks have never allowed millions of Negroes and Indians to vote in this country, and in this modern day and age still have not gotten around to protecting so basic a democratic right as the ballot in states south of Washington.

Our white folks accuse Russia of unjustly putting to death political prisoners. Well, God knows a poor Negro in Georgia does not have to attain the stature of a political prisoner to get put to death there within or without the law. Look at the two black men and the two black women lynched at Monroe, Georgia.

Our white folks who can find red spies working in secret cannot, however, find and convict lynchers who work in the open. And the new type of lynching where the police beat you to death in jail proves that Negroes do not have to be political prisoners to get their heads whipped, even unto death. Woodward was a soldier of the United States, but the law gouged out his eyes.

Who hollered *Boo!* at our white folks? Maybe they are scared and jumpy because they have guilt in their souls. Surely they must know it is not right to behave toward any human beings as they have behaved toward Negro Americans for the last three hundred years. Of course, some few know it and, through the kindness of their hearts, try to remedy the situation.

But the vast majority of American white folks go blissfully on suppressing the ballot in the South and Jim Crowing in the North. They have time to spend days and weeks and months in Congress talking about Europe and China and the Reds, but they never have time to weather a filibuster when an Anti-Lynching Bill comes up for consideration. Congress then has to go home on a vacation.

Have Time to Fight Civil Rights

Southern governors have time to meet and re-meet to combat the President's Civil Rights message, but no time in their respective states to begin—

to even begin—to straighten out the out-moded Hitlerian practices of whites toward Negroes. Yet they have time to rear up on their hind legs and denounce Russia for trying to work out a treaty with Finland, four thousand miles across the ocean. That is what really puzzles us about our white folks.

They claim Russia said, *Boo!* to Finland. And they get so worked up about it. But there are almost as many Negroes in Mississippi as there are Finns in Finland. We are beat to our feet—but they don't get worked up about us. It is only when Russia says Boo! thousands of miles across the Atlantic that the moral indignation of our white folks really rises.

Those Little Things

July 24, 1948

White folks are frequently claiming that they "know the Negro." But certain little nuances are always proving that they don't. For instance, a short time ago in Los Angeles late at night a white passenger happened to be passing as two Negroes were burglarizing a shop. The two robbers emerged at the moment the man approached, whereupon one said to the other, "Beat it, daddy!" And they ran down an alley.

The white man reported what he had seen and heard to the police. The robbers were not caught, but the next morning the papers reporting the robbery stated that the colored thieves must have been father and son because one of them was heard to call the other *daddy!*

During the war I remember hearing about a Southern Negro war worker being picked up on suspicion of the murder of a white woman. The police found among the Negro's belongings in his dresser drawer several knotted ends of women's silk stockings. In vain did the poor colored prisoner explain that he wore these stocking caps on his head—for the stocking ends had been taken by the court as possible evidence of some shocking sex perversion. The Negro got the death sentence. Yet anybody acquainted with adult Negro males knows why they wear stocking caps on their heads—and it has nothing to do with the Kinsey Report either.

I wonder if, when the Kinsey Report gets around to Negroes, it will take up the subject of "the dozens"—that fabulous game few whites seem to comprehend, even on the simplest level. I once knew a colored chauffeur who told me that one morning he had used his people's car to do a little shopping on his own, since the boss was not going out until noon. The chauffeur forgot to remove some of his parcels from the back seat where he had placed them, as the dog had been riding in front.

At noon when the boss emerged from the house to get in the car, he demanded in a rather sharp tone, "Whose things are these on the back seat here?"

The way he spoke made the Negro mad. So, feeling evil anyhow, the chauffeur replied, "Your mama's."

"Not at all," said the white man. "Mother has not been out this morning."

Fortunately, a complete lack of understanding of the little nuances involved prevented the chauffeur from getting fired. Sometimes Negroes, too, misunderstand white nuances. For instance, take the word *darkie*. To many white persons that word has a nice affectionate connotation, especially in the South. Frequently when they use it, white people mean no offense. But to us all the overtones of the word are condescension and patronizing insult.

Normally nobody minds the use of the words *boy* or *girl* as a form of address among acquaintances. But a white person had better be careful if he uses either term to Negroes. To us the words take on overtones of caste— for a servant is *boy* or *girl* up to the age of a hundred. But there are many well-meaning white people who do not know of this sensitivity on our part.

You never know or understand a people until you understand the little things about them. Those little things count an awful lot. Some of the Negro leaders called in for that Armed Forces Conference with Defense Secretary Forrestal and Army Secretary Kenneth Royall told me that the conference got off to a bad start from the very beginning because of a few unconscious phrases that Royall used which he probably did not know rubbed Negroes the wrong way.[5]

Of course, if white folks were not so clannish and stand-offish and did not segregate themselves from us, they would understand us better. But then how can a man like Royall understand Negroes when more than likely he never sits down to hold a conversation, let alone a conference, with a Negro unless he wants something. And you don't have to hold a conference with the hired help in the South. You just say, "Boy, do that." If there's anything that makes a Negro leader mad these days, it's that uncompromising tone of voice. By now one would think that at least high government white folks would know those little things.

Harlem's Bitter Laughter

October 2, 1948

Harlem, the world's largest Negro urban community, can sometimes laugh at the dog-gonest things. But its laughter is often a bitter laughter—the kind of laughter that, I imagine, reverberates through Dante's hell when the devil suddenly slips on his own hot pavements and burns his sitter-downer.

It amused Harlem no end a week or so ago when our white folks in Washington suddenly tore their diplomatic pants by asking the brownskin Minister from Ethiopia, the Honorable Ras Imru, to leave his box in Jim Crow Constitution Hall just as the President of the United States was entering to attend the American Association for the Advancement of Sciences.

"*American* it sure is," said one Negro loudly in a restaurant, "but *Association* it sure ain't, if they would invite even the Ethiopian Minister out of his seat for being colored."

"*Advancement of Science,*" said another. "Them crackers in Washington don't believe in science. Science teaches that all races are the same. Look at the Red Cross during the War, they didn't believe in science, separating colored blood just like Hitler."

"It says here that they sent expressions of 'profound regret' and also 'acute embarrassment' to the Imperial Ethiopian Legation," said the first man, "but you know white folks is just like Mrs. O'Leary's cow, they will turn around and kick the milk right over again as sure as tooting." And all the fellows at the table laughed.

During that same week our white folks, racially speaking, kicked over the milk several times, according to the headlines in the daily press. 3 NEGRO EDUCATORS FLEE GEORGIA TOWN—Had Mingled with White Officials at Meeting—read one headline topping an article telling how the colored presidents of Fort Valley State College, Georgia State College, and Albany State College had to leave Milledgeville, Georgia's state educational meeting under cover of night, even though they had violated no "accepted rules of the Southern behavior pattern in regard to race problems."

In the same paper the same day it was front-paged: 5 G.I.S DIE AS B-29S MISS BOMB TARGET—29 Injured In Maneuver Accident in Florida. "All of the dead and all but one of the injured were Negroes," said the paper, quoting a public relations officer as saying, "The troops were in the right place, but the bombs weren't." Further down in the article it stated that the bombers were based in Texas.

"When them Texas crackers looked down and saw all them Negroes bunched together, they just couldn't help wiping a few of them out," said a colored ex-G.I. with a wry smile, proceeding to give several examples from his own army days of battles between Southern white soldiers and Negroes. "That is why the army should not train Negro boys in the South; it is too much of a strain for them crackers."

While the colored weeklies were featuring the story of how the Mayor of Albany, Georgia, did not shake hands with the colored woman Olympic team champion at the official city celebration held in Jim Crow fashion, the New York dailies carried the story of the arrest in Virginia of the Negro Olympic boxer, Norvell Lee, for sitting in the wrong seat in a train, evidently not the Jim Crow seat.[6] REFUSE GLASS OF MILK TO LAWYER AT AIRPORT read another headline that same week, describing how the distinguished Mrs. Sadie Alexander of the President's Committee on Civil Rights was denied service at the Washington air terminal.[7]

"Ethiopian Minister, lawyer, Olympic star, it makes no difference to them crackers who you are," said Harlem. "When they say, 'Take low,' they mean *take low*—black, get back! 'You-all Negras ought-a know better,'" imitating that high whining Southern drawl. And then laughing. Harlem laughing.

That is why many white people do not understand how Negroes can laugh at the stupid indignities so often heaped upon them, from low to high, in this American country of ours. The indignities themselves are not funny. But there is something so pitifully absurd about the racial stupidities of some of our white folks, something in such awkward bad taste indicative of such provincial bad manners, that it is hard to keep from laughing at them. They make such clowns of themselves. "The troops were in the right place, but the bombs weren't." Ha! Ha! says Harlem. "Acute embarrassment" over the ejection of the Ethiopian Minister from his box. Ha! Ha! says Harlem. "They knew Constitution Hall was a Jim Crow Hall all the time. Can Marian Anderson sing there? Why did they invite the Ethiopian Minister there if they didn't want to suffer 'acute embarrassment'? These white folks make me laugh."

Maybe it is this wry laughter that has kept us going all these years, from slavery's denial of the draught of freedom up to the Washington airport's denial of a glass of milk. Maybe it is just a way of saying, "To defeat us you must defeat our laughter."

[handwritten annotations: 1. general characterization of white people he speaks of 3. How does he use humor + what should response of black people be to particular concerns of what whites does humor do. have a raced dimension.]

The Folk Lore of Race Relations

February 8, 1958

In the days of slavery, the folk tales and jokes concerning the master-slave relationship were numerous, and often humorous with the wry, dry kind of humor that Negro stories frequently have.

Today's crop of race-relations anecdotes and jokes is growing apace, and a new folk lore concerning the old problem of whites and Negroes is springing up. Just last week I heard a new little rhyme which might be called "Dixie Mother Goose" which stated:

> Mary had a little lamb
> Its fleas were white as snow—
> For everywhere that Mary went
> Only white fleas could go.

Of course, by now everyone has heard the story of the Southern senator in Washington who became unduly friendly toward a colored lady typist in one of the government offices. When his Dixie cronies reproached him about it, he said, "But I don't want to go to school with her. I just want to have a date."

And another one going the round lately concerns young Herman Talmadge, son of the late governor of Georgia, who got so worried about integration after the Supreme Court decreed schools and buses and everything had to be mixed, that he did not know what to do.[8]

He decided to get in touch with his father in the spirit world about these problems, since the old man had had such a great reputation for handling "Nigras."[9]

It took young Talmadge quite a long time to make contact with his parent in the other world, but finally he got through to Old Gene.

"Father," the son said, "I have been trying to get in touch with you for the longest."

Gene replied, "I have been trying to get in touch with you, son, for a mighty long time, too, because I am catching hell down here."

Herman said, "Pappy, we are catching hell in Georgia, too, and what I want to know is, what shall we do about these 'Nigras?'"

Old Gene answered, "Son, please don't be too hard on them at home—because the head devil down here is a 'Nigra' and I am catching enough hell now!"

One of my favorite race-relations stories concerns a radio program in Mississippi back in the days of World War II. It seems that in those times of burgeoning democracy, even the white folks in Mississippi began to be somewhat worried about so much criticism from the rest of the world concerning the way they treated Negroes.

So it was decided to put the nicest old Negro they knew on an international hook-up to tell the world how happy he was in Mississippi. Uncle Mose agreed that this was a good idea and accepted the little speech which they wrote out for him to say and which was to take only three minutes. In front of the white folks, Uncle Mose practiced for three hours.

The radio show was advertised in all the newspapers all over the world. On the day of the broadcast, the white folks sent a squad car and two policemen in full regalia to escort Uncle Mose to the radio station, and they had a big audience of distinguished white folks in the auditorium to listen to his testimony.

In the studio just before the switch was turned on, the announcer told Uncle Mose that his voice was going to be heard all over the state of Mississippi, and all over the United States. In fact, all over the world. Uncle Mose expressed surprise.

"You mean to tell me that folks are gonna hear me all over Mississippi and all over the United States and all over the world, too?"

"Yes, indeed," said the announcer.

"Do you mean all over the whole world?"

"All over the whole world," the announcer assured him. "And when I turn this switch and announce your name, I want you to speak right up."

"Yes, sir," said the old man.

"Now, Uncle Mose, you have the mike. Say what you want to say."

"All I want to say," the old man's voice boomed, "is HELP! HELP! HELP! HELP!"

Part 5

Brazenness of Empire

America after the War

May 22, 1943

When the war we are fighting now is over, America is going to be a paradise. We are fighting for democracy, and democracy is what we intend to have. Naturally, then there will be no more grandfather clauses in the constitutions of Southern states, and no more poll-taxes, and everybody can vote.

Anybody can hold office, too, if elected to office by popular vote. So there will be a number of Negroes in the House and Senate at Washington, particularly from those states like Mississippi and Georgia where the Negro population is heavy. Those Negro statesmen will represent everybody, not just the Negro segment of the populations of their states.

In Washington's various departments, also, there will be a real integration of Negroes into governmental machinery. They won't, as now, be simply advisors. Truman Gibson will be Assistant Secretary of War, not a mere advisor on Negro affairs. Mr. Gibson will advise and work on all affairs having to do with all Americans. And Judge William Hastie will probably by then be on the bench of the United States Supreme Court, judging all cases that come before it.[1]

No More Jim Crow

There won't be any more Jim Crow in Washington after the war, since we are fighting for democracy. The capital of a great democratic nation will no longer permit segregation in the very departments of the government itself, nor in its restaurants, nor on any of the buses or trains that run out of Washington.

There will no longer be any Jim Crow schools there, either. Negro and white teachers will teach pupils of all racial derivations. After this war, having put forward democratic slogans for the whole world, naturally Washington will be ashamed to have segregation any longer right in the District of Columbia, under the very dome of freedom. Nor will Washington permit segregation anywhere else in America.

That will be a good thing, for then colored people will no longer have to ride in over-crowded Jim Crow cars. They will no longer have to take the back seat over the wheels in buses, nor be limited as to where they may sit in street cars in the South.

The South will be ashamed of all that sort of thing after we win this struggle for democracy. No more going up dark alleys to side entrances to theaters if you are colored, then having to climb three flights to the top gallery. No more public places denying service to Negroes. No more hospitals refusing to treat Negro patients, or to have Negro doctors and nurses on their staffs.

Making Up for Mistakes

When the lights come on again all over the world, nobody will be left in the dark, scorned and humiliated. Hitlerian race theories will all be wiped off the books of American democracy. Semi-official organizations like the Red Cross and the Boy Scouts, appealing as they do for contributions from all peoples, will be ashamed of their past record of prejudice and Jim Crowism.

The Red Cross will regret its strange, unscientific custom of once having segregated its blood donors, marking Jim Crow cans for Negro blood. They will regret, too, the way they carried segregation abroad in their Red Cross clubs in lands where Jim Crow had not been the custom before.

When the Lord gets through passing the ammunition, the D.A.R. will be delighted to have Marian Anderson sing any time she wants to in their once lily-white Constitution Hall. Hollywood will be glad to give good Negro actors good roles as decent human beings in the new pictures Hollywood will make when Hollywood really understands what democracy is all about—as, of course, Hollywood will when we all get through fighting for democracy. Then the jazz bands will no longer insult Negro Christians by jazzing up their spirituals for people to dance by, nor will any more songs like "De Glory Road" be written.

Lots of past mistakes will be rectified when this war is over and democracy really comes into being. The Scottsboro boys, whom everybody has forgotten at the moment, will be freed.

American citizens of Japanese parentage will be released from their concentration camps—non-citizen Germans or Italians were not so treated. Chinese in Mississippi won't have to go to separate schools, nor will Negroes.

Mexicans, in the Southwest, will receive the same courtesy in public places, parks and swimming pools as do any other citizens. Color won't matter anymore. It's really going to be fine all over America when everybody will be decent to everybody else after the war.

Am I dreaming? Well, isn't it better for a person to be dreaming than to have a nightmare? Huh?

The World after the War

May 29, 1943

After this war is over and millions of people are through fighting for democracy, this world will be a wonderful world to live in. A great many men will have died to make it wonderful—white and black, Chinese and English, Jewish and Gentile. Out of respect for those men, no one land or government, of those now allied together for democracy, will ever again brow-beat or mistreat the men of another race or land.

Of course, after this war, India will be free to set up her own government and run her own affairs. No longer will outsiders imprison her great leaders like Nehru or Gandhi. No longer will foreign soldiers machine-gun her people, nor beat them with lathis. No longer will there be Jim Crow cars on the Indian railroads, nor Jim Crow clubs and schools in Bombay and Calcutta.

After this war is won, Africa also will be free. The Belgians will no longer force black men to do unpaid labor in the Congo. The French will no longer put Frenchmen over the Senegalese in Senegal. The Senegalese will choose their own rulers from among their own people. The British, without doubt, will withdraw their reign of reaction and color prejudice from Sierra Leone, Nigeria and Kenya. In Capetown all Jim Crow will be ended. No one will any longer dare be so undemocratic or boorish as to Jim Crow an African in his own country. This war is being fought for democracy, of course, and naturally Africa will benefit.

A Free China Too

China will then control her own rivers and her own ports when this war is done. Singapore will belong to the Malayans. Java and Bali and all those pretty little islands of spice and rubber will be no longer under the rule of Dutch imperialism. Holland is a member of the United Nations and Holland is fighting for democracy, not exploitation anymore. How wonderful it will be when the brown people of the South Seas are free!

Australia then will let down her color bars and no longer insult her neighbors in Asia as she does now. Australia will realize the value of friendly cooperation, rather than a policy of haughty Nordic isolationism. A few million people will not try to hog a whole continent, with a FOR WHITES ONLY sign up at every port.

In our own hemisphere, Mexico and Haiti, Peru and Venezuela, in fact all of Latin America will no longer be suspicious and afraid of the great Yankee Colossus to the North. The United States will no longer wield the big stick of economic force over our neighbors. All our own schemes of power and exploitation will be forgotten. Not domination but cooperation will become the basis of our Inter-American relationships. North and South, America will be friends. No longer will the mixed-bloods, the Indians and the Negroes of South America fear the Jim Crow customs of the United States.

Dreams vs. Nightmares

No longer will the bad racial manners of the Texas border seep over into Mexico to the detriment of Mexico's own dark citizens. No longer will our tourists dare go to Havana and draw the color line against the Cubans themselves—for, after this war, the citizens of the United States will be decent to colored peoples everywhere. So will the British and the Dutch. So will the Belgians and the French.

This world is going to be a pretty swell place after the war.

Am I dreaming? Well, if I am, isn't it better to dream than have nightmares all the time? I ask you!

The Detroit Blues

September 11, 1943

An old colored man in Detroit was sitting on the front stoop of a ramshackle rooming house around the corner from Hastings street a few days after the riots.[2] The tune of an ancient Clara Smith record kept running through his head as he hunched over in the warm sunshine.[3]

After awhile the old man started to hum, then very softly to sing. He wasn't singing the words Clara Smith sang on the record. He made up his own words, keeping only her refrain, "This Morning." His words were about the riots he had just experienced.

One or two other roomers, who drifted out on the porch to watch the white militia going by, heard the old man sing to himself:

> My only son is in the war
> This morning.
> My only son is in the war
> This morning.
> My only son is in the war,
> Don't know what he's fighting for.
> My only son is in the war
> This morning.

His words echoed an old troubling doubt in the minds of thousands of Negroes who had survived the fury of the riots, the iron pipes of the mob, and the bullets of the police.

> My only child is Over There
> This morning.
> My only child is Over There
> This morning.
> My only child is Over There,
> Don't know why, don't know where.
> My only child is Over There
> This morning.

Mournfully, the old man repeated that verse several times, with its troubling why, its minor puzzlement, its quaver of loneliness. Then his voice rose as he sang about the recent and woeful goings-on that had made a shambles of Hastings street.

> White folks, black folks, running mad
> This morning.
> White folks, black folks, running mad
> This morning.
> White folks, black folks, running mad—
> Beating and killing! Lawd, it's sad!
> White folks, black folks, running mad
> This morning.

They Always Wins

"I can't stand that song much longer, dad," one of the roomers on the porch said. "It makes me feel bad, bad, bad. I don't like it."

The old man hummed awhile, then new words spread over the surface of his tune:

> I got them sad Detroit blues
> This morning.
> I got them sad Detroit blues
> This morning.
> I got them sad Detroit blues—
> If the white folks win, the black folks lose.
> I got them sad Detroit blues
> This morning.

"They always wins," said a roomer on the porch. "They always wins because they got the police, and the militias, and the money—so they always wins."

> Um-um-um-ummm! Um-um-umm!
> This um-ummmmmm!

Somebody has got to answer that old man about the why and the wherefore of this war that keeps on saying it's for decency and freedom and democracy, yet can't make these bad people in Detroit behave. Somebody's got to be responsible for that old man's son Over There and explain to him what the current confusion in race relations in America is about. And somebody has got to tell that old man that he shouldn't be singing songs like: "If the white folks win, the black folks lose . . ." because that sounds as if it could easily be turned into something overly-racial, pro-Japanese, and wrong.

Somebody ought to explain to him that it isn't good to think in terms of white folks and black folks, anyhow.

Time for FDR to Speak

It's hard for an American Negro to untangle the word WHITE out of all this mess, and keep it pure—because it looks like to a Negro, when he doesn't stop to think, that the bad people are white, the Klan is white, the Fascists are white, so:

If the white folks win, the black folks lose . . . Maybe if the President himself would just explain these things to the old man on that ramshackle porch in Detroit and to the rest of the confused colored people in America—to the whites, as well, for that matter—all of us would understand better that it is the Fascist-minded here in THIS country as well as abroad we must fight in order to win this war in any real sense. Certainly it is time for the President to speak out and say that Fascist-Klan Jim Crow conditions are not American, not decent, not WHITE, not compatible with our war aims, and America is not going to stand them any more.

Such a declaration might not be "good politics" in terms of the Southern lily-white vote, but it would give heart to all the fighters for real democracy all over the world, black and white. And it would surely help that old man on Hastings street who keeps singing:

> I got them sad Detroit blues
> This morning.

Photographs from Teheran

December 18, 1943

In the news photographs from Teheran, Churchill and Roosevelt pictured with Stalin look just as if they sat down with me—colored! What I mean by that is, they look ill at ease like most liberal white folks do when taking a photograph with a Negro.

Either they are too earnest and too serious and too determined to look like they mean well, or else their smile is too broad. In other words, they are self-conscious. They don't take it natural. White folks are just not used to sitting down with Negroes—or Russians.

Stalin represents one-sixth of the earth's surface, spanning both Europe and Asia, and containing a large portion of the earth's inhabitants, white, yellow, and brown.

Churchill and Roosevelt primarily represent white folks alone, for the colored folks under them are all in subordinate positions. The Negroes in America still ride in Jim Crow cars and have their blood segregated by the Red Cross. The Negroes in British Africa are still very much ground down, do not vote, and have no part in the running of the Empire. Neither do the Indians in India.

But the yellow and brown people in Stalin's Soviet Asia have as much to say about what goes on in the Soviet Union as the next one, colored or white. The Soviet Union has no color lines, no Jim Crow cars, and no distinctions based on race or previous condition of servitude. The British Empire and the United States of America are riddled by such distinctions. I just got off a Jim Crow car in Virginia myself, and I am an American citizen.

What Stalin Represents

It is very hard for a white American to sit down and have his picture taken with a colored American and look natural. It must be very hard for a white American or a white Britisher to sit down and have his picture taken with Stalin and look natural. Stalin represents all that such an American or Britisher does not. First of all, Stalin represents ALL of his citizens, with no poll-tax or color lines in the way of such representation. Under Stalin there are no colonies like India, no Nigeria, or Jamaica, or Trinidad, or Puerto Rico or the Canal Zone where the people have no real voice in the government. Under Stalin there are no poll-tax states, no lily-white primaries like Texas, no frightful regions like Mississippi where Ku Klux Klans and Bilbos are allowed to run wild. Under Stalin there are no Jim Crow trains and no Gandhis or Nehrus or Scottsboro boys in jail.

Stalin represents the working people of his country, for they are the people who run his country.

I think it is a very wonderful thing for Mr. Stalin to have his picture taken with Mr. Roosevelt and Mr. Churchill—for maybe some quite wonderful thoughts came into the minds of our President and the British Premier during the process. Maybe Mr. Roosevelt thought how bad it is not to get rid of the poll-tax in America, and how bad it is to have colonies like Puerto Rico where the people have no real say in the government under which they live, and how bad it is to be ALL this time granting the Filipinos independence— until after the Japanese have got them. And maybe Mr. Churchill thought how bad it is to run Africa as though the Africans were slaves and have no sense, and to run India as though the Indians were babies and have no mother-wit, and to run all the dark world under the British Empire as though colored people were inferior to whites and not deserving of a voice in the Empire that their labor and money help support, and for whose existence their sons die in battle just as die the sons of England proper and Scotland and Wales.

A Political War Too

Maybe I am reading thoughts into those pictures in the papers last week of Roosevelt, Churchill, and Stalin. But to me the only man in the pictures who looked really at ease was Mr. Stalin. He didn't look like he was worried about having his picture taken. He didn't look like he was in the wrong place. He looked perfectly serene and at home with the aging power diplomats from across the seas. Churchill and Roosevelt are the ones who look like, "Since this has to be done, let's make the best of it."

It would have been nice, while those pictures were being made, if Mr. Stalin had told Mr. Roosevelt and Mr. Churchill something about how his government has solved the problems of race and poverty in the USSR. But I do not suppose he did. After all, Stalin is fighting a political war, too, as well as a military one.

God knows I will be glad when every Jim Crow railroad station is level with the ground! I am an American citizen and I do not think it is right that I should have to go through a Jim Crow waiting room to a Jim Crow car, segregated and inconvenienced, because I am colored. I have just come out of the South and as I looked at the pictures of Churchill and Roosevelt being photographed with Stalin, I thought they looked just like two Caucasian citizens of Dixie who, for political reasons, were taking their picture with a Negro. I hope I am wrong. I hope they both felt better than that. God help and God bless them!

Colored Lived There Once

January 27, 1944

This morning's radio news advised me that out in Asia, high-ranking Japanese officers and officials, anticipating an American siege, are moving out of the fine hotels and apartment houses in Manila, capital of the Philippines.

When the British shortly lay siege to Hong Kong, and we Allies soon attack Singapore in full force, I can visualize high-ranking Japanese officers and officials moving out of the fine hotels in Hong Kong and Singapore, too. They will leave the deluxe apartment houses of the European Quarters there and hie themselves hence. Such an exodus will likewise take place in Java, leaving palatial Dutch apartments and hotels empty of Japanese families.

But the natives of Java, and the natives of China, and the native Malayans, and the native Filipinos are never going to forget that in those fine hotels built for and formerly occupied only by white people, for three or four years during World War II, there colored people lived. These colored people—Japanese and wealthy natives—lived there because the Japanese had taken Manila and Hong Kong and Singapore away from the white people by force.

Naturally, the Americans and the British are going to take their former possessions back. But when they do, those great cities of the East will never be the same again. The brownskin natives will look at those tall European-style buildings and say, "Colored people lived there once!" And in their minds they will think, "We have a right to live there again."

Brazenness of Empire

That is the thought that will eventually shake the British Empire down to the dust. That thought will shake Dixie's teeth loose, too, and crack the joints of Jim Crow South Africa. The colored peoples of the world are getting very tired indeed of white hotels and white apartment houses and white governors and white viceroys and white generals set down in the midst of their own colored communities, arrogantly demanding respect and special privileges and white rights.

Imagine South Africa, segregation worse than Georgia or Mississippi, passing laws that keep you from moving about at will if you are colored, black labor unionism crushed, Negro newspapers suppressed, white supremacy upheld with a vengeance!

ALL of Africa is more or less that way. ALL of Asia used to be more or less that way, too, except for Japan, the far interior of China, and Soviet Asia. Shanghai, Hong Kong, Manila, Singapore, Sumatra, Bombay, all cities where white foreigners had the gall to draw the color line *even in a colored country!*

In China before this war, I saw hotels for white only. I even saw a Y.M.C.A. for whites. (The "C" in Y.M.C.A., incidentally, means "Christian.") I saw clubs in China that did not admit Chinese. I saw restaurants that did not desire their patronage. Oh, most amazing and audacious nerve of some white folk! They will come into a man's own house and take the best room and put a sign up on it, COLORED NOT ADMITTED. These old-fashioned imperialists are indeed an astounding and brazen tribe! But things will never be the same for them in Asia again.

Ill Wind Blows Good

It is an ill wind that blows nobody good! War is an ugly thing. Fascism is an ugly thing. White or black war, white or black fascism, slaughter of whatever color, or autocracy of whatever color is ugly. I hold no brief for Japanese fascism. I do not want a murderous and fascist-minded world for mine—yellow, brown, black or white. But one good thing this war has done is that it has begun to weaken the unmitigated gall of white imperialism around the world, and it has awakened the colored peoples of the earth to the glaring paradox of Christian democratic pronouncements as contrasted with actual official practices.

Japanese imperialism is just as bad as any other—except that the Japanese do not draw the color line. How could they, being colored themselves? Their little clash at arms with the British and Americans will, I think, profoundly change the future pattern of life in Asia. The British, no doubt, will take back Hong Kong, just as we will take back Manila. The big fine European-style hotels and apartment houses will again go white. White admirals and generals and viceroys and over-lords and bankers and missionaries and whores will again move in. They will think they are living swell.

Passing in the sunlit streets outside, the brown and yellow natives will look up at those fine buildings FOR WHITE ONLY. They will say, "Colored lived there once!" Then silently to themselves they will think, *"We will live there again!"* And each such thought will be a coffin-nail in the stinking little old black box of Western imperialism.

Invasion!!!!

June 17, 1944

The invasion has begun! American troops are in France. The Hitler armies are being driven back, back, back toward Berlin, across the soil of France. France—that has never known color prejudice. The France where a Negro could be a man before Hitler came. The France of the great mulatto writer, Dumas. The France that made Felix Eboué a Governor General in Africa.[4] The France that ever welcomed Negro students and artists and musicians and tourists. The France that made our own dusky Josephine Baker one of the great stars of its popular theater. The France of the Revolution, of the Bastile, of the fighting Marseillaise—that France is the beachhead of our Invasion against Hitler.

American Negroes are a part of that Invasion moving in blood and death and determination into Europe. Men from Harlem and Chicago's South Side and Pittsburgh's Hill and Savannah's Yamacraw and Rampart street and Tuskegee and Dallas and Los Angeles and Seventh street in Oakland and Beale street in Memphis and U street in Washington are moving with the American Army into Europe. Colored women Red Cross workers will follow, or perhaps have already gone across the Channel.

We Are There Today

We are there on the French Coast today—you and I. We are there because people we know and love are there—blood of our blood and bone of our bone. Maybe your son, or your daughter, maybe your brother or sister, husband or cousin, or sweetheart, or friends. Negro and white neighbors are there—so we are there, too.

We are there through the equipment that those of us who work in war plants from Brooklyn to San Diego have helped make—or through the ships that those of us who work in the yards have helped build—or on docks have helped load—or helped to man and sail if we are in the Merchant Marine as are thousands of Negroes. We are there on the Invasion Coast in the shells and bombs and landing barges our money—through War Bonds and taxes—have helped buy. We are there through the blood plasma (in the plainly and deliberately marked *Afro-American* packages) that we have given from our veins to the Red Cross.

Blood to replace in wounded bodies the blood that Hitler spills. Segregated blood—that in the heat of battle no doctor worth his salt cares whether it be segregated or not. Blood that may and does save a white life as quickly as it does a black life. *Blood that saves American lives.* Our blood on the Invasion Coast of Europe, in the veins of men who fall driving Hitler back to Berlin—and death—and yesterday.

Among the First to Land

Jim Crowed at home, you say? Sure, we are Jim Crowed at home. Jim Crowed in the Army? Sure, we are Jim Crowed in the Army. Very few of us in fighting units, you say? That is true. But Negro Engineers were among the first to land in France. Labor Battalions, Service Troops, Quartermasters, or those who load and unload ships under shell fire and air bombardment are in just as dangerous a plight, and are doing just as useful a task as those in infantry or paratroop or glider units. Without the men BEHIND the lines passing on ammunition, there would be no front lines. Without the men ON THE BEACH unloading ships, there would be no beachhead steadily moving inland.

Whatever our job, we are of great value to the Invasion Army of which we are a part. Are you ashamed that some of us are Jim Crowed into not fighting—only working? The shame is not ours. It is up to those who still believe in racial separation—in spite of Hitler's horrible example of death and decay from which they should by now have learned a lesson. It is up to those white Americans who haven't yet understood what a waste of energy and morale goes into segregation. It is up to them to be ashamed—not for you or I.

This is our War because we are dying in it. This is our country because we are dying for it. This is our Invasion because we never did believe in slavery and race hatred and the strong-arm methods of subjugation that Hitler and others like him believe in. The new world that will come out of this war will be *our* world—and a decent world—because we intend to help make it so. Otherwise, we would be unworthy of the Americans—white and black—who push ahead under fire—from the coast of the Invasion toward the heart of tomorrow.

Over-Ripe Apple

August 19, 1944

Adolph Hitler wrote in 1938, "A defeated nation can even better than a victorious nation be trained and prepared for the day of final victory. It may happen that I cannot win victory at once in this coming war. We may be forced to interrupt it . . . But after some years, when the weak and inefficient democracies will have utterly failed to solve the world's post-war problems, then we will suddenly break loose from underground and our stupefied enemies will discover too late that millions of their own youth, misguided by weak education, disappointed by democracy's failure, will be on our side. Victory in this third world's war will be quick and easy. It will be in our pocket like a ripe apple we take from the falling tree of democracy." So spoke Hitler.

Certainly we American Negro citizens know that Jim Crow is one of the over-ripe apples of democracy. The problems of the Negro people in relation to democratic theory have been too long neglected by our federal and state governments, and by our churches and our schools. Government, church, and school have all practiced Jim Crow themselves.

Millions of American children have been brought up full of the idea of white supremacy. Just as millions have been brought up poor and undernourished. Poverty and the race problem are two of America's most over-ripe apples, tainting the whole barrel with their stench.

Hitler Calls Shots

One of the amazing things about Hitler is that he called his own shots well in advance, but nobody believed him. His *Mein Kampf* is full of predictions that he said he would fulfill—and he did. The world took *Mein Kampf* as lightly as America has taken the Ku Klux Klan, America First, Bilbo and Rankin. When these latter gentlemen arise in the Senate and talk just like Hitler about Negroes and Jews, other senators sit silent and say nothing, or else go out and smoke a cigarette, and grin. It is up to America to elect senators who will not keep silent before colleagues who talk like Hitler.

The Philadelphia street car and bus strike, because Negroes are employed to run cars and buses in a city desperately in need of such workers, is a case in point illustrating America's over-ripe apple. If the Philadelphia churches were Christian, and if the Philadelphia schools taught democracy, it would not be a city whose street car conductors, motormen, and whose bus drivers would be so indecent as to strike because fellow-citizens of color are given jobs.

"Weak Education"

Hitler's phrase, "misguided by weak education" is all too apt in regard to our American educational systems. Even now, today, some of our most distinguished universities, both state and private, both Christian and non-sectarian, refuse to admit Negro students. They thus set a most undemocratic example from the word, "Go!" Because starting off like that, they cannot go very far along the democratic road. Princeton is one. The University of Missouri is another. Notre Dame is another.

How can these colleges teach their students decent race relations when they have no decent race relations themselves? Can street car conductors be expected to know more about democracy than college men and women? Either, it seems to me, could see, however, that when manpower is needed to get war workers to their jobs, it is stupid to strike because men are employed who can do the job—but are black.

It seems to me, too, that college men and women, and college presidents and professors, would be smart enough to know that educated people of whatever race are better citizens than are ignorant ones. And that therefore, for the sake of improving all the citizenry, colored students should be admitted to all our schools just as white, Chinese, Jewish, and Latin-American citizens and non-citizens are admitted.

I think it might behoove America to pay more attention to Hitler's threat about that "ripe-apple" that he says a defeated Germany will put in its pocket. It is time we get wise to the fact that Hitler wages not only a military war but a war of ideas, like white supremacy and Nordic blood (for which our unscientific Red Cross has fallen). He also wages a political war, in which he certainly has the help of many of our Southern legislators.

We shall beat Hitler soon on the battle field. We must lick him *and all his ideas* at home, too. Or else that Third World War of which he is already talking, might be not just a phrase in the mouth of a demagogue. Decent Americans, Negro and white, want NO Third World War. Let's get together and pick the rotting, over-ripe, undemocratic apple of segregation out of America's apple barrel.

The Animals Must Wonder

February 3, 1945

Once I saw a man and a woman, who loved each other, quarrel. There were bitter words and the threat of blows. Bursts of anger punctuated minutes of silent defiance. It was sad for an outsider to see. But equally sad to observe was the hurt fright of their dog, his wonder, dumb fear, and terror at the strange loud violence of the two human beings he loved.

At first the animal trotted nervously about the house. He got under his master's feet and was shoved away. His mistress paid him no mind, being too busy yelling at her husband. Finally the dog sat trembling in a corner thinking, perhaps, that both were mad.

A recent dispatch from the European front reports how frightened and panic-stricken domestic animals in the war zones are, caught in the cross-current of battle between the Nazis and the Allied lines. As the armies of human beings go at each other with all the explosive weapons of death at our command, as the skies fill with the roar of bombers, the earth shakes with the bursts of shells, and the very air crackles with gun-fire—unprotected in their terror, the dogs, cats, horses, cows, and sheep must wonder if man, their superior and civilized master, has gone mad.

Panic of Animals

Newspaper men report lost and homeless dogs wandering cold and hungry through wrecked villages where the armies have passed. They report wild-eyed farm horses on stampede, crazed by tanks and planes, cows caught in an artillery barrage, dropping premature calves in snowy fields, sheep and pigs running in circles as if pursued by furies.

Animals, of course, do not know the difference between Nazis and Allies. To a gentle old plow horse deserted by his fleeing owners in the Aachen sector of the Western Front, the guns of both sides must sound like the very roar of hell itself. To a herd of sheep whose pasture is suddenly invaded by flame-throwing tanks, it must seem as if the world has gone mad. The animals in the war zones must be as puzzled as the precocious child whom one of the New York columnists reports as having written a most penetrating little verse to the effect that "in this world of ours wonders never cease! All the civilized peoples are at war—while the savages are at peace."

To the dogs, cats, parrots, and canaries of cities like Warsaw, Budapest, Bitche, or Manila, all human beings must suddenly seem like demons. As bad as life is for barnyard animals caught in the cross-fire of explosive warfare, things must be even worse for household pets accustomed to closer and more intimate contacts with mankind.

To suddenly be deserted in an empty house on a day when the very air explodes like thunder, aviation roars overhead, shells burst in the street, snipers' bullets shatter window panes, and steel tanks crush fences and gardens . . . on such a day, left-lonesome cats and dogs and birds in cages must think the end of time has come.

The S.P.C.A. Is Powerless

I have not read anywhere that the Society for the Prevention of Cruelty to Animals is taking up this current problem of animals and war. But then I suppose this estimable society would be just as impotent to deal with so vast a problem now as was the League of Nations to deal with the problem of human beings and war when Mussolini invaded Ethiopia.[5]

If human beings do not care enough about each other to work out ways of preventing wars before they happen, one could hardly expect them to be considerate of cats, dogs, parrots, canaries, horses, cows, pigs, or sheep. The human race has long claimed superiority over beasts. However, at the moment, from the Rhine to Burma, animals must wonder if this is true.

Given a chance, a cat might eat a canary, but he would not first bomb the canary's house, shell his cage, strafe his perch, snipe at him from ambush, shoot flames at him, then run him down with a tank . . . before slitting his gullet with a bayonet. Neither would a cat use a robot bomb to scare the birdseed out of him. If cats were ever to start doing such things, all vertebrates from canaries to Churchill would swear cats had gone mad. Not only would they be declared as crazy as loons . . . but as crazy as men! Then indeed would cats have lost their minds!

And if the canaries would suddenly start firing back at the cats, we would know the universe had gone mad!

The Fall of Berlin

May 12, 1945

The Lord works in mysterious ways his wonders to perform! It is right and fitting that Berlin should be captured for the Allies by Moscow, rather than by the armies of London or Washington. Berlin was the capital of all the race-haters in the world, the apex-city of white supremacy, the center of the Hitler Aryan blood theory that influenced even our American Red Cross. Moscow is at the opposite end of the poles in terms of race relations. Moscow teaches that all races of men are brothers—and practices it as well. There is no Jim Crow in the Red Armies that took Berlin.

The afternoon that Berlin fell, I was riding in a Jim Crow car through Oklahoma, separated and segregated from the rest of my fellow Americans because I happen to be colored. All the remainder of the long train was for white people. A third of a coach at the end next to the baggage car was set aside for me. The white conductor with his ticket box took up one set of double seats, the brakeman took up another, leaving only eight seats for the colored passengers. There was one toilet for men and women, no smoking compartment—all typical of the disgraceful travel arrangements imposed by law upon Negro citizens in the South.

When I got off the train at Tulsa, almost the first words I heard as I stood waiting for a colored cab—white cabs being capricious about taking Negro passengers—was from a colored man saying, "Berlin has just fallen!" A long ways from Moscow, deep in the Jim Crow country, a Negro said, "Berlin has just fallen! The Russians have just taken Berlin, and the radio says Hitler has committed suicide!"

Hitler's Dead

Hitler, the man who wrote in *Mein Kampf* that you had just as well try to educate an ape as to educate a Negro! Hitler, the man who lynched thousands of Jews! Hitler, the man who supported Mussolini in his invasion of Ethiopia! Hitler, the man who put forth the unscientific theory of the superiority of Nordic blood for which the American Red Cross fell! Hitler, who yelled like Rankin and believed in Jim Crow for all the world! Hitler has committed suicide in the face of the approaching Red Armies!

It is most right and fitting that Moscow should take Berlin first—rather than Paris, London, or Washington. It is fitting that the greatest race-hating city in the world should fall to the armies of a city that has no race-hatred at all. It is both practical and poetic justice that the crooked swastika should fall before the young red star!

Paris, charming, cultured, cosmopolitan center of a Europe that believed in colonies and economic exploitation. Paris, urbane city with too much sophistication to draw harsh racial lines—yet a city where deluxe hotels and restaurants and places of public amusement could still refuse a Negro or an Arab or a Jew because other guests resented such company. Paris, whose gloved oppression of African colonies differed basically not at all from the franker and more brutally expressed oppression of the Anglo-Saxon and Fascist countries. It is well that Paris did not first capture Hitler's Berlin.

New World Center

London, center of the world's most gigantic colonial system—Africa, India, Hong Kong, Jamaica. London, city where color lines are sometimes drawn as blatantly as in Chicago. London, with millions of voteless natives under its command. London, that keeps Gandhi under surveillance, Nehru in jail, and Roger Mais, brilliant young Negro writer of the West Indies, imprisoned. London that says the Atlantic Charter is not meant for colored peoples. It is well that London did not first capture Hitler's Berlin.

Washington, center of the world's democracy, yet the city where, on the trains from the North and East, the conductor comes through the cars and says, "Washington! Colored passengers change to the COLORED COACH ahead." (The capitol of our democracy is where Jim Crow cars begin for Negro Americans.) Washington, where Marian Anderson was barred out of Constitution Hall. It is well that Washington did not first capture Hitler's Berlin.

Paris has colonies. London has colonies. Washington has Jim Crow armies. Paris has voteless Negroes in Africa. London has colored intellectuals in jail for wanting democracy. Washington has a Red Cross blood donors center that practices the Hitlerian blood theory. Paris, London, and Washington still practice the inequalities of peoples based on race. But the Soviet Union's capitol is the world's new center, poles away from all that Berlin stood for, with ourselves in the middle. It is well then that it was Moscow that first captured Hitler's Berlin. Moscow has no colonies, no voteless citizens, and no Jim Crow cars. Moscow will support NONE of Hitler's policies in Berlin.

Part 6

Segregation-Fatigue

He'd Leave Him Dying

December 19, 1942

In the December 5 issue of *The Nation,* Joseph Julian, in his article, "Jim Crow Goes Abroad," quotes a Negro soldier in England as saying that many of his white American comrades in arms over there seem to be doing their best to make life miserable for him, asking the British not to associate with him, leaving pubs when he comes in, changing their seats if he happens to sit beside them in a movie show, and otherwise showing their provincial contempt for fellow American citizens of color in the uniform of the United States Army.[1]

The soldier says he spoke to his white commanding officer about it, saying suppose sometime he came across some of these white soldiers lying bleeding and dying on the battlefield and they needed a drink of water from his flask. The soldier reports the white officer as replying that he should just leave them alone and not touch them. So the Negro soldier, according to Joseph Julian, says that he will do just that—leave his white fellow soldiers lying there on the battlefield bleeding and dying.

Moton Dropped His Arms

This reminds me of a story I once heard the late Robert Russa Moton, then president of Tuskegee, relate to his entire student body during chapel there.[2] In the early morning he was changing trains at Atlanta. He had just stepped down from the train to the platform when he heard a scream behind him. Turning quickly, he saw that a woman had apparently caught her heel on the train step and was about to fall. His first impulse was to stretch out his arms and catch her, but, looking up and seeing that she was white—in the middle of the South—he let his arms fall.

At this point, the students laughed loud and long. Dr. Moton laughed, too. It was a good joke with which to open a chapel program. But to me it seemed one of the saddest stories I had ever heard. A Negro could not afford to be seen catching a white woman in his arms in Atlanta. Naturally, the woman fell on her face on the concrete platform.

A classmate of mine at Lincoln once told me a similar tale. During the summer he worked as a waiter at a white beach hotel in the prejudiced sector of South Jersey. The restaurant was managed by a white woman whose husband was a Southerner. Most of the colored waiters were from the South, too. One day in the pantry as the waiters were preparing the salads, butter, and silver in preparation for dinner, the woman and her husband got into a quarrel, and the man began to beat his wife. None of the colored waiters standing around dared put their hands on the white man to protect his wife. The best they could do was plead, "Don't beat the madam! Sir, please don't beat the madam!" The man said, "You black so-and-so's stay out of this!" They did. Result: the lady got an excellent beating.

I imagine something like that happened in Malaya when the Japanese came. The natives simply let their white folks—as did Dr. Moton—fall flat on their faces.

Here in the United States today legal and customary segregation still prevents colored Americans from using their strength to the full to help save our country from the enemy. Lots of colored Americans, unfortunately, have gotten to the point where they don't care about trying very hard anyway. Which is just another way of saying civilian morale among the Negro section of our population is none too good, in spite of the fact that we want it to be good.

I heard a fellow say in a shoeshine stand in Harlem one day, "The way they are treating the colored soldiers down South is a shame! Segregating them! Dragging them off buses and beating them—just for being colored— and they in uniform, too. I hope old Hitler sails right up the Mississippi as far as Memphis. Maybe he'd teach those crackers some sense. 'Course I don't want him to get as far as Harlem, though. Man, I'll fight to protect Harlem." I gathered from the latter statement that we could put him down as being 50 per cent behind the war effort.

Texas in U.S. Too

I asked a Negro soldier on furlough the other day in Chicago how he liked Texas. He said, "Like a Jew likes Germany."

Texas is a part of the United States. Things ought to be fixed up down there so a colored boy could like Texas a little better than that. In fact, I very greatly wish that the government would begin immediately, right now, a program of pro-democratic education for the whole South aimed at those of our citizens who seemingly do not understand yet how absurd it is to speak of fighting a war for freedom when (in those sections where education is needed most) a Negro is not even free to go in a movie show, unless he wants to enter by way of the alley and sit in the top gallery. When it comes to things more important than movies, like jobs, education, and travel, the line is just as sharply drawn.

And physical terror is still such that a man of Dr. Moton's standing, president of the largest Negro school in the world, would, were he living today, probably still be afraid to catch a falling white woman in his arms to save her from breaking her neck. I judge, however, from the way some of the Southerners are talking in public—from Ethridge to Arnall—that they would rather have their necks broken than act decent.[3]

That is more than I can understand. If I were white, I wouldn't want my neck broken. Would you?

Ask for Everything

January 30, 1943

The late Lincoln Steffens, great American journalist, friend and neighbor of mine when I lived in California, used to say, "The trouble with the colored people is that they never ask for enough. They should ask for everything—then they might get something."[4]

Certainly, if Lincoln Steffens were alive today, I do not believe he would agree with the hush-hush policy advocated for the Negro press by the Dabneys, Graves, and Browns lately writing on the subject, and implying that now is no time for Negroes to ask for freedom and democracy and equal rights.

If now is not the time, then there never was a time. Now is when all the conquered nations of Europe are asking for freedom. Now is when the Jews are asking for it. Now is when America is fighting to keep it. Now is when Nehru and Gandhi are sitting in jail silently demanding it for India. All the papers are full of editorials about it. And the radio is loaded down with it as a part of our war aims. How anybody can expect American Negroes not to catch the freedom fever, too, is beyond me—unless they think we are deaf, dumb, stupid, and blind.

When I read about the signs up in Germany, ARYANS ONLY, that exclude Jews from restaurants and other public places, I think it is pretty bad. But I think it is equally bad when I see signs up in America separating Negroes from whites, or barring out Negroes altogether. And I do see them from New York to California.

Army Sets Bad Example

I think the Negro press is right in demanding an end to segregation in the armed forces of the United States. From the segregated regiment it is naturally no step at all to segregated tables for Negro and white officers, Jim Crow seats for Negroes in the post movies, COLORED and WHITE toilets, and unscientific cans of Jim Crow blood via the Red Cross. When the Army sets the pattern, then with logic the railroads, private employers, and ordinary citizens can say, "To the Jim Crow with you, black boy. To the labor gang. To the segregated union local. Up the back stairs to the movies. You go to a Jim Crow army. Why shouldn't we segregate you in civilian life?"

That's one good reason why there should be no segregation in a democratic American army fighting to preserve and extend democracy. It sets a bad example for the rest of the country, and it doesn't fit the pattern of our war aims.

Not long ago a dozen young Negro draftees, according to a story told me by a passenger on the bus with them, were going from Beaumont to Houston. Only the back seat of the bus had been allotted for Negroes. That seat was full and most of the boys were standing in the aisle as the bus pulled out. The few seats vacant beside white passengers, they were not allowed to take. The boys began to complain, and loudly. They began to question audibly the kind of democracy that did not even permit them to sit down beside their fellow-citizens. They sent a delegation up to talk to the driver. It had its effect. At the next bus stop, the driver telephoned the company. The company sent a whole bus for the Negro passengers with plenty of seats for all. Had those boys kept meekly quiet, they would have stood all the way from Beaumont to Houston. They didn't keep quiet. They got results—even in Texas.

An Immediate Program

The Jim Crow car, and the Jim Crow seats in buses, are a disgrace to the American way of life and should be done away with. Substitute a system of first, second, and third class coaches, if need be, such as has long been customary in Europe—then if there are some people who simply cannot ride with poor Negroes, let them pay more to ride first class where they will probably find only a very few wealthy colored people like Chicago's Jones brothers. Or maybe Rochester.

I agree with the Southern liberals that the Negro problem cannot be solved overnight. But certainly some of its most obnoxious features could be gotten rid of at once, and to nobody's detriment.

So I hope the Negro press will go right on writing and fighting for the right to vote for ALL people, for the abolition of the Jim Crow car and all forms of biracial travel, and for the end of segregation in the Army, the Navy, and the Air Force. No decent American, black or white, thinks these things are right. And nobody would oppose an end to them except the dyed-in-the-wool reactionaries, the deep deep Southerners, and the paid Uncle Toms.

How wonderful it would be for America to be able to say to the rest of the world, "Look here! We have a land where nobody is kept down because of race or color. Look here! We have a land where everybody can vote, and it's not a Ya vote, either. Look here, Asia! Look here, Europe! We have democracy, and we know how to make it work. Here nobody can kick anybody else in the face unjustly and get away with it. We have a great big land, a united land, 'with liberty and justice for all.' See that man there—that's Joe Louis, and he doesn't have to go into a Jim Crow regiment! See that fellow there—that's Clark Gable, who got his wings at Tuskegee![5] See that woman there—that's Mary McLeod Bethune. And she's not just head of the Negro Youth Division of the NYA—she's head of the whole NYA."

> Wait a minute, Jack! Are you dreaming?
> If I am, I'm dreaming about DEMOCRACY.

If Dixie Invades Europe

July 24, 1943

One of the differences between America and Europe is that, over there, they are just a little more used to everything. Things have been going on in a big way for several thousand years, not just a few hundred.

For instance, in Harlem recently, lots of people have been gossiping about an aging front-pager who has taken unto himself a gay young mistress—having had, for many years, a faithful wife. He bought his youthful lady friend a fur coat. It seemed that that shocked Harlem—also his wife. But in Europe not even the wife would have been shocked, let alone the rest of the community—such goings on have been going on so long.

Now, take Negroes and their place in life. In Europe before Hitler came to power, nobody paid much attention to Negroes one way or another, except maybe to stare discreetly if they hadn't seen one for a long time. Here in the U.S.A. folks have seen us everyday for three hundred years, but they still look at us as if we were out of place. Europe is just more used to people in general, white or colored.

Now, let us take war. Europe is so used to wars that they don't think the human race is on the brink of destruction every time a few years of fierce fighting come along. It's the same way with social change. Systems of government can rise or fall without their thinking that mankind has reached his end. Practically no political party in Europe wants to keep things as they are. All of them want to go forward—or backward. But here in America lots of politicians, deathly afraid of change, just want to stand still. That is especially so in regard to political attitudes on the race problem.

Prejudice for Export

One of the things that worries me about race is that when the Allies invade Europe, the American forces might take with them onto the Continent more race prejudice than Hitler and Mussolini together have been able to manufacture in the last decade. Unless many of our army officers, troops, and Red Cross workers have changed since they left home, our conquering armies will carry along Jim Crow units, separate clubs for service men, and Jim Crow cans of blood.

That blood business, of course, will delight Hitler. He, no doubt, will find quite a bond between himself and the American Red Cross—because the premise of Hitler's whole superiority complex is the Aryan blood theory which the Red Cross also supports 100 per cent.

One hope that American race prejudice will not spread over Europe with the coming of the doughboys lies in the possibility that the Russians may meet the Allies half-way—so that part of occupied Europe will be red instead of Jim Crow.

Paris, Milan, Berlin, Prague, and Copenhagen were all nice cities, racially speaking, before the spread of the Fascist powers and the coming of war. When we liberate those once charming cities, it would be a shame for our armies to promulgate there our own fascist-like racial policies toward colored peoples. Jim Crowism is most certainly fascist-minded, although we have been practicing it in America much longer than Hitler.

Step Backwards

Negroes may not attend a single downtown theater in Washington, nor stop at the Mayfair hotel, nor attend the state-supported University of Maryland, nor belong to the Democratic Party in Texas, nor live in certain towns in the South. For the Grand Opera at Paris to send Negroes to the gallery, or the Cafe de la Paix to refuse to serve colored people a meal because the invading Americans bringing democracy might not like it, would certainly be a step backwards in civilization for the Europeans. Yet if we get there before the Red Armies, that is very likely to happen.

Because segregation, separate blood banks, and all that sort of thing is so closely related to Hitlerite practice, America ought to change it. Surely we ought not to allow it to spread over the world any further than it has spread. But when we have it so strongly entrenched at home, there is no way to keep it from being taken abroad. So we have got to start out right here and clean house, providing we can persuade the Washington powers-that-be to turn their democratic brooms into our own dark corners while our military powers are cleaning up Europe and Asia.

Clearly if, in the fighting field, a Second Front on the Continent is important, equally important in the civilian field here is a federal attack on racial division—a Second Front against Jim Crowism, anti-Semitism, Mexican-baiting, and all such anti-democratic carryings on at home, lest we cannot resist taking such attitudes abroad. For our American Army to pack up these antiquated racial policies of ours, knapsack, bag and baggage, and transport them to Europe would be a pity, indeed.

If we march into Berlin playing DIXIE in our hearts, instead of THE STAR SPANGLED BANNER, as far as colored people are concerned, Hitler had almost just as well stay there himself. God knows I don't like Hitler or Jim Crowism either. I think both of them ought to go!

Gall and Glory

October 23, 1943

I haven't seen a Negro yet about to be inducted into the army who did not say, "I hope they don't send me down South." Being sent to North Africa or New Guinea doesn't seem to phase them. Even those who are raring to go, and anxious to escape a none too secure civilian life, say, "The only thing I hate about going into the army is they'll probably send me down South for my basic. And I do not want to go down South."

The stories colored soldiers bring back on furlough, and the letters they write home, and to the newspapers, certainly do not give a very inviting picture of life in the South for colored troops. An example:

A young colored soldier inducted in New York (which is a pretty decent city, racially speaking) was on maneuvers in a Southern state. Troop operations took them through a small town on a broiling hot day. The white officers and soldiers and WACs went into the various restaurants for refreshments and food. There were no colored restaurants about and the Negro soldiers knew they could not eat or drink in the white ones. The Negro staff sergeant, however, sent the young colored soldier from New York into a cafe to bring out some cold drinks for the boys.

The soldier was standing at the counter waiting for the bottles to take out when a white civilian stepped up and said, "Get away from this counter. You can't stand here."

The colored soldier stepped back against the wall. But that did not satisfy the white customer. He said, "Get on out the door and wait for your stuff out there."

The colored soldier said, "I was sent in here by my sergeant to buy something. I know I cannot eat in here, but why do I have to go out before I get what I was sent for?"

The white man replied, "Because you're a Negro, that's why!" Only he didn't say "Negro," but rather the traditional Southern variation.

This made the colored soldier angry. He was not used to the discourtesy of Southern gentlemen. He answered, "I am in the uniform of the United States Army. If you don't respect me as an American citizen because I am colored, at least you ought to respect the uniform of your Army."

"You're a Negro," the man replied, "so get outside."

The soldier said, "YOU have no right to order me outside."

Whereupon a white lieutenant came up to the colored soldier and ordered him to go out, saying that he personally was sorry and he realized what the colored boys had to put up with, but to keep down trouble, "go out!" Not one white officer, not one white soldier, not one white WAC stood up for the Negro soldier. Not one said anything to the white man who so insultingly denied even the courtesy of decent address to one of Uncle Sam's fighters. Not one cared enough about the colored soldiers outside—in the hot sun with no right to a cool drink on a hot day in the middle of an ungracious town—to rebuff that ill-mannered racial bigot.

On the Jim Crow Car

Another story: The half coach of the Jim Crow car is crowded, so crowded that even women with babies are forced to ride on the platform between the coaches, and in the toilets which are given over to seating space. Many soldiers are standing.

There are some fifteen cars on the train for the white passengers and these cars are not so crowded. One of the colored soldiers begins to talk. He says, "This is a shame, all of us crowded into one half of a hot coach, with all those other coaches behind where people are not standing. But our women with children have to ride on the platforms and in the toilets. We are fighting for democracy, too, and this is a no-good shame!"

A trainman calls a white MP to make the Negro soldier stop talking about the undemocratic tradition of the Jim Crow coach. The white MP comes into the car. The Negro soldier says to the white MP, "Wouldn't you be angry, too, if you had to ride a hundred miles standing up when there are seats in the next coach? And wouldn't you be less than a man if you didn't object to your women and your children riding in toilets, and on smoky platforms when other people paying the same fare ride in air-cooled coaches?"

The MP, who must have been a decent guy, flushed and did not answer.

Not Ashamed Enough

The white lieutenant at the counter was sorry about the colored soldier who was put out of the cafe. The white MP on the train was ashamed of the crowded Jim Crow car. But neither of them was sorry ENOUGH, or ashamed ENOUGH, to do anything about the immediate situation.

Another story: A colored soldier is walking down the streets of Savannah with his wife who has come from a Northern city to visit him. Officers stop him and demand of the woman a health card, usually demanded of prostitutes. The soldier explains that she is his wife. He is accused of lying. One word brings on another. Both are arrested.

So it goes, woeful tale after tale of the inequalities of segregation and Jim Crowism as it affects our soldiers. For a Negro, serving Uncle Sam in Dixie is indeed glory mixed with gall.

Hey, Doc! I Got Jim Crow Shock!

February 26, 1944

One of the things that puzzled me in Spain, when I was there during the Civil War as a reporter for the *Baltimore Afro-American*, was the treatment of shell-shocked soldiers, particularly those who had run away under heavy fire or after several days of air bombardment such as troops experienced at the Battle of Brunete. Some of these men were put in hospitals for treatment. Others were court-martialled as cowards.

According to the newspaper *PM*, our present American army is handling such cases of shell-shock, currently termed battle-fatigue, more intelligently than ever before. Modern psychiatric methods are being employed, accompanied by the latest sleep and rest treatments known to science, designed to make men forget images of fright.

PM did not say, however, whether some men who run away under stress of battle are still court-martialled as cowards or not. Just who gets treatment in a hospital for shattered nerves, and who gets punishment in a stockade for cowardice, and how that is decided, I do not know. Some day I hope to find out.

Segregation-Fatigue

At any rate, the other day I heard of the case of a Negro soldier who did not run away in battle. For a year he had been in the South Pacific in a dangerous theater of action.

He was sent back to the United States for further training, and placed in an army camp in the deep South. He came through the dangers of the South Pacific all right, but here in our own Dixieland, Jim Crow got the best of him. He went off the beam, so the story runs, struck a white officer, and is now in a military prison.

It seems to me that his case might have been merely a case of Jim Crow shock, too much discrimination—segregation-fatigue which, to a sensitive

Negro, can be just as damaging as days of heavy air bombardment or a continuous barrage of artillery fire. To fight for one's country for months on some dangerous and vital front, then come home and be subjected to the irritations and humiliations of Southern Jim Crowisms, Dixie scorn, the back seats if any in buses, is enough—I should think—to easily drive a sensitive patriotic colored American soldier NUTS.

In my opinion, the American army should take up seriously—and at once—the problem of segregation-fatigue on the home front in relation to its Negro fighting men returned from overseas. The best of psychiatric treatment should be given them to prevent their developing discrimination-neuroses as a result of Jim Crow.

I gather from our weekly press that the average white old-line officer in the army is none too sympathetic to the problems of Jim Crowism in the military forces, simply taking such a set-up for granted. Even the Negro Colonel Benjamin Davis Sr., from newspaper reports, appears to be not too understanding.[6] (Perhaps he has been a colonel so long he has forgotten what it feels like to be just a colored private somewhere in Dixie.)

But, since I understand that now almost every large army post has on its medical staff trained psychiatrists, and since psychiatry recognizes the damage that harsh emotional stresses can render the physical body as well as the mind, I should think that officers in charge of Negro troops in the South should inform their men that if one feels segregation-fatigue coming on, with nerves taut to the breaking point from his personal battle with Jim Crow, he should at once report to the army psychiatrist.

Color Line Complexes

At least, from a good psychiatrist he might get hospital attention in case a Jim Crow breakdown developed into discrimination-neurosis, rather than several months in the stockade from a court-martial which sees only military infraction of rules. Before going over the hill from inability to stand any more Jim Crow, or before hauling off and hitting some Dixie white man with Civil War complexes, or before cussing out some "down-home" officer—all of which is wrong from a military viewpoint when done in one's right mind, but definitely neurotic from a psychiatric viewpoint when done under stress of emotional breakdown—I should think before letting these things happen, it would behoove a colored soldier feeling segregation-fatigue coming on to rush to the post hospital right away and get some expert advice from a psychiatrist.

Southern whites who are members of the military personnel and who suffer from color-domination complexes should also be treated by psychiatric methods.

But when they impose their neuroses on defenseless Negroes, emotionally for a Negro it is often like a ton of bombs falling a few hundred yards away. A Negro's mental and nervous system can be just as gravely injured by Jim Crow shock as it can be injured by the contusion of explosives.

Until a more decent pattern of life is forthcoming in the South, perhaps psychiatry might help repair some of the mental ills inevitably resulting from our present color stupidities. Certainly these ills should not be permitted to plague our soldiers. They have a war to win.

Fifty Young Negroes

December 2, 1944

It is Sunday morning, November 19, 1944. Over the radio this early morning comes reports from San Francisco that fifty young American Negro sailors have been found guilty of mutiny for refusing to load ammunition after the Port Chicago explosion that killed three hundred and twenty-three seamen, mostly Negro Navy sailor-stevedores. These fifty young Negroes have been given terms ranging from eight to fifteen years.

I go out into the Harlem streets to buy the morning papers to see if the news is true. Sure enough, it is there in the Sunday papers. I wonder if Negro Americans all across America are thinking what the old colored man, who sold me the papers at his combination bootblack-newsstand, implied when he said, "White folks tried them boys."

I am constantly amazed at some of the things white Americans do to their Negro fellow-citizens. I once wrote an article in *Common Ground* called, "White Folks Do the Funniest Things." But much of what they do to us is not funny at all. This morning I keep thinking of Alabama's famous Scottsboro trials—nine Negro kids tried and retried for their lives on the flimsy charge of raping two white girls in a coal car on a moving train between two stations not twenty minutes apart. They were put in the death house and kept there for months. None were killed but now, after a dozen years, some of those boys are still in prison. "White folks tried them boys."

What Do They Think We Are?

I remember a few weeks ago seeing in the newspapers a photograph released by the Navy of the court-martial of these fifty Negro sailors. It was a very strange and most unwise picture for our Navy's propaganda department to release. There, on the front page of the paper in which I saw it, were pictured a mass of Negro sailors on trial and, in front of them at the judicial tables, the judges and accusers ALL were white. Not a Negro among the officials sitting in judgment, according to this picture!

What do white folks think we are—imbeciles, morons, dolts, complete fools—that we do not notice these things? For so long in this country it has been the same old story—judge and jury ALL white. That old story has given us a sort of helpless, hopeless feeling about American justice in relation to Negro citizens. At this stage of crisis on the war fronts, it seemed to me most unwise to release on the front pages of our papers a visual version of such justice.

Perhaps many white Americans in power do not care what American Negroes think, or how we feel. In its issue of November 1, the *New York Times* reports from Italy that Major General Edward M. Almond of Luray, Virginia, commanding the all-Negro Ninety-second Division there, says that he does not ever "foresee the time when his outfit will include Negro junior officers outranking white junior officers." In other words, in the Ninety-second Division of this democratic American army of ours, white officers will *always* outrank Negroes, will *always* command Negroes, no matter how brilliant Negro officers may become in the tactics of warfare. What a fine statement to come from a top-flight officer in an army for which we pay taxes, too, and in which our men also die.

Negroes Cry in Vain

Roi Ottley's recent cable from Paris to the newspaper *PM* is headlined, WANT COMBAT DUTY, NEGROES CRY IN VAIN.[7] In France, Ottley reports the Negro soldier is doing little more than most Negroes are permitted to do in civilian life back home—heave bales and tote bags. Ottley quotes that great colored track star and brilliant college man, Lieutenant Ben Johnson—who is in a trucking unit—as saying we have officers in our army who do not believe the Negro can be made into a first-class soldier, and that they don't even give him a chance.[8]

Again it is a case in which, "White folks try them boys." I suppose as long as prejudiced, undemocratic whites dominate our army and navy, whites who are not ashamed to picture and speak their lack of democracy in the public prints, the Negro will continue to be largely officered by men like General Almond. And Negro soldiers and sailors will continue to mostly drive trucks, stevedore, load ammunition, tote supplies—rather than fight.

I wonder, did those sitting in judgment on the fifty Negro sailors in California judge only the fact that they are alleged to have refused to load ammunition after the explosion that killed hundreds of their comrades and shattered the nerves and morale of those men who remained alive? Or did they take into consideration that which goes much deeper into their lives than the explosion—the years of humiliation, insult, and Jim Crowism through which all American Negroes have gone since birth and that still shatters our nerves and morale every day—be we soldiers, sailors, or civilians? Did the white men "who tried them boys" look at the mote in their own eyes before sending a black man to jail for fifteen years?

The Purple Heart

March 24, 1945

This is the winter when the war began to come close to me. It began before winter set in with a distant cousin whom I never knew who was killed in the 99th Pursuit Squadron over Italy. It came closer in the fall when I learned belatedly that a friend died on the Anzio beachhead, a friend I had not thought about much for a long time—but his dying made me think of him again.

Then I began one of my annual lecture trips, this time from Wisconsin to Georgia. I stopped overnight in various homes—some white, some colored. In nearly every home, my hosts would show me a picture of a boy or girl in the services, a son or daughter overseas, at sea, or far off in camp. Sometimes my room would have been the son's room when he was home—tennis rackets still around, sports coats still in the closet.

The other day on a train heading Southward to Birmingham, they kept adding coaches at the end. I kept seeing groups of young men—15 to 30— saying goodbye to people on station platforms through Virginia and Tennessee. Draftees heading for an induction center down the line. Men going off to war. Relatives saying goodbye.

As the train pulled out some cried—men and women. They were all white, these draftees, as were the older men and women left on the station platform. Poor whites mostly, poorly dressed, red faced, with deep lines in their necks and stringy hair—"crackers," traditional enemies of the Negro.

"They would not feel sorry for me," I thought, "if I were lynched."

Better to Be Friends

I remember how at breakfast that morning in a crowded dining car I had had a whole four-chair table to myself because people like these were not willing to eat with a Negro. I saw at every station—usually off on the side, the South's traditional COLORED WAITING ROOM sign—their version of Hitlerism adopted long before Hitler. Now their sons were going away to war.

"They would not feel sorry for me if I were lynched—these 'cracker' parents in this Jim Crow state," I thought. Why did I feel sorry for them? Deep and lined were the wrinkles in an old man's neck just beneath my window as he embraced a young man—a stocky, red, embarrassed, poor white young man whose eyes were red, too.

"These are the people who hate Negroes," I kept saying to myself as the train gathered speed. But the thought would not come through clear and clean. "If I could help you, I would," kept getting tangled up with the thought that these people would not care if I were lynched.

"It would be better if we could be friends," I thought. "It would be better if we could find a way to stop hating anybody, and to learn how to get along together. It would be better if nobody had to send their sons off to war. You are the people who hate Negroes. Sometimes I have seen you look at my face in a car window and laugh. Today, as the train pulls out, you are not looking at any window except the window where your boy's face is. I see your tears, and I am sorry."

No Color Line in Death

That evening I stayed at the home of a Negro college president whose only son had just been killed on the Italian front. His son, after death, had been awarded the Purple Heart. The college president and his wife showed it to me, with its rolled, diploma-like citation from the President of our country. I had never seen a Purple Heart before.

I took it in my hand in its satin-lined box, a beautiful heart of purple and gold on a purple ribbon. On the back it said: "For military merit." The citation added: "For wounds received in action."

"For wounds received on the cross of human frailty," I thought, "of all our failing to create a world where young men do not need to go off to kill each other."

I thought of the rows of "crackers" on the village platforms my train had passed all afternoon. I remembered their tears at their sons' departure. I thought of the groups of poor-white young men going down the line to war—to "wounds received in action"—maybe to a Purple Heart—maybe to death. For some are sure to die.

They will die for me, I thought, just as the Negro son from this home died for them. There is no color line in death. *In spite of each other,* we die for each other—poor-whites—Negroes—soldiers—sons—heroes of the Purple Heart "for wounds received in action." Eligible for medals, eligible for tears at death—as at departure. Eligible to shake hands tomorrow—when we grow big enough to know how to live for each other. Eligible for friendship then—not hate.

War and a Sorry Fear

June 23, 1945

I have been away from home for ten weeks in Alabama and Georgia, Louisiana and Texas, reading my poems to people a long ways from Harlem where I live. While I was away the President died, Berlin fell to the Russians, the European war ended, the taverns ceased closing at midnight, and the neon signs came on again. When I got back to Harlem last night, I found the lights blazing, and the old fear deepening in Harlem minds that the war would end too soon.

Of course, for all folks in the war, or who have sons in the war, it cannot end too soon. But for some colored civilians who have only acquaintances or friends in the war, the feeling seems to be that it is ending too soon—that is, too soon for the white folks to have learned their lesson. As an American, I deeply regret this feeling. As a Negro American I understand it, but I regret it right on. No war can end too soon.

Out of this war have come some of Negro America's greatest gains. Our late President issued his famous Order 8802 outlawing discrimination in war plants. The Navy dropped its bars against Negroes being other than flunkies. The Army spoke out against discriminations on Army posts. Almost all thinking America became conscious of our racial derelictions. Hitler pointed up very sharply what "Nordic supremacy" means. But Negro America wants a whole lot more out of this war before it ends. Perhaps that is why Harlem did not celebrate V-J day with any great outburst of emotion.

War Lesson Not Learned

Negro America wants ALL of America to learn that it is NOT right to continue the poll tax, to deny the vote to millions on account of color, to continue the segregated set-up of the armed forces, to Jim Crow blood in the Red Cross, to keep segregated trains and buses running, to permit restricted covenants in housing. Negro America hoped white America would learn these things out of this war. Now seeping into Negro America is the fear that the war is ending too soon. The neon signs have come on too rapidly. The curfew is over too quickly. White America has not learned what it should have learned from this war.

As an American I am deeply sorry this is so. I would have my country know that what we have here of Hitler should have gone long ago. I would have my country know that there is no truth in the false differences of blood, and no democracy in the false limitation of opportunities because of race, and no justice in segregated buses and trains, and no decency in a separate Army and Navy. I regret my country did not learn more quickly, but I never really expected bullets and bombs three thousand miles away to be good teachers. The dead never know what hit them, and the wounded seldom realize that their own collective failings at home helped make the bullets that struck them down.

Domestic wars have to be fought at home—and not with bullets, but with persuasion—unless we want Civil War, which no good American wishes. How can you and I—ordinary Negro Americans—not big shots (because most of us are not big shots) help our white fellow Americans realize it is not good for them to keep on segregating, limiting, mistreating, and being rude to colored citizens here at home? So far the war, and the big shots, and all the inter-racial committees put together have failed to make white America as a whole realize this. How can we help do it?

Explain to White Americans

Maybe we could help do it if each and every Negro who knows a white person, or who works with or under a white person, would simply say to-day to *each* white person he or she knows or works with or under, "Listen, I want you to know, and to tell everybody you know, that it is time for you and all your friends to help make an America where nobody will be afraid of Hitler here, or the shadow of Hitler here, or the likes of Hitler in people who *think* like Hitler here. Listen, it is time for you to help me get rid of Jim Crow cars, and jobs on the basis of color rather than ability, and segregation in public places and schools and the Army. Listen, it is time for you to help make America mean what America is supposed to mean."

Tell that drug store on the corner, "I want to be able to buy a coke at the counter just like anybody else." And tell that ten-cent store, "I want my daughter to be able to get a job in here just like anybody else when you need clerks."

Explain to your white fellow American, "Hitler isn't just a foreigner. Hitler is you and me when we don't act right to each other. And Hitler is no good anywhere in the world, neither in Berlin nor Birmingham, Tokyo nor Topeka. So let's start being Americans, not Nazis, or Fascists, or Mikados. Shake! Let's go drink a coke together at the next corner and talk it over! Let's be friends, you and me! Understand, America?"

V-J Night in Harlem

August 25, 1945

In the early days of the war, there was a good deal of mumbling and grumbling around Harlem about "this is a white man's war," reinforced, of course, by military segregation and the Red Cross blood bank policy. But the way

Harlem celebrated V-J night when the news came that the war was finally over, indicated that Harlem had long since accepted the war as its own, too.

A few seconds after the radio carried its first flash that Truman had received the Japanese surrender note, bits of paper began to snow down from Harlem windows, just as all over New York. Within a few minutes the streets were full of people, auto horns were blowing, and kids were beating on garbage pail tops. The first person I recognized on my corner was a woman with tears in her eyes. "I am so glad!" she said. "It means my husband can come home from New Guinea."

As darkness deepened, Seventh avenue, Harlem's main street, became like a carnival or a summer-time New Year's Eve. Autos raced up and down, cut-outs wide open, horns blowing, flags and streamers flying, and folks clinging to running boards. Crowds overflowed the sidewalks. Musical instruments and noise-makers rent the air. One man put his victrola on a baby carriage and pushed it down the street playing records. Pretty girls were grabbed and kissed by groups of unknown men. And a fellow had painted himself a big sign, influenced by Father Divine: PEACE—THAT'S ALL.[9]

Mixed Pairs of Cops

Cops in pairs were on every corner. But it was different from that tense week some years ago when Italy invaded Ethiopia and the police department flooded Harlem with men. Then they were almost entirely white cops who glared at the Negroes and were glared at by the colored people. This time, V-J night, nearly every pair of cops was a mixed pair, one white, one colored. And whenever a situation developed that required police attention, it was the colored cop who took the initiative. New York's police department learned something from the last riot.

Downtown in the Times Square district where half of New York poured from the subways to celebrate, Negroes poured, too, up into the hilarious mass of people there. It was a great good-natured typically New York kind of celebration, all races and all classes pushing and yelling and cheering.

When I returned to Harlem, one man sitting in front of my house said, when I asked him why he wasn't out celebrating, "Why should I celebrate? Prejudice now is just as bad as it ever was."

Another man asked me if I had ever worked in a hotel. I said, "Yes." He said, "Well then tell me what does a houseman have to do? They laid me off my war job yesterday, so I saw an ad for a houseman and I think I will apply. You don't have to deliver no mail to guests or anything like that, do you? I ain't much at reading. I only had a second grade education down South."

Definition of Fascism

I told him a houseman didn't have anything to do with mail in a hotel, but with cleaning and handy-man work and anything too heavy for a maid to do. So when I went to bed I kept thinking of these two colored men, and how fascism really hasn't been beaten in the world yet, only defeated in its boldest military form—for fascism is the kind of thing that made one Harlemite not celebrate, and another handicapped for life because the South had given him only a second grade education.

Fascism is Bilbo and Rankin and Eastland who don't want Negroes or Jews or Italian-Americans to have job protection. Fascism is the president of Dartmouth college who doesn't want minorities to have an equal chance at education. Fascism is our Red Cross that follows Hitler's blood policy. Fascism is the force that would keep people ignorant and helpless in the face of economic greed, and that gathers its educational, economic, or military power to support its suppression of the people.

The war in Europe and the war in Asia is won, militarily speaking. Plenty of people are dead and cannot shoot any more, and the atom bomb has terrified the heart of man. Death has beaten death, force has beaten force. Those of us triumphant who belong to the victorious United Nations from London to Harlem, Melbourne to Chicago's South Side, Paris to Yamakraw have now the urgent duty of winning the war in our own lands and our own hearts, to put an end to the forces and the feelings that give cause to any man to question, "Why should I celebrate?" Or ask, "Does a houseman's job have anything to do with the mail? I only went to the second grade."

This war will be won only when EVERYBODY can celebrate being alive on a basis of equality with everyone else alive, when there is education and economic security for everyone, and our billions of dollars are spent on *life*, NOT death, on *human well-being*, NOT atom bombs.

North, South, and the Army

October 27, 1945

The other night in a crowded New York cafeteria I heard a little story that illustrates most graphically the whole racial situation in these United States. The story demonstrates that white-Negro relations are a national problem affecting both civilian and military life. It illustrates how the army has helped to worsen these relations. It proves wrong those Southerners, both white and Negro, who say that Southern Jim Crow is a "Southern" problem having nothing to do with the North. And it shows that often to achieve even the simplest things, Negroes must make an abnormal effort, and put up a fight, or show of fight, that other citizens do not have to be bothered with.

It was a funny little story, but a very sad little story, too. I heard it by pure accident because, looking for a place at which to sit with my tray of food, I happened to sit down at a table where, a few minutes later, a colored taxi cab driver with a big plate of baked beans also came to eat. There was a friend with him and the taxi driver started to tell the friend about an incident that had taken place that day.

The taxi cab driver said, "A man got into my cab downtown this afternoon and told me," and here he imitated a deep South cracker drawl, "'Boy, take me to 59th and Fifth avenue.'"

A Memory Explodes

We at the table laughed at the way he imitated a Southern white mode of speech. The taxi driver went on, "I told him, 'I ain't gonna take you nowhere. You get out of my cab—and damn quick!'"

The astonished Southerner asked, "Why?" and the Negro taxi driver said, "Because I don't like you, that's why! You crackers treated me so mean when I was in the army down South that I don't never want to see none of you no more!" The white man called a policeman to make the Negro driver take him to his destination, whereupon the Negro proceeded to tell the cop how badly colored soldiers are treated in Mississippi. The cop advised the white Southerner to take another cab.

These are the preliminaries to the little tale that capped the climax. But even this much of the story, I think, illustrates that what the South does racially affects the North—for here was a New York cab driver of color still so mad about his treatment months before in Mississippi that he was taking it out on an unknown, strange white man visiting in New York—just because the man was white and had a Southern accent.

As the taxi driver ate his beans, he went on to tell us of the painful months he spent in a Mississippi training camp before his recent release from the service. He told us about buses that left Negro soldiers standing hour after hour at the camp gates until all the white men on leave were carried into town. He told us about brutal civilian police in Jackson and Meridian. He said there had been a lynching near his camp with the body left hanging three days as a warning to Northern Negroes on how to behave in the South. Then he told about that last straw that made him go get a gun one day to fight and die, if need be, on American soil for his democratic rights. That the single right involved was so basically primitive and simple makes his story all the more symbolic of our American racial situation.

A Soldier Sits

Said the taxi driver, as he finished his beans, "They sent me to do some work in the white part of the camp that day. My bladder was always weak, so I had to go to the latrine no sooner than I got there. Everything is separate in Mississippi, even latrines. But there wasn't any COLORED latrines anywhere around, so I started to go in the one marked WHITE. A cracker MP yelled at me to halt, and when I didn't halt—because I couldn't—he drew his gun on me and cocked it. He threatened to shoot me if I went in that WHITE latrine.

"Well, he made me so mad, I walked all the way back to my barracks and got a gun myself. I came back and I walked up to that white MP. I threw my gun on him and I said, 'Neither you nor me will never see no Germans nor no Japs if you try to stop me from going in this latrine this morning.' That white boy didn't try to stop me. I went in. But by that time I was so mad I decided not to do what I started to do in the beginning. I decided to sit down and stay awhile. So I did. With my gun on my lap, I just sat—and every time a white soldier came in, I cocked the trigger. Ain't nobody said a word. They just looked at me and walked out. I stayed there as long as I wanted to— black as I am—in that WHITE latrine."

He pushed his empty plate away and stood up. As he left he said, "Down in Mississippi a colored soldier has to have a gun even to go to the toilet! That is why I will not ride no white crackers in my cab in New York today."

Part 7

Are You a Communist?

The Red Army

March 6, 1943

The Soviet Union and the rest of the Allied nations have just finished celebrating the 25th anniversary of the Red Army. Ten years ago when I was in the Soviet Union, the Red Army had not yet been called upon to test its strength, but everywhere throughout the Socialist Soviet Republics you could feel it gathering strength, and see how the energies of the people were directed toward the nurturing and perfecting of their army.

Food was rationed in the Soviet Union then (there I first got used to rationing books). Sometimes there was no sugar to be had, no tea, or very little bread. Should you complain or seem puzzled about this, you would be told, "But it is going to the Red Army." Or, "It is being stored for the army."

When a visiting tourist was driven nearly mad by the extremely bad service at Intourist, the Soviet Travel Bureau's offices which must have been run for the most part by ill-bred bureaucrats or intentionally rude saboteurs, sympathetic citizens would explain, "But, comrade, you don't understand—the best brains we have are all working for the Red Army. Our best translators, who speak good English and French, are working with the government or for the army—so please forgive the bad service at Intourist."

A Real People's Army

As a foreign writer, on several occasions I was invited to visit the barracks, clubs, and camps of the Red Army, and many Red Army men became my friends. I dined with them, read Negro poetry to them, spoke to them about America, our current problems, and the Scottsboro boys.

At one camp I was honored by suddenly being tossed two or three dozen times high in the air in a blanket—by a company of soldiers who assured me that that playful rough house salute was only given to friends.

In Askhabad, the capital of Turkmenia, during the fall I spent there, my best friend was an Asiatic Red Army man as dark as I am, on furlough after

two years in the High Pamirs on the Soviet-Chinese border. He had many
strange tales to tell about the ways of life and love in those mighty moun-
tains, and about how the old customs were disappearing and new ways of
life coming into being there in the heart of Asia—along with the teachers
and doctors and nurses and books in native languages never before put down,
that the Soviets were bringing to people nobody else had paid any decent
attention to or ever given a damn about how they got along.

What interested me most about the Red Army was its close contact with
the people, and the people with it. Everywhere there seemed the greatest
sense of friendship between soldiers and civilians. In Moscow, the Red Army
theater was crowded by people who didn't belong to the army. Civilian clubs
and schools had a way of adopting units of the army, writing them letters,
sending them gifts, and seeing that the men were entertained.

In Ashkhabad, way down in the Turkmenian desert, one high school had
adopted the whole crew of a ship of the Red Fleet. While I was there the
children were entertaining a delegation of sailors who came all the way from
the Baltic Sea to the Persian border to visit their young god-parents who had
written them so often, and sent them presents from that far-off Asiatic out-
post of the Soviet Union. The sailors who came were all Russian Slavic boys,
blond-haired, some of them. The young people whose comrades and guests
they were, were all yellow-brown Turkmenians with the straight black hair
of Asia. These children had never seen the sea, or a battleship—but they
adopted a battleship. It was their own, and its sailors were their friends.

Son of Toiling People

Often at night, in the big cities of Russia, you could hear truck loads of
soldiers going through the streets, singing in that deep Russian bass that
vibrates in the air like a drum. On the Seventh of November in the Red
Square—the Soviet's Fourth of July—I saw thousands of these soldiers lined
up as Marshall Voroshilov dashed from the gates of the Kremlin to ride past
them on his horse.

A great rolling cheer broke out at one end of the massed companies and
swept in an ever increasing roar across the ranks as the Marshall passed. Then
he returned to the center of the Square and, before the massed troops, ad-
ministered the stirring Oath of Allegiance of the Red Army that begins, "I, a
son of the toiling people . . ."

Son of the toiling people, that is the Red Army! Created from and by the
workers of the Soviet Union—the only land in the world that truly belongs
to the toiling people—controlled by and for those who work.

The strength of all the working arms of the Soviet Union is behind these
fighting arms of the Red Army. Peasants, workers, and soldiers—together
the toiling people and their sons are strong. Look, world! See how strong is

the strength of the toiling people! The Red Army is only 25 years old! Only 25 years old—yet see how strong it is because it springs from the strength and faith of the working people determined to guard the only land in the world belonging to the workers.

To you, Red Army, on your birthday, a salute from Negro America. We, too, are working people. I, a son of the toiling people, know that you fight for me.

Army of Liberation

July 15, 1944

So the Red Army is rolling across Poland!

I remember when I was a kid out in Kansas and the paper boy would pass on his bicycle and throw the evening paper up on the front porch with a thud against the screen door, my grandmother would maybe read bits of news aloud after supper. Sometimes there would be an item about pogroms in Poland. I learned very early in life that Poland was a country where the Jews were treated as a shunned people, segregated, humiliated, and killed by mobs. It seemed to me then that Poland must be, in relation to Jews, somewhat like America in relation to Negroes.

Later when I came East to Ohio to go to high school, and there were many children of foreign born parents in my high school, I learned more about the Jews in Poland. From the sons and daughters of emigrant German Jews and Russian Jews and Roumanian Jews, I learned that the Polish Jews were (so they said) the dirtiest and most uncouth of all European Jewery. Some of my schoolmates were Polish Jews, and they did not seem uncouth to me. But the Jews from more decent and prosperous parts of Europe looked down their noses at the Polish Jews—an attitude not unlike that of Boston Negroes toward Negroes from Georgia.

From the Polish Gentile kids in my high school, I heard how all Jews were no good, and how in Poland Jews lived in ghettoes away from the rest of the people. I thought, that is how I, a Negro, live in Cleveland.

Poland's Black Eye

Years later when I went to Europe, I found in France and Italy before Hitler that Jews lived more or less like other citizens. And in Soviet Russia I learned that there were laws that worked against any sort of racial discrimination. There Jews were guaranteed in practice as well as theory, equal rights with all Soviet citizens. But in Poland—a land I did not visit—in the '20's and '30's,

I heard that life for Jewish people was still difficult, still full of Jim Crow and humiliation.

Even now in this year of our Lord, 1944, American papers have carried stories of segregation and mistreatment of Jewish soldiers in the armies of the Polish Government-in-Exile. Anti-semitism is to Poland what the Negro problem is to the U.S.A.—a big black eye on its nice white face.

Now the Red Armies are marching across Poland! And the Polish Government-in-Exile is howling to high heaven. But it will be, I think, a happy day for Poland, when the Red Armies have marched all the way across that racially backward country and gone on into Germany—for the Red Army is the one great army in Europe that carries with it no racial prejudice, and its march across Poland should purify that unhappy land of anti-semitism.

Army without Jim Crow

Our own American Army, unfortunately, according to returned soldiers and members of the Merchant Marine, condones if it does not actually encourage segregation of American Negro soldiers in public places in Italy and North Africa—lands where previously there was no anti-Negro feeling. We are, of course, as everybody knows, segregated in the American Army itself. But the Red Army has within its ranks yellow men and brown men from Soviet Asia and Jews from all over the Soviet Republics, and it does not segregate anybody.

The soldiers of the Red Army come from a land that knows that the segregation racially of any peoples does not pay, does not create unity, and has no place in modern life. If the Red Army soldiers spread that knowledge across Poland, it will do more to knock the props out from under anti-semitism than anything else that has happened in my day and generation. Fortunately, the Red Army is not just a fighting army. It carries the democratic example with it, within its own ranks. Perhaps that inner democracy is what makes the Red Army SO great a fighting army.

When my grandmother picked up the evening paper from the front porch long ago in Kansas and read to me about the mob-slaughter of Jews in Poland, I did not know, of course, that years later I would be writing for a great Chicago paper about the liberation of those same Polish Jews by the Soviet Army—for when I was a kid there was no Soviet Army, and the *Chicago Defender* was full of stories of the mob-murder of Negroes in the South—which made me think Poland must be like our own land.

Now the Red Army is marching across Poland. I am glad there is an army marching across Poland that does not believe in the segregation or humiliation of any peoples because of their color or creed or race. Such an army is truly an army of liberation.

There are still a mighty lot of people in the world who need liberating.

The Soviet Union

June 1, 1946

There is one country in the world that has NO JIM CROW of any sort, NO UNEMPLOYMENT of any sort, NO PROSTITUTION or demeaning of the human personality through poverty, NO LACK OF EDUCATIONAL FACILITIES for all of its young people, and NO LACK OF SICK CARE or dental care for everybody. That country is the Soviet Union.

In 1947 the Soviet union will be 30 years old as a political entity. Emerging from the feudalism of the Russian Tzarist Empire with its serfdom, ignorance, and Asiatic slavery, in a quarter of a century the peoples of the Soviet Union have achieved these world-shaking social improvements—which puts it well ahead of every other country in the world in so far as human decency stemming from government goes.

I have been in the Soviet Union, so I am not speaking from theory or long distance information read in books. I have never been a member of the Communist Party so I am not speaking (as some may be inclined to accuse) from political bias. I do not claim that the Soviet Union is a paradise. It is not. But the steps toward an earthly paradise reach higher today on the soil of the Soviet Union than they do anywhere else in this troubled world. And the future of the Soviet Union is based on more concrete modern social achievements than that of any other existing state.

Series on USSR

I intend to write in this space a series of columns on the Soviet Union. I am tremendously impressed by the fact that this country, comprising one-sixth of the earth's surface and almost two hundred different nationalities of varying colors, has NO Jim Crow, NO anti-semitism, and NO racial prejudice. That alone is enough to attract toward the Soviet the sympathies of colored peoples the world over.

As a poor man myself working many hours a day all my life for a meagre living, I am tremendously impressed by a country that has no unemployment, where people need not be afraid of starvation because there may not be (often as here in our America) any work for them to do. Remembering well, as I do, the days of our great depression with members of my own family on home relief, WPA, and in CCC camps, with the streets of the Negro sections of Los Angeles, Chicago, and New York shadowed by women selling their bodies for the price of a cheap meal, I am tremendously impressed by a country where body and soul destroying depressions no longer take place, and where what food resources they have are more or less equally distributed.

During my lifetime, I have seen relatives and friends go for months without proper medical attention simply because they did not have the money to pay for it. I have seen persons wearing ill-fitted glasses because there was no cash for new ones, and others suffering aching teeth because they had no funds for emergency dental care. So I was deeply impressed in the Soviet Union to see suffering people receive medical attention immediately WITHOUT CHARGE.

Criticism from Dixie

When I saw these things in the Soviet Union, they seemed almost like miracles to me. I had never seen anything like that in Jim Crow Kansas where I grew up, or in Cleveland or Harlem where I later lived, or in Boston or Birmingham or San Antonio or Hollywood where I traveled. And no place in America had I ever been absolutely sure that I, a Negro, could go into any restaurant or public place and buy a meal. But there was never any doubt of such service in the Soviet Union.

That is perhaps why I was so amazed and shocked the other day to hear at the annual assembly of the American Academy of Arts and Letters in New York, where I was awarded a grant, a Senator from Arkansas, the Honorable J. William Fulbright, jump on the Soviet Union with both feet, stating in his address against Russia that ". . . we are willing and able to fight whenever we believe any power threatens the right and opportunity of men to live as free individuals under a government of their own choice."[1] (As if such freedom existed in Arkansas.)

Senator Fulbright's attack on the one country in the world that has equality for all races, seemed to me to come with ill grace from a white lawmaker from one of our most illiterate and color prejudiced states in poll-tax Dixie where the basic right of the ballot is still largely denied colored citizens. But I have seen all around the world from Africa to China, the gall of white Nordics who segregate in Nigeria, set up Jim Crow YMCAs in Shanghai, and draw the color line on India. So I should not have been amazed at our Senator from Arkansas. Perhaps he is so willing to fight the Soviet Union because he knows that once Soviet ideas spread over the world, people will get tired of poor schools, Jim Crow—and Senator Fulbright.

The Soviet Union and Jews

June 8, 1946

Years ago when I was a child in Kansas, summer evenings on the front porch or winter evenings by the stove in the kitchen, my grandmother used to read to me from the daily paper or from the Negro weeklies that we took, usually the *Topeka Plain-Dealer* or the *Chicago Defender.*

Very early in life, it seemed to me that there was a relationship between the problems of the Negro people in America and the Jewish people in Russia, and that the Jewish people's problems were worse than ours. In my child mind, I think the relationship came about in this way. Ever so often my grandmother would read a headline in the Negro press stating that a Negro had been lynched in Georgia, or two Negroes had been lynched in Louisiana, or three Negroes had been lynched in Texas.

From our daily paper ever so often she would read an item that a dozen Jews had been ridden down by the horses of the Cossacks in the Ukraine, or 50 Jews killed in a pogrom in Old Russia, or a hundred Jews killed and injured by a mob in Poland. So, I thought, here in our American South we Negroes were lynched by ones or twos or threes, but in Tzarist Russia and Poland they killed Jews by the dozens, or even the hundreds.

As I grew older, and went to high school in Cleveland, and mingled with Jewish students of Russian parentage, I learned that in Old Russia there were many schools to which Jews could not go—just as we have schools in America to which Negroes may not go. I learned that there were even towns and cities where Jews could not live—just as we have towns where Negroes cannot live. I learned that the police of Old Russia and Poland gave Jewish people very little protection from mob violence—just as American police give but little protection to the Negro people.

Changes after Revolution

While I was in high school the Russian Revolution took place and the Soviets took power. Among the Jewish students in my American high school there was much jubilation because, they said, the Soviets did not believe in anti-semitism, and that there were Jews high in the government now. In 1932 when I went to Russia, I was curious to see what real changes had taken place in the status of the Jewish people since Tzarist days. I knew that the Jewish problem in Old Russia must have been as deep-seated as is the Negro problem in my own country.

In the new Soviet Union I found no Jewish problem. I found no towns or cities from which Jews were still barred. I found no schools that refused to admit them. I found no more pogroms against Jews, and no one who dared openly insult or spit on Jews as was done in the old days. In *less than fifteen years,* I found that Soviet Russia had gotten rid of the Jewish problem.

Jews attended schools and taught in the schools just as other Soviet citizens might do. Jews voted and were elected to office equally with other citizens. Many leading Soviet officials were Jews. Many high in the arts and professions were Jews. Gone were the days of insults and pogroms because one was not a Nordic and a gentile. Gone—in *less than fifteen years*—was the Jewish problem!

Opposed to Race Hate

In Moscow I asked how these things were achieved. I was told that the whole theory of the Communist state was opposed to the separation of peoples on religious or racial grounds, and that workers had no strength divided up into warring camps. I was told the Soviet schools taught that all men are equal.

I said, "The theory of our American democracy is that all men are equal, too—except that where I live it does not seem to work out that way. Theories are all right—but how do you make them work in Russia?"

"Here we have laws against racial intolerance," they said.

I said, "We have such laws in some of our American cities, too, but often the laws do not work."

The Russians said, "In the Soviet Union, we *make* them work. Here nobody dares insult or spit on or hurt a Jew simply because he is a Jew any more. If any one does that, he is put in jail. After he stays in jail a while, he does not come out and soon insult or harm a Jew again, not very likely. But if a person persists in his racial prejudice, then he is put in jail for a *long* time. So people have stopped insulting Jews here—that is, the people who still might wish to do so. But no Communist, no real Soviet citizen would think of doing so anyway, nor would any child educated in our schools. Such a thing would be uncomradely—not to speak of being bad manners."

So I learned that the Soviet government had not only made laws and enforced them against racial intolerance, but had also taught people good manners, which seemed to me a wonderful thing to be doing. In Washington, D.C., in this year of our Lord, 1946, not even the grand ladies of the D.A.R. know how to behave politely.

The Soviet Union and Color

June 15, 1946

A quarter of a century ago just after World War I, speaking of his visit to the Soviet Union, the great American journalist, Lincoln Steffens, said, "I have seen the future—and it works!"

In 1943 in his book, *One World,* the late Wendell Willkie wrote of his trip throughout the Soviet Republics, "Russia is an effective society. It works."[2]

One of the things that impressed me most deeply when I was in the Soviet Union is that their laws against race prejudice really work. Before the Soviet Revolution in 1917 the Jews were treated much as Hitler treated them in Nazi Germany, and the colored subjects of the Tzar were Jim Crowed as I am Jim Crowed in America. Today all of that stupid racism is gone in the Soviet Republics. In less than 30 years anti-semitism and color prejudice have all disappeared over one-sixth of the earth's surface.

The Russians and the Ukranians are white, but there are many colored peoples in the Soviet Union. The Yakuts in the North are colored, and the Uzbeks, the Turkomens, the Tajiks in the South are colored. By our American standards even the Tartars might be Jim Crowed south of Washington, D.C. And certainly the Mongols would be treated in California as badly as Americans treat Japanese or Filipinos or Negroes. In Old Russia and its colonies, the Tzars treated these peoples badly, too.

Jim Crow Trolley

When I was in Tashkent, the regional capital of the Republics of Soviet Central Asia, there were funny little old street cars running about the size of the cable cars in San Francisco. I noticed a partition at the center of these street cars, and asked a brownskin Uzbek friend why it was there. He explained to me that in the old Tzarist days, the partition separated the Europeans from the Asiatics.

I said, "You mean the white people from the colored people?"

He said, "Yes, before the Revolution, we would have to sit in the back. But now everybody sits anywhere."

I thought to myself how many white Americans say it will take a hundred years, or two or three generations, to wipe out segregation in the South. But in Tashkent it had taken only a few years—and a willingness on the part of the government to enforce decent racial laws.

In a museum in Ashkhabad, capital of Turkmenia, I saw signs on the wall as curiosities for the school kids to look at: SARTS KEEP OUT, in both the Turkomen and Russian language. I was told that in the old days these signs were at the entrances of the big beautiful public park in the heart of Ashkhabad. In Tzarist times that park was only for Europeans—white people, not for the native peoples whom the whites contemptuously termed "sarts," a word equivalent to our worst anti-Negro terms.

As I stood looking at these signs in a museum now, but once very real barriers to the colored peoples of Turkmenia, I remembered parks I had seen in my own America where I could not enter—public parks in cities like Charleston and Memphis and Dallas. Even today after a great world war for democracy, such parks still exist in our United States. They are gone in the Soviet Union.

Does Not Take 100 Years

As in India today, or South Africa, there were formerly humiliating and difficult travel restrictions and educational and political limitations applied by the Tzarist Russians against their Asiatic colonies.

The Soviet government has wiped out all of these restrictions. People who less than 30 years ago had to travel under Jim Crow conditions, now travel as freely as anyone else. People who could not vote because of their race or colonial status, now vote as freely as others, and elect members of their own group to all of the Soviet law-making bodies. Whole groups of people whom the Tzars never permitted to have schools, now have schools—even colleges and medical schools.

In his *One World,* Willkie reported that the Yakuts were formerly only two per cent literate—just a few could read and write. But by 1940 education had made such progress that the figures were reversed—now there are only two per cent that cannot read and write.

So from Jim Crow cars to freedom, from helplessness to the ballot, from ignorance to schools, from scorn—"sarts"—to decency and respect as Soviet citizens, from being nobodies, serfs and semi-slaves to having a part in their own government—that is how far the colored peoples of the Soviet Union have come in a little over 25 years. So there is a clear example in the world to prove to our American "experts" in race relations that it DOES NOT TAKE A HUNDRED YEARS, it does NOT take generations to get rid of ugly, evil, antiquated, stupid Jim Crow practices—if a country really wants to get rid of them.

The Soviet Union and Women

June 29, 1946

Even more impressive than the changes for the better in race relations in the Soviet Union, is the vast improvement in the position of women there. In both the Asiatic and European portions of the Union since the revolution, the level of women has been lifted greatly.

Work for all, state educational funds for the young and old-age pensions for the aged have wiped out prostitution completely. There is no longer any need for any woman to sell her body through hunger, or the desire to go to college, or to care for herself when age is creeping on. In many great cities of the capitalist world, I have seen poor girls of high school age selling their favors as cheaply as a pair of stockings. And I have seen women too old to be appealing to men still trying to earn a few dollars with their bodies. During the American depression, the streets of our big cities were full of such women. Poverty, the economic root of prostitution, is gone in the Soviet Union.

In the Tzarist days in Russia, only women of the top middle and upper classes received an education. It was almost unheard of for poor working girls to have a chance to go to school. Educational opportunities for poor people were far more limited in Imperial Russia than they are even in Mississippi today. And when a family could afford to send one child to school, it was the boy who got the chance, not the girl. Now all that is changed, and girls are educated equally with boys in the Soviet Republics. Jews and colored Asiatics, formerly hindered by quotas or no-admittance policies in Tzarist schools, are no longer so restricted, which means that women and men of minority groups have the same educational advantages as other Soviet citizens.

Asiatic Change Leads European

The change in the position of women in the republics of Soviet Asia is even more striking than in European Russia. In Uzbekistan and Turkmenistan before 1924—when the British armies withdrew and permitted Soviet ideals to penetrate those former Tzarist colonies—women were virtual slaves. Men kept harems and women were bought and sold. The daughters of poor families were purchased by rich men for their harems. A poor man had a hard time getting a wife at all since only the ugliest, oldest, and least desirable women were left for his poor price.

Once in a harem, women could leave—even to do a little shopping—only when the lord and master permitted. Then they were always guarded by older women and servants. Harem life was very dull, so I was told by former harem inmates in Tashkent and Samarkand. Having no education, the women could not read. Most of the time they simply sat around the courtyard combing each other's hair, or quarreling. And that courtyard, by the way, was a sort of backyard corral—the front of the house and its fine gardens being largely reserved for the men of the family.

Uzbek women were formerly among the most heavily veiled in the Orient. The thin little half-veils of Turkey and Arabia were not for them. In Uzbekistan, before the Soviets came to power, all grown women had to wear the "paranja," a heavy black horse-hair veil from head to foot, through which their faces could not be seen, and through which they themselves could scarcely see. In Uzbekistan today some of the older women still wear this veil through custom or fear of their husbands, but Soviet law permits them to cast it aside if they wish, and no young women wear veils any more. One of the oldest customs of the Orient has thus been broken by the new Soviet freedoms for women in Central Asia.

Tzarist Theater for Men Only

As in the old Chinese and Japanese theaters, only men appeared as actors and dancers in Tzarist Asia before the revolution. Art and culture were not for women. Custom did not permit them to appear in public except heavily veiled. A woman was only for her husband's harem pleasure. But today the stage and concert halls are open to women throughout the Sovietized parts of Asia. Tamara Khanum, whom I met and interviewed, was the first unveiled female Uzbek dancer to dance on the stage in the late 1920s. This was such an innovation in cities like Bukhara and Samarkand that the state had to supply a company of soldiers to guard her to keep the reactionary men-folks from tearing her from the stage. But today hundreds of women take part in Uzbek plays and concerts, so soldiers are no longer necessary.

Most of the women of Soviet Central Asia now have thrown away their veils, are no longer bought and sold, are free of harems, and are being educated in Soviet schools in ideals of freedom for all. From a land of Jim Crow, exploitation, and harems, Soviet Central Asia has become the most advanced portion of the Orient and an equal part of the entire great Soviet Union.

The Soviet Union and Health

July 20, 1946

When I was in the Soviet Union, with Arthur Kessler, then a Berlin newspaper reporter (now better known as the author of *Darkness at Noon* and other famous novels), I paid a visit to a collective farm in a remote corner of the Republic of Uzbekistan. The farm was way down in the heart of Asia near the Afghanistan border, not far from where the northern-most tip of India almost touches Soviet territory.

Over the Soviet borders there was a steady trickle of immigrants from Afghanistan and India, mostly poor peasants from Beluchistan. These immigrants had heard that in the Soviet Union no beys or emirs or princes or colonial overlords robbed the poor of the fruits of their labor. They had heard that there the irrigation ditches were not controlled by the rich, and that no man had to till another man's fields in order to have the use of a little water for his own. The collective farm that Kessler and I visited was peopled entirely by turbaned Beluchi tribesmen.

The men and women there were as brown as I am—in other words, a definitely colored people. The only white person on that farm—in fact, the only European for miles around—was a young and quite beautiful Russian nurse. She was in charge of the clinic and all of the health work for these Indian peasant farmers. She delivered their babies, nursed their sick, cured malaria, and fought inherited venereal disease. She taught them that modern science and hygiene are better than old customs and superstitions—such as putting an axe under the bed to hasten child-birth, or washing new born babies in sand.

Deeply Impressed

I was deeply impressed with efforts such as this which the Soviet Government was making everywhere I went to care for the health of even the most backward of its peoples. But I was even more impressed later when, having a toothache myself, I received treatment without charge, simply by showing my card as a guest-member of the Soviet Writers' Union. I learned that all workers in the Soviet Union were entitled to such health service. And I could not help remembering how in my America one often went without treatment for lack of money.

All over the Soviet Union medical schools were open to all without regard to race or color. There is no quota system for Jews or non-white peoples such as we still have here in the United States. In Samarkand and other Asiatic cities, great medical centers were being built for people who under the Tzars and Emirs, had not even had grade schools, let alone medical schools.

Hospitals were not closed to patients on account of race. A few years before I went to Russia, a great Negro woman YWCA worker, Juliette Derricotte, known and respected by Negro youth all across America, had died in the South because, after an automobile accident, no hospitals along the road where she was injured would admit her since she was not white.

A few months ago, since our war for democracy was fought, I was the guest of a Negro physician during my Southern lecture tour. His charming and cultured wife had recently been taken suddenly ill, requiring emergency attention. But the only hospital bed that could be secured for her in that town was in the damp and mouldy basement of the local hospital—for it was in the basement that ALL Negro patients were placed, with only a screen between the men and the women. And no Negro physician could practice in that hospital. Negro doctors could not attend their own patients there. Prejudiced white nurses slapped and abused colored patients at will.

No Color Line in USSR

Nothing like that goes on in the Soviet Union. The color line in health, as in all other walks of life, has disappeared there. In the hospital at Tashkent, I saw Europeans and Asiatics together in the same wards. And there were both Russians and Uzbek physicians in attendance.

There is still a very great need for skilled doctors and surgeons in our United States. But this very summer of 1946, the New York papers have carried news of investigations of several of our great medical schools that either bar entirely or have very small quotas for Americans of Jewish, Negro, or Italian descent. There is a great need in America for nurses, but many nursing schools will not admit colored girls. Jim Crow is like a dagger in the back of America's health program.

We are a great and a rich country. There is no good reason why anybody should have to live with the toothache for lack of money. There is no reason why anybody should be denied treatment or hospitalization because of race. There is no good reason why an American Jew or Italian or Japanese or Negro should be limited to only a hand full of hospitals at which such minority citizens may intern after finishing medical school—if they are ever lucky enough to get into medical school under our segregated quota systems. From the Soviet Union our country can learn much concerning the morals of medicine.

Faults of the Soviet Union

August 3, 1946

The Soviet Union is not a perfect country. It is not a paradise on earth. It is by no means peopled by angels. Its peoples are human beings just as we are. They make mistakes. They do wrong. They have not created as yet a heaven here on this terrestrial globe. But they are not as bad as some of the books published in this country and many of our newspapers have made them out to be.

The American standard of living, even for poor people, is higher than that of most other countries of the world. Years ago when I traveled about the world as a seaman, I learned that little things like a radio, or a kodak, or a wristwatch were luxuries in many lands, whereas in our own country even the poorest person can manage to get hold of one or the other without trying too hard. And a Ford car—well you just about have to be rich to own a car of any sort in Europe or Asia. That, of course, is why immigrants have flocked to America from all over the world.

Americans are notoriously bad travelers and complain loudly about the inconveniences they encounter abroad. They get mad when they cannot find orange juice in Europe or Coca Colas in Asia. And nowhere else on earth do you find that marvelous institution, the American drug store, with everything from an aspirin to apple pie, an alarm clock to a dictionary.

I do not believe there was an orange in the whole Soviet Union when I was there, nor even orange juice in a can. Certainly there was no apple pie, and I do not believe you could buy an alarm clock anywhere. One could not purchase a pencil, either, that would write more than 20 words without wearing down to the wood, or breaking off. Coca Colas were unheard of. Little physical lacks such as these irritated many American visitors very much, and I think even turned some completely anti-Soviet.

Newspapers Lacking

Great big bulky newspapers with news from all over the world, sports, a condensed novel, comics, and lots of pictures every day, are missing, too. And Soviet radio programs, when I was there, were as monotonous as their restaurant menus. Just as they lacked a wide variety of foods, so they lacked the Lone Ranger, Backstage Wife, Bing Crosby, and the Ford Hour, not to mention commercials. Soviet street cars and trains were as crowded as ours during wartime. And theater tickets anywhere were as hard to secure as they are for hit shows on Broadway. Houses and apartments were hard to get, too. In fact, almost everything was scarce—but what there was was made to go around more or less equally to everyone.

Freedom of speech in the American sense was lacking in the Soviet Union. You could not get up in public and make a speech denouncing the heads of the government, nor could you publicly denounce Jews and Negroes as Bilbo, Rankin, and Talmadge do in our country. For doing such over there you would be put in jail and locked up good. Soviet newspapers do not go in for crime news, nor for items derogatory to any racial group. Nice juicy murders and big black brutes are both missing from their pages. Soviet headlines are not as exciting in a sensational way as ours.

The Soviet Union is far from being a communist country in a theoretical or practical sense. At the moment socialism is what they have achieved. Salaries and living conditions are still unequal. But nobody can profit from or exploit the labor of another. What one makes must be made from one's own labor, initiative, and intelligence. And nobody much can make a million dollars—just as very few in our own country can make a million—although millions here still suffer that illusion. But in the Soviet Union nobody need fear poverty, either, since all basic human needs, food, health care, jobs, childcare, education, are planned for by the state to benefit ALL the people.

Last in Series

My next column will, I think, be my last in this series about the Soviet Union. I have written in this space mostly about the things I liked about the Soviets, because they far overbalance the things I didn't like, and because I

think our America can learn some good things about race relations, democratic education and health programs, and insurance against poverty from
the Soviet people. I would also like to see our country and their country be
friends, not enemies.

Naturally, I have been asked the question, "Well, if you like Russia so
much, why don't you go there and stay?" Here is my answer: I don't go there
and stay because this is my home, the U.S.A. I was born in the very middle
of it. It is mine—faults and all—and I had rather stay here and help my
country get rid of its faults—race prejudice, economic inequalities, and Bilbo—than to run away.

Light and the Soviet Union

August 10, 1946

One of my most vivid memories from my year in the Soviet Union is the
memory of a visit to Chirchikstroy—meaning the Chirchik River Dam—one
chilly evening. Chirchikstroy is in the deep heart of Soviet Central Asia not
far from the borders of India and China—way down in the storied region of
Samarkand and Bokhara.

As a foreign writer visiting in a nearby city, I was the especially invited
guest to what might seem to many a very humble celebration in a remote
rural region. The celebration was the opening of the first workers' barracks
at the site where the new dam, Chirchikstroy, was to be constructed. Since
it was a damp chilly day, and since I have never cared too much about the
country even under ideal weather conditions, I was almost on the verge of
declining the invitation to go and look at nothing more than a workers' barracks. Had the dam been built, perhaps I might want to see that—but a
barracks, well, I was doubtful.

I am eternally glad that I went, however, because in my short visit to the
banks of the Chirchik River, I found the whole human meaning of the Soviet Union and its material and spiritual significance to the world of tomorrow. An uneducated young worker there put into five short words the entire meaning of the Union of Socialist Soviet Republics—and his five short
words took in the whole world, not just his own people or his own land.

In the late afternoon, about the time when, had it not been drizzling rain,
the more faithful of the Mussulmen could have been seen bowing down in
the dust toward Mecca, we left the big Oriental city in a rickety car headed
for Chirchikstroy. As we drove over the country roads past mud huts and

country Chai-hanas (tea houses) decorated with red bunting and pictures of Soviet heroes, I thought about the Uzbek past of autocratic beys and emirs, Tzarist military overlords, serfs, harems, veiled women, human beings bought and sold, dirt, poverty, and disease.

New Schools, Hospitals

In Ashkhabad, Merv, Samarkand, I had seen new schools, hospitals, youth clubs where Soviet teachers and officials were fighting against the old ugly heritage of the past. I had seen young people impatient that the standards of a thousand years were not changing fast enough, impatient that not all women had discarded their ancient horsehair veils and thrown off the shackles of the harems, that not all men had given up their ideas of tyranny and the feudal age. In Soviet Central Asia I had seen a land and a people in transition more marked even than that of European Russia. At the end of my rickety auto ride I was to hear in five short symbolic words the meaning of all that projected around the world and forward into time beyond our day.

The fellow who wrapped it all up into five words was an unpreposing looking little guy of unknown ancestry, maybe Tartar, maybe Tajik. He was short and stocky and homely. His skin was a kind of dirty yellow and his short wiry hair was the same color. American Negroes would call him "meriney." He looked like he might be 16 or 17 years old. He was a member of the Reception Committee that greeted me at the door of a long wooden hut on a barren stretch of ground as our car drove up in the pitch black of a country night. A country village and a few mud huts, vague shapes of machinery—steam shovels, perhaps—I had seen nearby in the darkness, but I could not see in the dark the river whose waters were to be dammed.

Festive Air

The eternal tea of the Orient was going around piping hot in its little bowls. There was a festive air, and though not a word of any of their language could I understand, my translator got over to me much of the conversation and the meaning of the folk songs that came later in the evening. But it was the little "meriney" guy who sort of took me in tow and who showed me every corner of the cleanly scrubbed barracks and the wooden bunks—all built, he said, by the men themselves in their spare time after work as their gift to the building of this new dam—the first modern dam in that part of Asia. And it was in speaking of the dam that the little guy said the five words that wrapped it all up.

He said, "Then there will be light." He told me how there was only candles and lanterns and tallow flares now, and most of the villagers in the mud huts scarcely had those. "But," he said, "when the dam is built, there will be

light! And not just for us," he said, "but for all the world, too, because this
dam will be so powerful that we can send light over the borders into India
and into China! That is why we do not mind giving our labor after hours to
build this first building here—this workers' barracks—and we will give many
extra hours to that dam, too—because when it is done—tell your people in
your America—when it is done, there will be light! Light to study by and to
see—and it won't be dark any more!"

Are You a Communist?

September 13, 1947

A distinguished-looking light-skinned Negro woman of my acquaintance,
a teacher in the New York public schools, was Harlem bound the other day
on a Fifth Avenue bus which she boarded in the shopping district. A nice
middle-aged well-dressed white woman sat down beside her and, as the bus
wended its way past Central Park, she began to chat with the colored teacher.

In the course of her conversation the white lady said that she had just
purchased some shoes in Sak's Fifth Avenue store. "And, don't you know,"
said the white woman indignantly, "a Negress came in and sat right down
beside me!"

"Quite a number of colored people trade at that shop," said the colored
teacher.

"I guess Negroes made so much money during the war," said the white lady,
"but if I were a clerk, I would hate to wait on them, particularly for shoes."

"Why?" asked the Negro teacher, realizing that the woman did not know
she was talking to a colored person. To try to understand her reasoning, she
continued to draw her out.

"Why," said the nice-looking elderly white lady, "Negroes are dirty."

"I suppose you mean poor Negroes," said my friend. "Sometimes poor
people of any race are not as clean as others because they often have no hot
water, no baths in their apartments perhaps."

"I think most Negroes are dirty," said the white lady, "and if I were a shoe
clerk, I would hate to wait on them. They ought to trade in their own shops."

"Don't you believe in equal rights?" asked the colored teacher.

"Oh, of course, I do!" exclaimed the nice white lady. "I'm an American
and I believe in fair play for everybody. I believe in Negroes having their own
places, their own schools and all. I have nothing against Negroes but, of
course, I'm not a Communist."

They Must Be Red

In this nice-looking elderly white lady's mind, people who really believed in equal rights for Negroes—in shops and elsewhere—*must* be Communists. In reverse, I heard another story last winter in the Middle West reflecting the same kind of attitude on the part of colored people.

In a city where I was giving a program of my poems, it seems a group of sincere and religious white Quakers—far from politically left-wing—decided they would like to do something helpful for the Negro community, further carrying out their workcamp ideal of practical usefulness. So several white young Quaker women went into the colored project homes offering without charge to care for the children of working mothers while the mothers were on the job, or to help Negro invalids keep their home clean. Although they were treated politely and a number of colored folks accepted their help, the general consensus of opinion as whispered about among the Negro project dwellers was, "Those white folks *must* be Communists!"

It seems strange to me that if—as I must admit happens all too rarely in America—people really believe in interracial friendship and decency, they just *have* to be Communists. Certainly, it is true that the Communist Soviet Union has abolished all racial lines and has succeeded (as even the most biased observers against the USSR admit) in making racial equality work. It is true, too, that the Communist Party in America has preached the complete political, economic, and social equality of all peoples. But it is also true that there are some Americans who are not Communist who believe in equality.

I Believe in Equality

I am not now, nor have I ever been a member of the Communist Party, *but I believe in equality.* Perhaps that is why the followers of Gerald L. K. Smith sometimes put out handbills against me, stating that I move in "high" white society, and that the Communists have assigned me to mislead the Negro intellectuals. Perhaps that is why the *Chicago Tribune* published my picture last Sunday as branded by the House Un-American Committee as a "member of the Communist Party." Both Mr. Smith and the Un-American Committee are wrong.

In a New England city where I was scheduled to speak some months ago, my lecture sponsors met me at the train with, "Somebody showed us a clipping that said you were a Communist, Mr. Hughes, and we got so afraid that we got in touch with the F.B.I. But the F.B.I. says you are not. So we are going ahead with our program." The next time the House Un-American Committee gets ready to call me a Communist, I respectfully suggest that they check with the F.B.I. That is, if the Committee wishes to keep the facts straight.

A Thorn in the Side

May 15, 1948

Gerald L. K. Smith, the Klan and others who think like them, evidently want me to retire from the American lecture platform—but they have another want coming. This season, evidently to intimidate my lecture sponsors, various reactionary organizations have dug up old left-wing poems of mine written back in the dire depression days of the late 1920's. Aided and abetted by the Hearst Press and the *Chicago Tribune,* they have front-paged from Coast to Coast that I am "a self-confessed card-carrying member of the Communist Party," which is not now and has never been true.

In California the Tenney Committee, and in Washington the Un-American Committee have written me into the record, so the newspapers allege, as a subversive and dangerous radical. A *Tribune* reporter phoned me asking in what country was I born, evidently thinking I must be a Russian.

The *Copley Press Leased Wire* quotes from an attack by Senator Albert W. Hawkes, Republican of New Jersey (without saying when or where the attack was delivered) to the effect that I am a "preacher of Red sedition." Also that I am reported to have taken a two-year course in Communism in the Soviet Union, returning to preach in our pulpits, colleges and high schools "at high rates of pay."

A Lie, Unadulterated

This is a plain unadulterated lie. But the persons and organizations who have gone out of their way this year to frighten my lecture sponsors, give nice liberal white ladies hysterics, and cause school boards where I have read poems to tremble, are not above lying. Evidently they go on the principles of Hitler that the bigger the lie the easier it is to have it believed. My nine published books, my hundreds of programs of my poems during the past fifteen years, the many hours put in at army camps and USO's during the war—the whole pro-democratic trend of my work—proves them liars.

However, if I felt that their attacks were personal attacks on me, I would not use the time of my readers with an answer in this column. But I am sure that I as an individual and a poet am not important enough to rate thousands of dollars worth of radio time, newspaper space, and legislative activity. Since when did poetry become that important? No. I feel that these attacks are the beginnings of attacks upon the whole forward movement of the Negro people, and particularly upon the increasingly effective work of the interracial organizations of Negroes and whites across the country for whom I often speak.

Then, too, the attacks are not limited to myself. Less than a year ago our reactionary papers published a long list of allegedly "communistic" or red-tainted Negro leaders including such distinguished persons as Reverend Benjamin Mays of Morehouse, Dr. Clement, President of Atlanta University, and our esteemed Mary McLeod Bethune—all people who have helped to weld together decent white and Negro Americans into forces working for the betterment of our democracy as a whole and particularly toward practical solutions of our racial problems.

Unfortunately, there are some Americans who do not wish our racial problems to be solved in a democratic way, who do not wish Negroes to vote, equality to be achieved in education, or black men and women to be given a square deal in housing or employment. These undemocratic Americans have now adopted the "red smear" technique to discredit liberal Negroes and whites who do not believe in Jim Crow and ghettoes.

The voices who cry "red" the loudest have never been known to be raised against segregation or color lines. In each case the persons or organizations who have opposed most strenuously my programs of poems in various communities from Akron to Los Angeles, are the very persons or organizations known to be the most anti-Negro, anti-Jewish and anti-labor in the community. In California they have opposed the relocation of Japanese-Americans.

From Douglass to White

From Frederick Douglass to Walter White, the value of Negro speakers and writers is that they have acted as a kind of thorn in the side of American democracy—not only working for *racial* equality but for real democracy for *all* the American people. The Klan-minded do not want democracy for anybody. Naturally, they would like to remove from American public life any whites or Negroes who favor democracy without regard to race, color, or creed.

If I were a Klansman I would try to keep myself from speaking, too, and I would work through such respectable organizations as the American Legion—which I believe the Klan-minded are now doing. Certainly, if I felt as Rankin or Gerald L. K. Smith feel, I would try to keep any and all democratic thorns out of my side. But as black as I am, there is no way for me to feel like Gerald L. K. Smith.

A Portent and a Warning to the Negro People from Hughes

February 5, 1949

The most important thing happening in America today is the trial of the 12 Communist leaders in New York City.[3] It is important because it is your trial—all who question the status quo—who question things as they are— all poor people, Negroes, Jews, un-white Americans, un-rich Americans are on trial. It is very serious to us as Negroes because it is exactly what happened in Germany. First Hitler locked up the Communists. The Jews were No. 2 on Hitler's list. In America the Negroes are No. 2 on bigotry's list. Hitler began with the Reichstag Fire Trial of the Communists. He ended by burning Jews alive in the ovens of Buchenwald.

At the moment in America they only burn fiery crosses on Negro lawns in Virginia, make us ride the back seats of buses in Mississippi and Alabama, lynch us in Georgia, and Jim Crow us in jobs in New York in spite of the nice law we have. If the 12 Communists are sent to jail—I am no prophet and was born with no veil over my face, but mark my words—if the twelve Communists are sent to jail, in a little while they will send Negroes to jail simply for being Negroes and to concentration camps just for being colored. Maybe you don't like Reds, but you had better be interested in what happens to the 12 Reds in New York City—because it is only a sign of what can happen to you.

Why are the 12 Communist leaders being tried in New York? They are being tried because they sit way out on the farthest limb of *accusation and questioning* of things as they are. They are being tried because they say it is wrong for anybody—Mexicans, Negroes, Chinese, Japanese, Jews, Armenians—to be segregated in America; because they say it is wrong for anybody to make millions of dollars from any business while the workers in that business do not make enough to save a few hundred dollars to live on when they get old and broken down and unable to work anymore; they are being tried because they do not believe in wars that kill millions of young men and make millions of dollars for those who already have millions of dollars; they are being tried because they believe it is better in peace time to build schools, hospitals, and public power projects than to build warplanes and battleships.

But aside from what the Communists believe, the seriousness of their trial lies in the fact that Communists are few, whereas white 100% Nordic Americans are many. The many are trying the few. Negroes are few. White 100% Nordic Americans do not like Negroes any better than they like Communists—perhaps not as well because most Communists are, at least, white. If the 12 Communist leaders go to jail, next on the jail-list are Negro American leaders—and after the leaders come the ordinary folks.

Of course, some American Negro leaders denounce Communists as resoundingly as Rankin. These Negroes will stay out of concentration camps only a few months longer than those who do not denounce Communists. There were Jews in Germany who joined with Hitler at the beginning. But Hitler got them in the end—and burned them dead up! Hitler harassed and humiliated their people all over the world from Berlin to Bronxville. At this moment the Jews of America have very little more protection than you and I—black—from the fiery cross.

Who are the people who might perhaps jail and burn Communists, Negroes, and Jews? They are very nice people. They are people who would not for the world be caught burning a fiery cross on anybody's lawn—but they let others burn it. They are nice people who would not themselves segregate me in the back row on the left at the movies—but they attend movies that segregate me and pretend not to notice my dark face when they pass the last row and see all the Negroes sitting there. They are people who will give a few dollars to a colored "Y" or settlement house, but will not give a factory job to a black man or woman. They are people who treat their Negro maids and yardmen very nice—but never do anything about the inferior fifty-year-old tumble-down fire-trap schools that the children of their Negro servants attend—while the white children go to a new half-million dollar school that the city has built.

The people who have the potential of killing, Christian people who are simply indifferent to Communists and Negroes and Jews, are very nice to minorities and their problems. This indifference lets the Klan burn crosses, and permits whomever will to do the jailing and the killing.

Old Ghost Appears before the Un-American Committee and Refuses to Remove His Hat

August 6, 1949

On the morning when Old Ghost appeared unannounced, also unsummoned, before the House Un-American Activities Committee in Washington, its chairman, Mr. Georgia, almost rose from his chair in astonishment. He had never seen a Negro ghost before, not even in Waycross. And since Jackie Robinson's speech, Negroes had no place on the Committee's agenda. Now all of a sudden here was this unexpected stranger as Negroid as the late Marcus Garvey.[4]

"Take off yore hat," commanded Chairman Georgia.

"I will not," said Old Ghost, standing on back-stanced legs on the witness stand, tall and dark as Paul Robeson and twice as cocky.

"I say, Nigra, take off yore hat!"

"I won't," said Old Ghost.

"I will cite you for contempt," said Chairman Georgia.

"Cite on!" said Old Ghost debonairly. "Cite on!"

"Boy, why are you here?" asked Chairman Georgia while the other Committee members sat dumfounded. "We have no Negras on the agenda today. You was not subpoenaed."

"I am here to insult you," said Old Ghost. "I can *see* that my black presence is not amenable to your comfort. And the fact that I wear a hat, not a bandanna, irks you. Therefore, I am pleased! I will not take off my hat except in the presence of ladies."

"You must be a radical," said Chairman Georgia.

"I am," said Old Ghost, "which is why I want to be called, 'Mister.' According to the dictionary, *radical* means *complete, thorough, extreme,* also *one who favors a basic change.* That is me! I am tired of being called, 'Boy.' I also would like to get at the root of a matter that, as a Southern tax-payer of color, has long had me puzzled: How come your committee can investigate everything from the reds to second basemen, and can't investigate the Ku Klux Klan which is so active in your home state of Georgia that I, a tax-payer, am even scared to vote in the rurals? Huh?"

"Do not say, 'Huh' to me," said Mr. Georgia. "Say 'Sir.' Respect my office! And take off yore hat!"

"I stand on my constitutional rights to do neither one nor the other," said Old Ghost. "Black though I be, I do have some rights of petition and redress of grievances."

"What are yore grievances?" asked Representative Georgia.

"My main one," said Old Ghost, "is that I will have to stay in Washington overnight. And you know neither Ralph Bunche nor I, being black Americans, are welcome at the Mayflower Hotel."

"This Committee has nothing to do with hotels," said Representative Georgia. "We are concerned with Russians."

"A Russian can sleep at the Mayflower," said Old Ghost. "Why can't I? I'm 100 and 2 per cent American."

"You know why you can't," said the Chairman of the House Un-American Activities Committee. "Why do you want to take up mah time with such questions?"

"Purely rhetorical," said Old Ghost, his dark face shining. "But this what I really want to know. Have you-all heard who Walter White married?"

Suddenly the whole Committee started talking at once. Blood boiled. The gavel banged. What was said cannot bear repeating. One Committee member choked on the first syllable of "inter-marriage" and, to Old Ghost, Mr. Georgia in particular sounded most Un-American. But the dusky spirit just laughed up his sleeve, having thrown the whole meeting into a state of confusion. Before he disappeared, Old Ghost swished his robes about his backstanced legs and said, "Gentlemen, I cannot permit myself to listen to tirades. I will return to Washington, however, Emancipation Day and shall be pleased to receive you in my ghostly suite at the Mayflower—since I go through keyholes. Au revoir, my dear Un-Americans, au revoir!"

The Accusers' Names Nobody Will Remember, but History Records Du Bois

October 6, 1951

If W. E. B. Du Bois goes to jail a wave of wonder will sweep around the world.[5] Europe will wonder and Africa will wonder and Asia will wonder, and no judge or jury will be able to answer the questions behind their wonder. The banner of American democracy will be lowered another notch, particularly in the eyes of the darker peoples of the earth. The hearts of millions will be angered and perturbed, steeled and strengthened.

They will not believe that it is right, for Dr. Du Bois is more than a man. He is all that he has stood for for over eighty years of life. The things that he has stood for are what millions of people of good will the world around desire, too—a world of decency, of no nation over another nation, of no color line, no more colonies, no more poverty, of education for all, of freedom and love and friendship and peace among men. For as long as I can remember, Dr. Du Bois has been writing and speaking and working for these things. He began way before I was born to put reason above passion, tolerance above prejudice, well-being above poverty, wisdom above ignorance, cooperation above strife, equality above Jim Crow, and peace above the bomb.

Today the books of W. E. B. Du Bois are on the shelves of thousands of libraries around the world, translated into many languages, known and read by scholars everywhere. The work of his youth, his monumental *Study of The African Slave Trade* is still the authoritative book on that nefarious traffic. His *The Souls of Black Folk, Dark Water,* and *The Quest of the Silver Fleece* are among the most beautiful and stirring of volumes about democracy's color problems ever written. Through those books in the first decades of this century the consciences of many young Americans were awakened.

As a co-founder of the National Association for the Advancement of Colored people, Dr. Du Bois gave America one of its greatest liberalizing organizations whose contributions to democracy through legal test cases and mass unity, history will list as invaluable. As the founder of the Pan-African Congress, he linked the hand of black America with Africa and Asia. As a teacher and lecturer in the colleges and forums of the nation, he has had an immeasurable influence for good upon young minds. As editor of *The Crisis* for many years, he developed the first distinguished, lasting journal of Negro opinion in the Western World. Dr. Du Bois is the dean of Negro scholars. But not only is he a great Negro, he is a great American, and one of the leading men of our century. At the age of eighty-three he is still a wellspring of knowledge, a fountain of courage, and a skyrocket for the great dreams of all mankind.

Somebody in Washington wants to put Dr. Du Bois in jail. Somebody in France wanted to put Voltaire in jail. Somebody in Franco's Spain sent Lorca, their greatest poet, to death before a firing squad. Somebody in Germany under Hitler burned the books, drove Thomas Mann into exile, and led their leading Jewish scholars to the gas chamber. Somebody in Greece long ago gave Socrates the hemlock to drink. Somebody at Golgotha erected a cross and somebody drove the nails into the hands of Christ. Somebody spat upon His garments. No one remembers their names.

Why Ill Winds and Dark Clouds Don't Scare Negroes Much

October 22, 1953

It is an ill wind that blows nobody good. Many New Yorkers consider the current Puerto Rican invasion bad. They say they lower wages, bring up a new racial and language problem. A quarter of a million new arrivals create terrible housing problems.

All this may be true, affecting Negroes as well as whites in Manhattan. But there is one good way in which it has affected Negroes. The Puerto Ricans, being colored (in the West Indian sense, meaning mixed bloods) or some entirely and purely Negro, have achieved housing all over New York City, including many areas which did not formerly rent to American Negroes. Being "foreigners" and speaking Spanish helps them.

But once the Puerto Ricans of many colors and complexions moved in, American Negroes followed. Result: Today in New York our own colored people have less trouble getting housing outside Harlem and the other Black Belts than they did before the Puerto Ricans came.

Another good result of the Puerto Rican migration to the Manhattan mainland is that it has once more put the slum problem on the front pages of American newspapers. It has again dramatically focused attention on the crying need for new housing for low-income groups. Not that anybody is going to do much about it.

Nationally, we no doubt will continue to spend billions on atom bombs, send other billions to far off places like Germany and Korea and keep on building bigger and better war planes and battleships instead of houses and schools.

But at least the prick of conscience will be irritated a little because the Puerto Ricans, living ten in a room, will be with us for some time—to point up how inadequate our big city housing is for almost everybody who is not rich.

It is an ill international wind indeed that blows nobody good. The whole democratic world is mad at Russia. But had it not been for Russia propagandizing the idea of racial equality all over the world for the last forty years, I doubt if Asia would be as wide awake as it is. Or if America herself would be so concerned with lip-service to equality as our politicians and radio commentators have become.

If some of these very same commentators or politicians were to find themselves living next door to a Negro they would probably move. Seated near one in the Stork Club, they'd be horrified. But on the air, oh, how eloquent they can wax concerning freedom, democracy, and equality for all.

At least, that is to the good. It does no harm to talk about decent things even if one does little more than talk. At least, the idea of goodness is planted, a seed is sown that might someday grow into reality.

Maybe the radio or TV networks will, even before Judgment comes, employ a Negro national commentator. Walter White would make a good one, or Charles S. Johnson, or Elmer Carter, or Marjorie McKenzie.[6]

It's an ill wind indeed that blows nobody any good. Current witch-hunting and book-burning has made a great many white folks realize what it means to have a book or an idea suppressed.

They often claimed they never knew at all before why Negroes were always complaining about prejudice in publishing, lack of opportunity to express racial aspirations in our big journals, and the paucity of books telling the truth about Negroes.

Some white liberals thought we were just complaining to be complaining. When their own books get banned, their own ideas barred from publication for being too liberal, their own reputations attacked, more and more nice white folks get some little inkling as to what it has meant to be colored, over a whole life time.

Not only Negro books have not been in many libraries, but Negroes themselves are even now not allowed inside the doors of hundreds of Southern libraries, in spite of the fact that most of these libraries are tax supported. We, *and our books* have been banned.

Censorship is not new to Negroes. It is good that more whites are becoming aware of how "undemocratic" it is.

Various ill winds are sweeping across the world these days. Tornadoes of them, in fact. And whole lots of great big dark clouds are floating in the sky. Negroes have known dark clouds and ill winds for generations.

They don't panic us anymore. We have learned that it is an awfully ill wind indeed that blows no one good, and a dark, dark cloud, for true, that doesn't have some sort of a silver lining. Sometimes it is the ill wind that blows the dark clouds out of the sky.

Part 8

Beating Out the Blues

Child of Charm

December 5, 1942

I stood just inside the stage entrance of the Folies Bergeres one summer night in Paris a few years ago, waiting for Josephine Baker. Before curtain time I had already been to her dressing room, but she was not there. Her maid told me in French, "Mlle. Baker never arrives until just before the moment she goes on the stage. If you plan to speak with her, it is best you await her at the very door itself, as she will have but little time." So I planted myself at the stage door. I was to interview the famous actress for an American newspaper I represented.

The music of the overture began and from my place just inside the stage door, I watched the dozens of near-nude French beauties of the chorus scamper into position in the wings. I heard a burst of applause as the curtain rose. I kept glancing out into the side street waiting for Miss Baker's car to arrive. As I waited, I thought back over the fifteen years since I had first seen Josephine Baker as a chorus girl, the end-girl, in the great New York Negro musical of the 1920's, *Shuffle Along*. Miss Baker's gay gawky antics had been a feature of that show, though she was only in the chorus.

Paris Fascinated

A year or two later she went to Paris with a small group of colored entertainers who introduced the Charleston to the French capital. Josephine was not the star of the group, but she made the biggest hit. She was then only about seventeen. Her lanky child's figure, her grotesque sense of rhythm, and the warm chocolate skin of the body that she used with such abandon, fascinated the Parisians. Almost overnight she was a star.

Great European managers vied with each other to sign her up for Berlin, Madrid, London.

Josephine Baker stayed in Europe where there was no color line.

She developed into a tall slender beautiful woman. She associated with counts and dukes, sultans and wealthy industrialists. She presided over the great annual Paris charity ball of the Petits Lits-Blanc. Dolls, beauty preparations, night clubs, railroad cars were named after her. Books were written about her. The great dressmakers, Poiret, Worth, Mainboucher, made her clothes.

Once she came back to New York to star at the Winter Follies. She danced with a white dancing partner then, startling Broadway. And she lived at the Waldorf-Astoria with her personal French maid in attendance.

New York Not Kind

A few years before, she had been just a gawky little colored girl from St. Louis. And she did not forget to go back to her home town to visit her parents. According to local memory, at that time she made her father a present of a new truck. But seemingly New York was none too kind to Josephine Baker. In her own country she was still "colored"—though Europe's most famous star in her genre—so she did not stay long. She went back to Europe where she was worshipped by thousands of theater-goers who had forgotten all about the novelty of her color long ago.

As I waited at the stage entrance, and the beautiful ladies of the French chorus swirled by me up and down the stairs to the dressing rooms, these things went through my mind about the woman I was to meet.

A long sedate car swept up to the curb. A chauffeur jumped out and opened the door. A slim brown girl, quietly dressed, emerged and hurried into the theater. I spoke. She said, "Bon soir." I told her of our appointment. Graciously, she said in French, "Come into my dressing room."

A Victim of Hitler

In a European theater, a visit with a great star during intermission is usually a treat reserved for a diplomat, a visiting prince, or some one of similar standing. After the first half of the lavish extravaganza was over, Miss Baker received me lying on a chaise-lounge in the floating veils of her gown as queen of a desert harem. She spoke to me only in French. I, too, spoke French as best I could.

But once when I did not understand—she was telling me about her plane and how well she had learned to fly—she switched into English, but with a decidedly French accent. She said, "I teel you how I fly zee plane, how I have learn zee loop-zee-loop. I love eet! I thrill eet!" Then she went back into French again.

St. Louis to Broadway to Paris! Poverty to stardom! Segregation to the adoration of the European world! Such was the path of Josephine Baker. Then came Hitler. The Nazis swept over Europe. Paris fell. Patterns of race-hatred as violent as Mississippi became official policy. Before the Nazi hordes, Josephine Baker fled into Spain, into Portugal, into North Africa—to Morocco itself where, perhaps, the Sultan who so admired her, gave her sanctuary. Her planes, her jewels, her chateau, her wealth were confiscated by the Nazis.

A few weeks ago, according to the papers, she died in Casablanca.[1] Josephine Baker, child of charm, dusky Cinderella-girl, ambassadress of beauty from Negro America to the world, buried now on foreign soil—as much a victim of Hitler as the soldiers who fall today in Africa fighting his armies. The Aryans drove Josephine away from her beloved Paris. At her death she was again just a little colored girl from St. Louis who didn't rate in Fascist Europe.

Music at Year's End

January 9, 1943

Memphis Minnie sits on top of the icebox at the 230 Club in Chicago and beats out blues on an electric guitar. A little dung-colored drummer who chews gum in tempo accompanies her, as the year's end—1942—flickers to nothing, and goes out like a melted candle.

Midnight. The electric guitar is very loud, science having magnified all its softness away. Memphis Minnie sings through a microphone and her voice—hard and strong anyhow for a little woman's—is made harder and stronger by scientific sound. The singing, the electric guitar, and the drums are so hard and so loud, amplified as they are by General Electric on top of the icebox, that sometimes the voice, the words, and the melody get lost under sheer noise, leaving only the rhythm to come through clear. The rhythm fills the 230 Club with a deep and dusky heartbeat that overrides all modern amplification. The rhythm is as old as Memphis Minnie's most remote ancestor.

Memphis Minnie's feet in her high-heeled shoes keep time to the music of her electric guitar. Her thin legs move like musical pistons. She is a slender, light-brown woman who looks like an old-maid school teacher with a sly sense of humor. She wears glasses that fail to hide her bright bird-like eyes. She dresses neatly and sits straight in her chair perched on top of the refrigerator where the beer is kept. Before she plays she cocks her head on one side like a bird, glances from her place on the box to the crowded bar below, frowns quizzically, and looks more than ever like a colored lady teacher in a neat Southern school about to say, "Children, the lesson is on page 14 today, paragraph 2."

Beating Out the Blues

But Memphis Minnie says nothing of the sort. Instead she grabs the microphone and yells, "Hey, now!" Then she hits a few deep chords at random, leans forward ever so slightly over her guitar, bows her head and begins to beat out a good old steady down-home rhythm on the strings—a rhythm so contagious that often it makes the crowd holler out loud.

Then Minnie smiles. Her gold teeth flash for a split second. Her ear-rings tremble. Her left hand with dark red nails moves up and down the strings of the guitar's neck. Her right hand with the dice ring on it picks out the tune, throbs out the rhythm, beats out the blues.

Then, through the smoke and racket of the noisy Chicago bar float Louisiana bayous, muddy old swamps, Mississippi dust and sun, cotton fields, lonesome roads, train whistles in the night, mosquitoes at dawn, and the Rural Free Delivery that never brings the right letter. All these things cry through the strings on Memphis Minnie's electric guitar, amplified to machine proportions—a musical version of electric welders plus a rolling mill.

Big rough old Delta cities float in the smoke, too. Also border cities, Northern cities, Relief, W.P.A., Muscle Shoals, the jooks, "Has Anybody Seen My Pigmeat On The Line," "See-See Rider," St. Louis, Antoine Street, Willow Run, folks on the move who leave and don't care. The hand with the dice-ring picks out music like this. Music with so much in it folks remember that sometimes it makes them holler out loud.

Folks Have Jobs

It was last year, 1941, that the war broke out, wasn't it? Before that there wasn't no defense work much. And the President hadn't told the factory bosses that they had to hire colored. Before that it was W.P.A. and the Relief. It was 1939 and 1935 and 1932 and 1928 and years that you don't remember when your clothes got shabby and the insurance relapsed. Now, it's 1942—and different. Folks have jobs. Money's circulating again. Relatives are in the Army with big insurances if they die.

Memphis Minnie, at year's end, picks up those nuances and tunes them into the strings of her guitar, weaves them into runs and trills and deep steady chords that come through the amplifiers like Negro heartbeats mixed with iron and steel. The way Memphis Minnie swings it sometimes makes folks snap their fingers, women get up and move their bodies, men holler, "Yes!" When they do, Minnie smiles.

But the men who run the place—they are not Negroes—never smile. They never snap their fingers, clap their hands, or move in time to the music. They just stand at the licker counter and ring up sales on the cash register. At this year's end the sales are better than they used to be. But Memphis Minnie's music is harder than the coins that roll across the counter. Does that mean she understands? Or is it just science that makes the guitar strings so hard and so loud?

The Duke Plays for Russia

February 6, 1943

There must be something wrong with a guy who feels like crying all the way through a concert by a jazz band. But that is the way I felt the other night when the Duke gave his first Carnegie Hall concert in New York in celebration of the twentieth anniversary of Duke Ellington's orchestra. The concert was for the benefit of Russian War Relief. Tickets were sold out a week in advance. Great crowds of people at both the front and back doors of Carnegie Hall were turned away. A fellow I know was offered $25.00 each for a pair of $2.20 seats he had. He would not sell them. There was a big sign in the lobby that said entirely sold out, no stage seats, no standing room. In other words, no nothing.

The audience seemed to be almost half-and-half—half colored and half white. The tiers of stage seats behind the musicians were jammed with all kinds and colors of people, and all mixed up, from blonds to our types of brunettes.

It was nice to see so many colored and white folks, famous and not famous folks, so mixed up and happy together—and nobody the worse for it. I couldn't help thinking about the more backward and barbarous regions of our country where people are prevented from sitting together in concert halls by law. And I thought, if they just knew what they're missing, seeing how happy people are here tonight at Duke's concert, they wouldn't be that way.

Folks Together

That was one of the things that got me to feeling like crying, thinking how a simple thing like music—and not high-brow music, but popular music—the people's music—could bring folks together, like at the Savoy Ballroom in Harlem where everybody dances with everybody else, white, West Indian, Filipino, Mexican, Negro, and nobody's the worse for it.

Then I got to thinking how this music was Negro music, and how Negro music had influenced all American music to such a great extent that it is now pretty hard to draw any color line at all in popular music. From George Gershwin up or down, white American composers have been influenced by, have improvised on and borrowed from the Negro composers and the folk

songs of the Negro people, until our American popular music is flavored
through and through with the sad-happy honey of the Negro soul.[2]

The Duke is not only conductor and arranger for his band (pianist, too)
but a great composer of popular music as well.

The band went into "Black and Tan Fantasy." Then, with scarcely a pause,
into a regular good old down home blues—by another name. Then into two
pieces by the Duke's son, Mercer Ellington, who was just inducted into the
army.[3] By that time, I was thinking about the army, anyhow, and how this
concert was being recorded by OWI for rebroadcast to our boys overseas.
And I got to thinking about some other boys—only somehow people never
say "boys" in referring to the Red Army—fighting on the coldest front in the
world—and the most active—the Russian Front, and how the Duke was here
playing his "Black and Tan Fantasy," his "Portrait of Bert Williams," his "Portrait of Florence Mills," and his "Jack the Bear" for Russian War Relief.

And I got to thinking how the Russians had lately driven the Nazis—who
hate Negroes—back from Leningrad. And how they had driven the Nazis—
who hate Jews—back from Stalingrad. And how they were driving the Nazis—who hate colored and white people sitting together listening to music—
back in the Caucasus, back, back, back, with their ideology of hate and
murder, toward Berlin. Back, back, back, in the cold and the snow of the
Russian night, under the dive bombers and artillery fire—the Russian people driving the enemy back with their own lives so that never again will they
be able to say, "Aryans over all! Hate and Hitler over all!"

Harlem to Stalingrad

About that time, the Duke and his band started to play a new composition of his own, a musical tone poem about the history of the American
Negro. And the first part of the music had in it slavery time and a little old
colored woman standing outside the windows of the white folks' church who
kept saying over and over to herself on the trumpet, "Jesus is my savior, too!"
She was not supposed to be near the slave-owners' church. Certainly they
wouldn't let her in. And the slave-owning preacher wasn't preaching for her.
But she kept saying over and over, anyhow, "Jesus is my savior, too! Decency and kindness and life and happiness are mine, too! My right, too! I can
sing, too! Live, too! Walk on the earth free, too!"

Democracy! Freedom! All the fine words in the papers and on the radio
today, the fine words that sometimes the insincere use so carelessly and so
cheaply—that even senators from Texas where I can't vote use—they are my
words, too! Freedom! Liberty! Democracy! Are my words, too. The guns on
the Russian Front driving the Nazis back, back, back into their own lair of
death and darkness, those guns speak for me, too.

And the Duke's music—music reaching down into the hearts of millions of all colors all over the world—affirms for me, and for Russia, and for the common people everywhere, the right to life and joy and happiness, too. Harlem to Stalingrad! From the Duke to Shastakovitch! From the mixed audience in Carnegie Hall to the great Republic of the USSR with its many varied races working and fighting together! A long way—but not so far in terms of the human heart, of human needs, and the basic unity of human beings.

On Leaping and Shouting

July 3, 1943

The young lady who leaped so high in the middle of Madison Square Garden a couple of weeks ago at the Negro Freedom Rally is named Miss Pearl Primus.[4] She was in the very middle of the Garden on a star-shaped stage, and twenty thousand people were sitting around her. Every time she leaped, folks felt like shouting. Some did. Some hollered out loud.

Pearl Primus is a dancer. She was doing a dance called "Jim Crow Train," and another dance called "Hard Time Blues," to records by Josh White and Waring Cuney.[5] She is a dark brown young lady. She got low down on the ground, walked, turned, twisted, then jumped way up in the air. The way she jumped was the same as a shout in church. She did not like the Jim Crow train, so she leaped way up into the air. And it was like a work-weary sister suddenly shouting out loud on a Sunday morning when the minister starts singing, "Jesus Knows Just How Much I Can Bear."

Outlet for Emotion

Dancing and shouting have a lot in common. Both are a kind of relief, an outlet for pent-up emotions, a savior from the psychiatrist. Rhythm is healing. Music is healing. Dancing and shouting are healing. Father Divine knows this, so does Rev. Cobb. Exhorters and gospel singers know it instinctively. Shouters know it in their souls. Folks who work hard all week, all year, all their lives and get nowhere, go to church on Sunday and shout—and they feel better. Colored, and poor, and maybe born in Mississippi, "Jesus Knows Just How Much I Can Bear," so you holler out loud sometimes and leap high in the air in your soul like Pearl Primus does when she dances "Jim Crow Train" which is a pretty hard thing to bear, especially when you got relatives fighting in North Africa or New Guinea, and you at home riding in a Jim Crow car.

"Lord, I wish this train wasn't Jim Crow!" the song cried on the record.

The guitar cried behind the words and suddenly the strings hit a hard and stubborn chord and Pearl Primus jumped straight up in the air! And folks cried out in the Garden—where there were twenty thousand people sitting in the great arena, having met for the cause of freedom.

Paul Robeson had just got through singing "Water Boy," "Joe Hill," and a Russian song which he dedicated to the Negro flyers who took off recently from the soil of Africa to bomb Italy, having ridden on the Jim Crow trains of Alabama themselves not so many weeks before. Robeson also sang "Old Man River" that keeps rolling through the heart of the South. Then the lights went out. When they came on again—centering on a star-shaped stage—there stood a brown-skin girl going down to the station to catch a Jim Crow train.

That Jim Crow Train

Did you ever ride on a Jim Crow train? Did you ever go to see your mother on a Jim Crow train? Did you ever go to college on a Jim Crow train—Fisk, Tuskegee, Talladega? Did you ever start your furlough on a Jim Crow train? Soldier boy, training to fight for freedom, on a Jim Crow train. Did you ever take your vacation on a Jim Crow train? War-worker from Detroit going home for a visit on a Jim Crow train. Did you feel it in your soul, that Jim Crow train?

Did you ever see a dancer dance a Jim Crow train? Dance the rocking motion of a Jim Crow train, coach up by the engine on a Jim Crow train, half the coach for baggage on a Jim Crow train, other half for Negroes on a Jim Crow train, white conductors, candy butchers, baggage men and brakemen taking up the seat room in the colored half-coach of a Jim Crow train, cussing, spitting, smoking, on a Jim Crow train, Uncle Sam's own soldiers Jim Crowed on a Jim Crow train, sign says, "This Coach For Colored" on a Jim Crow train, colored women Jim Crowed on a Jim Crow train, Washington, D.C., change to the Jim Crow train, Pearl Primus dancing on a Jim Crow train, dancing she don't like no Jim Crow train, jumping in the air about a Jim Crow train, shouting in her soul God help that Jim Crow train!

Where is freedom going on a Jim Crow train?

Art and Integrity

October 20, 1945

In politics it is sometimes expedient to lie. In art, as in science, it is just the other way around. For the artist it is never expedient to bring into being anything other than the truth as he sees it. Most politicians of necessity suppress or distort facts, lie outright or by implication, and put their best foot forward for their own cause even when they know their toes are covered with corns inside the beautiful campaign shoes they wear. If scientists did that you never would find out how to cure cancer. If most artists and writers did it, politicians would have no civilization left to lie about.

In practical life, I admit, it is occasionally expedient to lie. Indeed, it is sometimes necessary, since lying is one of the survival virtues. Many a Negro in slavery days would not have escaped North to freedom had he not said to the patrollers that he was "just gwine down to de mill to bring back massa's corn"— when in reality he was headed up the broad highway to liberty.

Art and Politics

Runaway slaves were a small, but significant, minority. Yet if writers on slavery were to put down that all Negroes caught off their masters' plantations were simply going to the mill to bring back corn, that would be not merely a slight *historical,* but mammoth *creative,* lie as well. The reason many books and plays about Negroes ring false and off-key is that, in spite of surface truth, the implications are that Negroes never aim at anything more than "massa's mill"—an untruth whose political value for reaction is most useful.

Unfortunately for the peace of mind of the artist, art *has* a political value. That is why, in times of stress, the politicians set up various open or covert censorships to try for their own ends to control art. In order to play safe, the bad artist often conforms to the political needs of the moment and creates a saleable tissue of conscious lies in order to keep his cupboard full.

Of course, there is also in art such a thing as unconscious lying. An acquired surface knowledge may lead a creative writer to *think* that the surface is all there is to a subject. Such errors have been made in science. But the careful scientist probes far beneath surface phenomena, likewise the careful artist. It is the *conscious* liar who becomes a shoddy and utterly unworthy artist.

Truth vs. Compromise

For every artist the old moral problem of truth and compromise frequently comes to the fore. Compromise often brings food and drink. Truth alone glorifies the spirit. Guile permits a lion to stalk a deer for food, or a Hitler to close in on a new country and therefore gain *more* food. But guile will never create a single book or a single picture or a single stained glass window that any human animal can contemplate with pride and say, "I, when not eating, made that."

The things of which man can be proud, the beauty that he can really enjoy, are born only of truth, or the attempt to attain truth. That is why art in its essence is a path to truth. Propaganda is a path toward more to eat. That the two may become inextricably mixed is not to be denied. That they may often be one and the same is certainly true. But that the greatest art is also the greatest truth—and at the same time therefore the greatest propaganda for a good life for *everybody*—is beyond the possibility of sane denial.

Those who wish to be good artists must face the problem and make a choice—with the knowledge that it is often a hungry choice if you choose the great side: *truth* whether there is food or not, *beauty* if there is temporal success or not, *your creation* if it is expedient or not. Taking the long view (which is the only view art can take), integrity is the sole expedient.

Art and the Heart

April 6, 1946

It is interesting, I think, to contemplate how art crosses color lines and gets around into places where the creators of the art themselves may not be welcome.

In traveling through our prejudiced Middle West, I was struck by the large number of records by Negro bands—Duke, Lionel, Louis Jordan, Cab, on juke boxes in cafes where Negroes are not served.[6] The patrons enjoy the music, and the proprietors of the places make money from the records of Duke Ellington, but Mr. Ellington himself could not drink a cup of coffee or sit at the counter in many a Kansas or Missouri cafe where his music is played.

In Salt Lake City, Utah, the public and the press recently acclaimed the great singing of Dorothy Maynor, but Miss Maynor stayed in a Negro home, not a first-class hotel. After her concert, many of Dorothy Maynor's hearers gathered for refreshments, to "oh!" and "ah!" over her music, in cocktail rooms and supper clubs that would not serve the great Miss Maynor (or any less famous member of her race) even so much as a pretzel.

In Amarillo, Texas, recently I saw an ad in the local paper for Ann Petry's new Harlem novel, *The Street.*[7] It was not on the back page, either. But Amarillo is strictly a Jim Crow town, and many Texas papers, so I am told, would not even carry news or photographs of local black men who died for their country in our late war. Art rates higher than life or death in Texas, I reckon, which hardly makes sense. But I guess it is a point in favor for art.

Through the Back Door

In Joplin, Missouri, a downtown shoe-shine parlor had a big poster in the window announcing my program of poems at the Bartlett School during

Negro History Week. But the colored shine boy employed inside said he was not permitted to shine my shoes! My picture on a poster concerning my poetry was welcomed in the shop, but not my patronage.

In a city in the South last season, I was told of a Negro radio group whose singing of spirituals delights thousands over the air on Sunday mornings. But the singers must use the alley entrance and the freight elevator of the hotel where the radio station is located in order to reach their broadcasts. Their songs do not go out the back door by way of the alley to the air lines, but the singers must come in that way with the ash cans and the freight.

Any Negro actor or artist who has toured the theaters or concert halls of this country can tell of hundreds of American cities that receive their art with applause, but will not give them a warm, decent place to sleep when the performance is over. Even some of our American army camps enjoying Negro USO talent, have been most discourteous to the artists. The men applauded warmly in the Post theaters but, in some cases, not even eating accommodations were offered visiting colored performers.

Members of Fletcher Henderson's orchestra reported recently having to sleep all night in a bus after playing an air base dance because the field had accommodations for whites only.[8] Yet those same whites danced to and applauded their music!

Art Like Religion

Art must be like religion—both can cross physical color lines with ease, but neither seems to have much effect on most white people's hearts and souls—at least not in this rude American country of ours. Or can it be that most American white folks have no hearts and no souls? I am really puzzled about this, ours being a Christian country, but with so many people who are not Christ-like toward their darker brothers.

As for art—Richard Wright is widely read and cordially applauded at lectures. Millions listen to Marian Anderson at concerts and on the air. *Carmen Jones* with Muriel Smith as Carmen, plays for months across America.[9] Everybody loves Duke Ellington. But on tour in many cities that applaud these artists, in so far as public accommodations are concerned—hotels, restaurants, shine parlors, taxi service—Richard Wright, Marian Anderson, Muriel Smith, or Duke Ellington, had just as well be dogs.

In most American hotels a guest may bring his dog without difficulty—but not a Negro, not even a great Negro, not even the greatest singer in the world or the greatest master of modern popular music.

Words to Remember: Stein's

January 8, 1949

The late Gertrude Stein said, "A rose is a rose is a rose," which very definitely made a rose *a rose*.[10] She also said, "When a thing is, it is," meaning, "What is, is," which is certainly true. So many people take refuge behind "if" and "ought," but they are very different from "is." "If" and "ought" are words of dreams, whereas "is" is a word of reality.

There ought not to be any racial prejudice in the world, but there is. There ought not to be any national conflicts, but there are. For example, a Negro is, Russians are. Segregate Negroes as much as you wish way over on the edge of town, but each living Negro still is. Battle with Russia as much as you choose, but when the atomic radiation is cleared away, there will still be some Russians left somewhere, I expect, though it be in the Arctic Circle. Just as "a rose is a rose is a rose is a rose," so a Negro is a Negro is a Negro is a Negro, also is a Russian is a Russian is a Russian is a Russian. Miss Gertrude Stein was a very wise old lady to state so simply and emphatically a basic truth.

It is always good to dream of an idyllic future, but as Miss Nannie Burroughs used to say in her speeches, one must also cope with "the nasty now."[11] Unfortunately for many white Americans, there are millions of people in the world that they do not care very much for: Russians, Orientals in general, Negroes, Indians. But there they *are,* and unless the good Lord or the atom bomb remove them (before we are removed ourselves) there they will be tomorrow. The wise thing for white Americans to do would be to recognize the "if" of the situation, and work out a decent way of living on the same globe with the rest of the folks Providence put here.

If Congress would only realize that desirability, perhaps it would then have time to pass some bills providing good housing for everybody in the U.S.A., and good schools, which in turn would cause the resulting construction to provide good jobs for many people for a long time to come, instead of Congress using up so much time and energy on the international situation and filibustering every time a bill comes before it that might benefit American Negroes. In spite of all the wasted motion and wasted words in Congress, Negroes will still be here to worry Congressmen. What is, is.

Take me, for instance, still colored after battling with prejudice for some forty years. When I was a child in Lawrence, Kansas, they barred all Negroes out of the one movie show in town. But in spite of that, I've seen thousands of movies and have even worked on a few in Hollywood. They would not let the colored boys participate on the track team in Lawrence, but in spite of that I became a championship high school relay runner in Cleveland.

When I got to college, they hemmed and hawed about letting me into the dormitory at Columbia, but I got in. Once when I wanted to take a trip to Havana, I was told that tourist regulations would not admit American Negroes, and an American steamship line would not sell me a ticket, so I went on and bought a ticket on a British boat, and went to Havana anyhow. Throughout my creative years, ever so often some white Broadway producer tells me Negro plays are great risks and so he turns mine down—but I keep on writing plays.

However, if white America had not taken up so much time making things harder for me, Negro, than for other Americans, I might perhaps have been able to contribute more books and more plays to American culture. If Americans would recognize the "is" of my being colored, and not the "if" of if Americans could keep me "in my place," it would surely be better for my white fellow citizens as well as for myself.

I am, no matter who doesn't like me to be. My Negro-ness *is*. Just as Gertrude Stein's "rose is a rose is a rose," so I am and I am and I am and I am! In fact had I not gone through school (in spite of all) I might even say, "I is." Or more positively still, "I'm is!" Or even, "I are." One thing is certain, whatever form the verb, *to be,* takes, a Negro is, and I am.

Return of the Native—Musically Speaking—the Drums Come to Harlem

June 21, 1952

Historians of American life will probably record this Spring of 1952 as the Spring when Eisenhower made his Abilene speech, as the Spring when the Supreme Court overruled President Truman in his seizure of the steel mills, as the Spring when Jersey Joe Walcott still hung onto his title by defeating Ezzard Charles, as the Spring when our troops were bogged down in Korea with Syngman Rhee acting more like a little Hitler than ever.[12] Not being a historian myself, I think I shall remember this Spring as the year when the drums came to Harlem.

Not that there haven't been drums in Harlem all along—but never before on such a community level, at least not to my knowledge, and I have lived in Harlem a long time. This Spring on the first warm nights of open windows and folks sitting on the stoops, sometimes far away, and sometimes very near, and sometimes all up and down the dusk-dark streets, you can hear drums beating. The teenagers have gone in for tom-toms, bongos, and even the big congo drums of Africa. There has been this year a kind of musical going home to the basic sources of rhythm. Through the open windows of tall tenements, from basement doorways, on street corners, and from the park and playground, comes the soft throbbing of drums, of the bare hand against the tightened skin of the drumhead, of the rhythm of the players' own hearts.

The drumbeat is only the heartbeat, embroidered upon by the variations of the drummer. The first music must have been pure rhythm, even before song came, or the minor melodies of the earliest ancient flutes, before the antelope horn was cut to make its first note, before the throat's cry turned into a tune. The first drum probably repeated only the steady rhythm of the human heart, before the heart's rhythm became monotony and some drummer added an extra beat, began to play with the possibilities of the hand's variations upon the taut drumhead—and the intricate rhythms of Asia and Africa came into being. Then, of course, nobody dreamed that out of the drumbeat thousands of years later jazz would be born, or that congo drums would be played in the Waldorf-Astoria.

The bass drum with its big stick, and the snare drum with its two little wooden sticks, were for a long time Europe and America's favorite kinds of drums. But, in the Western World, drumming with the bare hands was kept alive in the islands of the West Indies, among the Negroes there, where the ways of Africa were not so quickly lost as on the mainland. In Haiti, in Trinidad, and in Cuba, the bongo, or the Congo drum heated over the open fire, and played by expert fingers, was all the music needed for a dance or religious ceremony. And if melody were required, the human voice lifted a song. But often the beat of drums alone was enough to set bare feet to dancing on the hard earth, or to kindle into shouting the ecstasy of the gods.

Behind the beguines, the congas, and the songs of the West Indies, there is always the bare-handed drumbeat, the human fingers beating out basic rhythms on the taut skins of animals stretched to cover an end of a hollow log. When the music of Cuba began to gain popularity in the United States and in Europe, along with it came the old ancient African drums played with the finger tips. And now those drums are a part of big Paris, London, and Broadway bands, and a part of the little trios, giving a base and a heartbeat to even the most trivial popular tune. Now the kids of Harlem have begun to save their quarters and dollars until they get enough to buy a set of bongos, or maybe even a big tall Congo drum. Three hundred years removed, they claim again from Africa, the rights of rhythm. And the Jimmys and Georges and Joes of Sugar Hill and Lenox Avenue, maybe thinking they have discovered something new, are beating out of their own hearts the ancient rhythms that preceded jazz and swing, bebop and the mambo by a thousand years. And the Harlem nights this Spring of 1952 are alive with the drums.

The Influence of Negro Music on American Entertainment

April 25, 1953

The Negro as a folk entertainer has always been accepted in America, but as a trained professional artist he has had a long hard way to go. It is one thing to listen to a black troubadour picking a guitar on a street corner and maybe drop a dime in his cap. But when you pay a dollar to see a picture, your prejudices as well as your risibilities must be tickled. The Negro began long ago tickling America's risibilities. In slavery he could hardly tickle anything else. It was fun listening to unorganized unprofessional Negro singing, hearing the absurd broken dialect spoken, watching the clop and buck and wing of slave dancers. It was so much fun that before the Civil War professional white entertainers borrowed these things from the Negro and made the famous and hilarious blackface minstrels. White actors even borrowed a comic version of the Negro's color—burnt cork. Eddie Cantor and the late Al Jolson only recently discarded it. Amos and Andy still wear it on their tongues.[13] In the movies there are some Negroes who do not have to wear it, burnt cork almost comes natural. Uncle Tom did not really die. He simply went to Hollywood. But even there, he is growing old.

Not all the slave songs were humorous. But it was the humorous ones that sold best, the minstrel men discovered. Not all the slave dancers were hilarious buck-and-wingers. But in the early 1800's who could sell the ache of the spirituals, or the frenzy and terror of Congo Square and its drums? Not all the things said in dialect were laughable. But the heartbreaking phrases had to wait until today for a dramatist like Theodore Ward to remember.[14] They were not for the minstrels. Thus long ago in America the stereotype of the Negro as a humorous clown was born. That shadow of the South is still over the Negro in professional entertainment. A superb dancer like the late Bill Robinson told jokes shaming his people because he danced in that shadow.[15]

Negro entertainers themselves in the 1880's began to imitate the white minstrels—they began to imitate the imitators of themselves. They, too, sang "coon" songs that the Negro people did not like, but which the whites paid money to hear. From the first colored "coon" of minstrel days to Stephin Fetchit on the screen there is a direct line.[16] Therein lies the tragedy of the Negro in American entertainment. For money he became a stereotype OF HIS OWN WHITE STEREOTYPE—and for so LITTLE money. The white Al Jolsons and the white Amoses and Andys made much more.

Fortunately there has been another and more truthful line from the folk art of the Negro past to the commercial entertainment of today. It, too, has had its humor, but it is the humor of the heart, not merely that of imitative tongues and burnt cork shadows. The vitality of Negro folk music from the slave songs to Broadway, and the inventiveness of the Negro dance from the plantation to Katherine Dunham, have been too great to be completely lost even when exploited most commercially.[17] The Negro has influenced all American popular music and dancing. And that influence has been, on the whole, joyous and sound.

The Broadway musical theater from the minstrels to *Porgy and Bess* has been enriched by Negro rhythms, thematic material, and Negro singers and dancers. White composers and lyricists from Stephen Foster to George Gershwin to Harold Arlen have utilized Negro folk sources for their inspirations. Negro song writers, too, have wisely gone back to these sources. In the minstrel days one of the greatest of the colored composers was James Bland of "Carry Me Back to Old Virginny" fame.[18]

Ragtime began as a folk art, became a conscious creation, turned into jazz, to swing, to be-bop, and took decisive hold on American popular music no matter what the composer's color. Given new vitality just before the First World War by the folk blues and the personal creations of W. C. Handy in blues form, Negro syncopation became the popular music of America. James Reese Europe created a stir with the first orchestral concert of syncopated music at Carnegie Hall in 1912.[19] Now Duke Ellington has an annual concert there. And Negro bands, white bands, and mixed bands play syncopated rhythms all over the country, not only for dancing, but for listening. Negro rhythms have begun to affect symphonic composers. American music is soaked in our rhythms.

How a Poem Was Born in a Jim Crow Car Rattling from Los Angeles to New Orleans

January 9, 1954

Negroes in Los Angeles say that the ticket agents at the station try their best not to sell seats to colored people on the Southern Pacific's crack streamliner to New Orleans, the Sunset Limited.

Negroes are told how much easier one can get out on the slower train, the Argonaut. Reservations on the Sunset must find themselves all together in Car 22 away up at the front of the train just behind the engine.

Streamliners leaving New York and Chicago for the South try the same tactics, too. They have worked out systems whereby most colored folks are segregated in Day coaches even before they leave the North. All this is done in spite of the Supreme Court decision that segregation in interstate travel is illegal. Even when tickets are ordered over the phone, it looks as if the agents can tell a Negro voice. Failing that, ticket agents may claim error and change the car number when colored passengers pick up their reservations.

Negroes still go through a lot of inconveniences in traveling that white people know nothing about.

From Texas to New Orleans last summer, I rode in a Jim Crow car on the Argonaut. When I boarded the train, the night was sweltering hot. But it was cool inside the crowded coach where, in spite of the number of colored passengers including mothers with babies, the white news butcher and candy vendors took up two whole seats at the back of the car, and the pillow vendor took up two more for his paraphernalia. This seems to be a custom in most Southern colored coaches, thus depriving the passengers of the extra room to spread out for comfortable sleeping at night.

I had not even gone to sleep before the air-cooling system in our coach ceased to function. Going through Louisiana, the car became stifling hot and the perspiration began to pour off of everyone. Folks began to fan with newspapers. Mothers took the clothes off their babies except diapers. The white brakeman, candy and pillow vendors left our car and went back into the white coach. There were about a dozen air-cooled coaches for whites on the train behind our car.

No Negro passengers moved. Several spoke to the porter who tinkered with the air-conditioning but could not make it work.

Finally, I said if the air cooling did not come on, I was going to move back into another car. The Negro porter just shrugged his shoulders. I spoke to the mother of three sweltering children in front of me who had gotten on the train in California. "Why don't we all move back into one of the other coaches where it is cool. We are interstate passengers, so the law permits us to do so."

The woman said, "Are you kidding? The law might permit it, but these white folks down here don't."

Finally, I got up and went into the next coach. I found the brakeman and told him if the air conditioning was not fixed in a few minutes I was going to move in where he was. He said he could not give me permission to move. I said, "I don't need your permission. I have the permission of the Supreme Court of the U.S.A. I am paying the same fare as anybody else on this train, so I have the right to sit anywhere. You, the pillow vendor, and the candy man stayed in the colored coach all day taking up room, but moved when it got too hot. Why should I stay in there and swelter?"

He said, "Don't tell me, see the conductor." So I demanded that he bring the conductor. I returned to my seat in the hot coach as he disappeared. Shortly the conductor and the brakeman came in.

A very old woman across the aisle from me (who, perhaps, had been riding Jim Crow cars all her life but not liking them ever) up to this point had said nothing. She just sat there wiping her sweating face. She did not say anything now when the conductor came into the car. But, I think, fearing a scene, perhaps thinking that I might be ejected from the train for protesting, as sometimes happens, or maybe not wanting to cry, she reached up and got her lunch-box from the shelf and began to eat, turning her face away from the conductor and myself. There was no scene. The conductor and the brakeman fixed the air-conditioning and left without saying a word. Shortly the car was cold enough to give everybody pneumonia.

But, as the train went on into the Southern night, I forgot the air-cooling, and about three o'clock in the morning between Lake Charles and New Orleans, remembering this old woman who took down her lunch-box and turned her face away from trouble and ate, I wrote this poem:

> Get out the lunch-box of your dreams
> And bite into the sandwich of your heart
> And ride the Jim Crow car until it screams
> And, like an atom bomb, it bursts apart.

Slavery and Leadbelly Are Gone, but the Old Songs Go Singing On

September 4, 1954

Well, I guess you know there was once a singer named Leadbelly, and he was a penitentiary boy, and he sang his way free.[20] I guess you know he got locked up again, but he got out singing. And he sang songs from here to yonder. He sang himself great. He sang himself famous. And he sang himself up on a lot of records. He died while other folks made money from his records. But that made no difference. He had lived! So he left his voice behind and his songs. One of Leadbelly's songs is "Ol' Riley." It is about freedom.

In 1963 we will be one hundred years free. Have you forgotten that you were once a slave? Is it a memory you do not want to remember? Maybe it was not you, not me—maybe it was somebody who came before you and me, some colored somebody else. So why remember? Don't—if you don't want to. Forget if you can. Forget—if you are not still a slave to segregation and Jim Crow and all the other leftover balls and chains of slavery. If you have escaped those, then forget. Don't be like Leadbelly remembering a song called "Ol' Riley."

The song is on a record you can buy in a pretty cover in a long playing edition containing eight of Leadbelly's famous folk songs, including "Irene." (Leadbelly Memorial Album, Volume I, Stinson SLP 17.) "Ol' Riley" is the last song on the first side. Maybe "Ol' Riley" is just kept alive out of spite to make us remember slavery. But there are some people who like the song, too, who think it's a great song, a Negro history ballad with music, a drastic folk poem. It's about a slave. It's also about a dog named Rattler—one of those Uncle Tom's bloodhound dogs who were trained to catch runaway slaves. Let's not even remember bloodhounds. Okay, sorry, let's not. Don't! I mean you! But somehow I have got to remember. Somehow, I think I still hear the bloodhounds barking when Talmadge talks, or Burns, or Malan, or the rocks fly through housing project windows in Chicago, or the spoons rattle in the Stork Club where Josephine Baker never got her steak. Somehow I think I hear the bloodhounds when the Urban League board starts fussing over who did what for what white folks. I swear I hear the bloodhounds!

Anyhow, the song goes like this:

> *Ol' Riley walked the water,*
> *In the long hot summer days . . .*

running away from slavery up the creek bed—in running water so the dogs couldn't smell his tracks. But there was an old dog named Rattler his master sent out to get him.

> *Here, Rattler! Here, Rattler!*
> *Here, Rattler, here! . . .*

But maybe I shouldn't tell you about this song. It is a very crude song, a folk song, which means not cultured, not smoothed up, not Billy Eckstine, Sara Vaughan or Eartha Kitt.[21] I'm sorry! It's not. It's about Old Riley who wanted just once in his life to be free, and about "Hey, Rattler," who was a vicious bloodhound trained to track Negroes who wanted to be free.

Did I hear you say there are no bloodhounds today? Why bring bloodhounds up? No fellowship, no foundations, no pay-offs with fangs? No dripping dog nozzles on the scholarship checks with the big name signatures; no bark when the number bankers pay off your sons in quick money? No bite in poverty? Sorry, I guess not. Anyhow, the song is about a slave and a dog. The slave's name is Old Riley and the dog's name is Rattler. It happened maybe a hundred years ago, before we got free. I don't know how Leadbelly, who died in New York in 1949, remembered the song so long. Maybe it was because he was a criminal and mean anyhow. Maybe he just remembered it out of pure evil, and made a record of it to leave behind as his legacy to us who have been 90 years free—and have forgotten what slavery was all about.

Such a long time free! We have forgotten! About to integrate—done so in the upper, and even in the lower brackets. God help the middle, though! God help the unintegrated! God help the great-grandsons of Old Riley who want to be free and aren't! But when he ran away, they sic'ed Rattler on him. Sic'ed a dog on him. A dog! We never had a dog sic'ed on us, did we? Not a real live dog. Just paycheck dogs, endorsed dogs, honorary degree dogs, fellowship dogs, gift check dogs, high rent dogs, low wages dogs, dogs with the long sharp white fangs of money. Can you find the running water? Get 'em, Rattler!!

Jazz: Its Yesterday, Today and Its Potential Tomorrow

July 28, 1956

To discuss jazz you can start anywhere with the music as the circle and you yourself the dot in the middle. I'll start with the Blues. I am not a Southerner. I never worked on a levee. I hardly ever saw a cotton field except from the highway. But women behave the same on Park Avenue as they do on a levee: when you've got hold of one part of them the other part escapes you. That's the Blues—love's labor lost.

A lot of commercial music nowadays comes out of the Brill Building. But life is as hard on Broadway as it is in the Blues-originating land. The Brill Building Blues is just as hungry as the Mississippi Levee Blues. One communicates to the other, brother! Some people are wont to declare that nothing that comes out of Tin Pan Alley is jazz. I disagree. Commercial, yes. But so was Storyville, so was Basin Street. What do you think Tony Jackson and Jelly Roll Morton and King Oliver and Louis Armstrong were playing for in the old days?[22] Peanuts? No, money, even in Dixieland. They were communicating for money. For fun, too—because they had fun. But the money helped the fun along.

To skip a half century and come right up to now, some folks say Rock and Roll isn't jazz. First, two or three years ago, there were all these songs about too young to know—*but* . . . etc. Well, the songs are right. You are never too young to know how bad it is to love and not have love come back to you. That is as basic as the Blues. And that is what Rock and Roll is musically—teenage *"Heartbreak Hotel."* The music goes way back to Blind Lemon and Leadbelly—Georgia Tom merging into the Gospel Songs—Ma Rainey, and the most primitive of the Blues.[23]

It borrows their gut-bucket heartache. It goes back to the jubilees and stepped up spirituals—Sister Tharpe—and borrows their I'm-gonna-be-happy-anyhow-in-spite-of-this-world kind of hope.[24] It goes back further and borrows the steady beat of Congo Square—that going on beat—and the Marching Bands' loud and blatant yes! Rock and Roll puts them all together and makes a music so basic it's like the meat cleaver the butcher uses—before the cook uses the knife—before you use the sterling silver at the table on the meat that by then has been rolled up into a commercial filet mignon.

A few more years and Rock and roll will no doubt be washed back half forgotten into the sea of jazz. Jazz is a great big sea. It washes up all kinds of fish and shells and spume and waves with a steady old beat, or off-beat. And Louis must be getting old if he thinks J. J. and Kai—and even Elvis—didn't come out of the same sea he came out of, too.[25] Some water has chlorine in it and some doesn't. There are all kinds of water. There's salt water and Saratoga water and Vichy water, Quinine water and Pluto water. And it's all water. Throw it all in the sea, and the sea would keep on rolling along toward shore and crashing and booming back into itself again. The sun pulls the moon. The moon pulls the sea. They also pull jazz and you and me. Back beyond Kai to Count to Lonnie, beyond June to Sarah to Billy to Bessie to Ma Rainey. And the Most is the IT—the all of it.

Jazz seeps into words—spelled out words. Nelson Algren is influenced by jazz. Ralph Ellison is, too. Sartre, too. Jacques Prevert. Most of the best writers today are. Look at the blues ending of the *Ballad of the Sad Cafe*.[26] Me, a dot in the middle. The first time I heard the Blues was on Independence Avenue in Kansas City. Then State Street in Chicago. Then Harlem in the twenties with J. P. and J. C. Johnson and Fats and Willie the Lion and Nappy playing piano—with the Blues running all up and down the keyboard through the ragtime and the jazz.[27] And I wrote my initial poems about that music, *The Weary Blues*.

When I first reached New York *Shuffle Along* was running with the Sissle and Blake tunes. A little later came *Runnin' Wild* followed by the Charleston beat, then Fletcher Henderson and Duke and Cab. Jimmie Lunceford, Chick Webb, and Ella. Tiny Parham in Chicago and Mary Lou in Kansas City. And at the end of the Depression times, what I heard at Minton's in Harlem—a young music coming out of young people—Billy—the male and the female of them—the Eckstine and the Holiday—Charlie Christian and Dizzy and Tad and the Monk[28]—came out in poems of mine in *Montage of a Dream Deferred*:

> I play it cool
> And dig all jive.
> That's the reason
> I stay alive.

My motto,
As I live and learn,
Is: DIG AND BE DUG
IN RETURN.

"House Rent Parties" Are Again Returning to Harlem

March 9, 1957

After the Stock Market crash of 1929, followed by the closing of many factories, shops, and banks, numbers of people in Harlem had no work. But they still wanted to have a little fun once in a while even during the Depression, so the custom of giving pay parties in some homes came into being, with a small charge made at the door, and also for refreshments inside. Such parties became very popular.

Sometimes, at the end of the month, people would give pay parties to help them get the rent together. So these parties came to be known as House Rent Parties, whether the purpose was always to help raise the rent or not. These parties were often announced by small printed cards given out to friends, put into neighborhood mail boxes, or stuck in the elevator grills of apartment houses. Often there would be a little verse at the top of the cards, sometimes partly in slang or "jive talk" like:

> Hop, Mr. Bunny!
> Skip, Mr. Bear!
> If you don't dig
> this party,
> You ain't nowhere!

To come into the party might be a dime or a quarter at that time. For fifteen or twenty cents a hot fish sandwich or a golden-brown chicken leg could be enjoyed. There was dancing, often to very good music. Some of the best piano players in Harlem played at House Rent Parties in the late Twenties and early Thirties—maybe J. P. Johnson, Willie "The Lion" Smith, Dan Burley, or Fats Waller, all of whom eventually became famous. At these parties young pianists developed their styles, had fun themselves, and worked out ways of playing that influenced other jazz pianists.

When I first came to Harlem, as a poet I was intrigued by the little rhymes at the top of most House Rent Party cards, so I saved them. Now I have quite a collection. Some of the cards were reproduced in the Harlem section of the first volume of my autobiography, *The Big Sea.* One card dated June 9, 1928, advised:

> *If Sweet Mama is running wild*
> *And you are looking for a*
> *Do-Right Child.*
> *Just come around and linger*
> *awhile*
> at a Social Whist Party given by Pinkney and Epps,
> 226 West 129th Street. Good Music. Refreshments.

A card announcing a September, 1929 party was headed:

> *Some wear pajamas,*
> *Some wear pants.*
> *What does it matter,*
> *Just so you can dance?*

And Lucille and Minnie's card dated November 2 of that year said:

> *Fall in line and watch*
> *your step—*
> *There'll be lots of browns*
> *With plenty of pep.*

And Mary Winston stated that at her party:

> *We've got yellow girls,*
> *We've got black and tan.*
> *Will you have a good time?*
> *YEAH, MAN!*

Usually a good time was had by all, with the piano playing well into the wee hours of the morning.

But with the passing of the Depression, such pay parties disappeared from the Harlem scene. Lately, they seem to be coming back into favor again. Maybe it is inflation today and the high cost of living that is causing the return of the pay-at-the-door and buy-your-refreshments parties. Only, unfortunately, instead of live music and all-night-long piano players, now, the juke box, the phonograph, or radios usually furnish the music.

The parties are not as much fun as they used to be when the guests contributed to impromptu entertainment with maybe a large lady singing the blues, or a young tap dancer hitting a series of steps just for fun, and perhaps somebody arriving at 3 A.M. with a guitar.

The current House Rent Party cards, however, are just as amusing as the old ones. And they are distributed indiscriminately to all and sundry, as before, handed out in bars, stuck in mail boxes, and dropped in elevators. A recent Harlem card asked:

> *Why stay home and look at*
> *the wall?*
> *Come on out and have a ball*
> *—at*
> a Party given by the 7 brothers Social Club, December 7, 1956.

But now, although there is no Depression such as we had in the Thirties, money does not buy what it used to buy, prices are high, and maybe for that reason, the pay-as-you-enter parties seem to be returning to Harlem—and who-ever-you-may-be can come, so long as you have money to spend. Not much money is needed. For just a little, you can have a ball at a House Rent Party.

That Sad, Happy Music Called Jazz

January 24, 1959

Danced to and laughed to and sung to all around the world now is the Negro's own music, jazz. Jazz is such happy music because it was born out of such great sadness. Its rhythms of joy grew from the heartbeats of sorrow, for it was born of bondage. A hundred and fifty years ago, Congo Square in New Orleans was one of the saddest happy places in the world.

It was there in that open dusty acreage that the slaves held their Sunday dances and all day long beat on their drums the rhythms of Africa. They made intricate wonderful happy music and shook their feet in gay abandon until the sundown warning sent them back to their slave quarters. While danc-ing many of them forgot their bondage.

Yet the music itself, for all its gaiety, remembered Africa, the ships of the Middle Passage, whips, chains, blood hounds, the slave markets, the life-times of work, past and to come, without pay and without freedom. So the rhythms of Congo Square in New Orleans became the first sad-happy rhythms destined to set the tempos of American jazz.

Soon came the field hollers of the plantations, the work songs of the South-ern roads and the Mississippi levees, the religious spirituals and jubilees with their undertow of drums and their melodies of sorrow and hope, sadness and faith, darkness and dawn, and hidden rebellion.

As the years went on, the blues came into being with their mighty music of despair and laughter, of trouble and determination to laugh in spite of troubles: "When you see me laughing, I'm laughing to keep from crying."

It is this combination of sadness and laughter that gives jazz its unique quality, that roots its deep syncopations in the human soul, that keeps it from ever being a frivolous or meaningless music or merely entertainment, no matter how much it is played for fun.

Certainly jazz is fun music. Its spontaneous improvisations, its syncopations, its infectious rhythm are all tributes to the play spirit in men and women, and to the will to laugh and live.

But behind the fun—in the beat of its drums, the cry of the trumpet or the wail of its sax—lie all the shadows of sorrow and suffering that at first were woven into the distant origins of this wonderful music.

Men and drums stolen from Africa, songs and drums held in the harshness of a new world, rhythms tangled in the tall cane, caught in the white bolls of the cotton, mired in the rice swamps, chained on the levees or in the heat of the Georgia roads, targets for the cross fire of the Civil War, crying in the poverty and terror of the Reconstruction, fleeing from the Ku Klux Klan, struggling Northward to work in the war plants of the great World Wars.

"Oh, how long, how long has that evening train been gone? How long? How long? How long?"

Underlying the lacy gaiety of ragtime, the rolling rumble of boogie woogie, the happy dignity of Dixieland bands playing for funerals, parades, dances, picnics, to the sway of swing, the satire of bebop, the heavy beat of rock-and-roll, through the cool sounds of a Charlie Mingus, there is in all this music something of the aching question deep in the heart, "How long, how long before men and women, races and nations, will learn to live together happily?"[29]

The cry and the question are ever present behind the gayest of jazz. It is this longing and this laughter combined that gives jazz its great basic human appeal and endows it with a kind of universality that causes it to be played and loved around the world.

The Negroes of the New World created jazz, but now it belongs to everybody—our gift of rhythm to all the peoples of the earth.

Part 9

Here to Yonder

Why and Wherefore

November 21, 1942

Things that happen away off yonder affect us here. The bombs that fell on some far-off Second Front in Asia rattle the dishes on your table in Chicago or New Orleans, cut down on your sugar, coffee, meat ration, and take the tires off your car. Right now Hitler is about to freeze your salary or your work, although his activities at the moment are centered around Stalingrad. But it is not so far from here to yonder.

For the last 20 years, half writer and half vagabond, I have traveled from here to yonder around the world and back again, up and down the African coast, through Russia, through Asia, back and forth across America and, in general, from pillar to post. One thing I learned is that Alabama and Africa have the same problems. Stalingrad and Chicago fight the same gangsters. Two 14-year-old boys are lynched at Shubuta Bridge and Harlem shudders—also Chungking.

What happens at the post affects the pillar, and vice versa. Here is yonder, and yonder is here. When you do wrong, it affects me. If I don't behave myself, it hurts you. When you do good it helps me. When I do good, I hope it aids you. When white folks do wrong, in the long run it lays as heavy a burden on them as it does on us. Witness India, witness Malaya, witness the poverty of the South and the sorry spectacle of Shubuta Bridge.

A year before the war in Paris, the summer of Munich, I saw the left and right literally—I mean factually—thumbing their noses at each other, shouting curses back and forth in the Place de l'Opera in the heart of the French capital—the workers and the fascists openly displaying that woeful gulf between them that brought about the fall of France and the Vichy collaboration that now sends your son, your brother, your friends, mine—and probably me—to fight on the European front to restore France to herself.

What happened that summer at Munich, in Paris, in the betrayal of Spain, and later at the Maginot Line—way over yonder—will make YOU cry right here, for some of the men we know, our relatives, friends, and fellow citizens, Negroes from Harlem and Chicago and Mississippi—some of those men will never come home again. Some will die way over yonder in Europe, in Asia, and Africa—thus forcefully and directly does the yonder reach into the here. It touches you. It touches me.

Guns, Not Shovels

The cat was taking his first physical, standing in line in front of me at the hospital where our draft board had sent us. He was talking and he didn't care who heard him. (Chalk up one point for the democracies—at least a man can talk, even a colored man.) He said, "I know they gonna send all us cats to a labor battalion. I'm a truck driver, and I know they gonna make me a truck driver in the army."

"How do you know?" I asked.

"All the guys I know from Harlem," he said, "have gone right straight to labor battalions. Look at the pictures you see of colored soldiers in the papers, always working, building roads, unloading ships, that's all. Labor battalions! I want to be a fighter!"

"I know a fellow who's gone to Officers School," I said. "And another one learning to fight paratroopers."

"I don't know none," he said. "And besides, if they don't hurry and take this blood test, I'm liable to lose my job. That Italian I work for don't care whether the draft board calls you or not, you better be to work on time. He ain't been in this country but six or seven years and owns a whole fleet of trucks, and best I can do is drive one of 'em for him. Foreigners can get ahead in this country. I can't."

"Some colored folks get ahead some," I said.

"You have to be a genius to do it," he argued.

Another man in the line spoke up, older, dark brownskin, quiet. "Between Hitler and the Japanese," the other man said, "these white folks are liable to change their minds. They're beginning to find out they need us colored people."

It was that third fellow who took the conversation all the way from the here of Manhattan Island to the yonder of Hitler, the Japanese, and the arena of struggle—that far-off yonder—including Africa, India and China, Gandhi and Chiang Kai-Shek—that yonder that, in spite of all, is changing our world in Harlem, on State street, and maybe even in Mississippi.

There was no chance to talk any more for the line moved on. He went in to the little room where the doctors were, had his blood drawn, and hurried off. I do not know his name. Probably our paths will never cross again. But I hope, since he wants to be a fighter, Uncle Sam will give him a gun, not a shovel or a truck. A gun would probably help his morale a little—now badly bent by the color line.

Your Folks and Mine

The afternoon paper that I bought as I came out of the hospital reported an unconfirmed rumor that Josephine Baker is slowly dying of consumption way over yonder in Casablanca on the coast of North Africa. That hit me almost as hard as the war news. I hope the report is not true, for the dusky brown girl from St. Louis is one of our greatest ambassadors of charm and beauty to the world.

Aubrey Pankey, young Negro singer from Sugar Hill, is giving concerts this week in Rio de Janeiro.

Chatwood Hall, former colored postal clerk from Minneapolis, is in Kuibyshev, U.S.S.R.

Arna Bontemps in Chicago is writing a new book. These are folks I know and shall write about in future columns.

I know lots of folks, whose names have never been in the newspapers— as interesting as those whose names have been in the papers. I shall write about them, also. Your folks and mine—as colored as me—scattered all over the world from here to yonder. From week to week, they—and you—shall be the subjects of this column. I got a feeling that you are me. And I know dog-gone well, HERE is YONDER. I even expect that in due time white will be black. Amen!

Don't Be a Food Sissy

April 3, 1943

Horse meat is excellent to eat. Goat is delicious. Camel is fine. A snail is no quail, but still it's eatable. Frog legs and eel are, of course, delicacies, but I have eaten them, too, and found them good indeed. I have never eaten rattlesnake, although I have known people who are not prejudiced against it and serve it at their cocktail parties. But I think I would not care to eat rattlesnake unless very hungry.

I was VERY hungry when I first ate snail. During the recent Spanish Civil War, I arrived in Madrid one night too late for dinner after a rough 14 hours by bus from Valencia. Very tired, I slept through a bombardment and woke up too late the next morning for breakfast. At the Writers Club where I was stopping, the last drop of coffee and the last crumb of bread was gone. By ten I was ravenous so I went in the street looking for food. There was nothing to be found in any store, restaurant, or public place—all bare. Madrid was under siege and Franco had cut all the railroad lines, trying to starve the people out.

Knowing some Spanish, I kept asking in the streets where I might buy something to eat. Finally someone told me of a bar off the Puerta del Sol where, at eleven every day, beer and hors d'oeuvres were sold—until both ran out. I was told to hurry. I did.

The bar was crowded long before the bartender began to draw beer. When he did, I grabbed a glass. (That was my fruit juice.) Shortly, a man arrived from the kitchen bearing an enormous tray piled high with small, steaming, mud-gray objects in curling shells. I looked hard. They were snails—free with beer.

The men at the bar fell upon them, using toothpicks to pull the snails from their shells, then eating them whole. Being hungry, too, I wasted no time in contemplation. I took a toothpick. I grabbed a snail. I ate it. And it was good! In fact, it tasted not unlike a clam if a clam didn't have a sea-flavor. I ate a dozen snails. They were my first breakfast in Madrid. Later, cooked in yellow rice, Valencian style, I found them delicious.

Horse Meat and Mule

During that summer in Madrid, I ate horse meat almost every day for dinner and, on occasion, mule. The horse meat tasted like a good beef pot-roast slightly overdone. The mule was tougher and stronger than horse, but either did right well when you were hungry. With gravy on it, mule looks just like beef, anyhow.

Camel meat, which I ate in Asia, is fat and greasy like pork or possum, especially if you get a chunk of hump. Goat, as eaten in Mexico and Italy, is excellent, like lamb. Frog and eel, of course, have long held high rank as table delicacies, although many Americans are prejudiced against them. They're fine as chicken. And when they are all sliced up and cooked, they don't look in the least like frogs or eels, if that is what worries you. After all, a pig is not a handsome animal, but we eat him.

I tell you about these foods because you're liable to have to eat almost anything soon, what with rationing increasing and meats becoming scarce. Don't be afraid. You'll survive. Many things you now think you don't like, you WILL like if you get real hungry. So my advice would be to take to new foods gracefully. Don't make life unpleasant for yourself and others by being too choosy at the war-time table. Don't grumble and grouch. Don't be finicky. Don't be a food sissy. Eat!

Barbecue Horse Ribs?

Chicago has some wonderful barbecue stands, much better than Harlem's. Next time I get out that way, I have visions of some good old short ribs of horse down on State street, crisp and brown, with hot sauce on them. And maybe Tony's will set a platter of snails up on the bar.

When I think about snails, I think about that other war, the Spanish War, where the people on the Loyalist side had much less to eat than most Americans have ever had, even during the worst days of our depression. In Madrid sometimes, not even mule meat was to be found. But they didn't kick. They wanted to win the war—against Germany and Italy and Franco. They wanted freedom and schools and the right to have labor unions MORE than they wanted food.

The Spanish people lost. We let them down that time, as did France and Great Britain. Then, so short a while ago, the democracies still thought they could appease Hitler and Mussolini and Franco. Now, we know better—a little. (Except for Franco, about whom we are still kidding ourselves.)

Now, we have our own war to win. The Spanish war spread all over the world, Spain's foes against us—those who would crush the poor, dissolve labor unions, the Jew-baiters and Negro haters, against us.

We have to win, even if it means eating horse meat, or mule meat—or none—until this war is won. So, if you can help by not being a food sissy, then don't be one!

On Missing a Train

July 31, 1943

The other day in New York I missed a train for the first time in years. It pulled out before my very eyes and left me standing there within reach, loaded down with bags and baggage. It was a nice, long, air-cooled, streamlined train, and the next train three hours later was a local with antiquated wooden coaches. That made me mad.

I knew well the day before that I had to catch an early morning train, so I don't know why I didn't go to bed early. I had to meet a deadline on a magazine article, but when I finished the article that evening, I should have packed, bathed, and gone to sleep to arise at six. Instead, about midnight, I went out to get a sandwich. And after I had eaten the sandwich, I heard a soldier and a girl arguing on the corner of 145th street.

"If you don't leave me alone," the girl said, "I will phone my husband."

"I don't care nothing about your husband," the soldier said. "It's MY money you've been spending tonight."

So I stopped to see how that came out. About then a friend of mine came up out of the subway so I stood and talked to him. We got into a long comparison of the relative merits of Bob Montgomery and Beau Jack, Henry Armstrong and Sugar Ray.[1] And after a while it was late.

Needed: A Secretary

When I got home I was about to start to pack my bags when I noticed suddenly how dusty my books were, and I got to thinking how everything of any value needs constant care, and here were my autographed books— Saroyan, Roland Hayes, Nancy Cunard, Jim Tully—getting all dusty. They had been dusty for weeks but just then, at 2 A.M., it occurred to me to wipe them off. So I did.

While unpacking the books from the shelves, I came across the recent autobiography of a friend of mine that I had never looked into, so I started to read it, and I kept looking to see if it mentioned me, and by the time I found the page where it did mention me, it was four o'clock in the morning. Then I had to put all the books back in the bookcase before I could pack my bags and bathe.

By then I was sleepy, so I got to thinking how an author should have a secretary to look after things for him, or at least a valet, or a housekeeper, or a wife. Somebody should dust his books, and pack his bags, and run his bath water. Anyhow, I was too sleepy to do any more myself, so I set the alarm and went to bed.

Next thing I knew, the alarm went off at six! BRRR-rrr-rr-r! But I didn't pay it any mind—except to turn it off—because I had had but two hours sleep and I needed a FEW minutes more. Those sweet few minutes turned into sixty. When I jumped up and looked at the clock, I had just an hour to bathe, shave, pack, and make the train. I made it—in time to see it streamline out of the station as I reached the platform.

Naturally, I blamed it on the fact that there were no taxis in Harlem at that hour of the morning. The street car was full of folks going to work, and slow.

A Boat in Shanghai

I was mad. I hate to miss trains, especially when it is my own fault. If I can blame it on somebody else, I don't feel so bad. Once in Shanghai I almost missed a boat to America because Teddy Weatherford and the boys in his jazz band wanted to entertain me with a farewell breakfast.[2]

The Japanese steamer on which I had booked passage was sailing at three. Teddy said he would come to take me to breakfast at ten. He came at eleven. He said, "We have to stop by the market and get the chickens." We stopped. He lived way out on the edge of Shanghai. When we got there it was noon. They served highballs for fruit juice. We forgot the time, but when the chickens were fried I knew I was hungry—and also late. As the gravy came on the table, I looked up and saw that it was two o'clock! But I had to sop just one biscuit! I also ate a leg. (It was so good I regret I never got the other one.)

Then we started rushing for the boat. But first I had to stop by my hotel and pack. The packing consisted of throwing everything I had in the bags by the armload with no kind of order. Result, bags would not shut. Things would not go in. Teddy and I gathered the rest of my clothes and manuscripts in our arms and dashed for the car. He drove like mad through and around rickshaws and diplomats. Coolies screamed. Police whistles blew. The Chinese had closed the pier gates and the Japanese sailors were pulling up the gangplank when I got to the docks. But I got on the ship.

The other day, though, trains having no gangplanks to delay them, I reached the station just in time to see the coaches gliding up the rails gathering speed with nothing I could latch onto to hold them back or pull myself up by. So I got left. And I couldn't blame no jazz band, neither could I blame a holiday. I could only blame me! That's what made me mad. There are many things in this world I do not understand. One of them is, when I KNOW I have to get up early to make a train, why don't I go to bed at a decent hour the night before? Can anybody answer me that?

Saturday Night

August 7, 1943

The usual Saturday night squalls and brawls were taking place on Harlem's Eighth avenue . . . A couple walked all staglegged . . . A lady came to take her husband home from the corner saloon and he didn't want to go . . . A fellow said he had paid for the last round of drinks and the bartender said he didn't . . . The squad car came by. Also the MP's . . . A midget stabbed a full grown man . . . Saturday night jumped.

"Forgive them, Father, for they know not what they do," said a Sanctified Lady, passing a group of sinners on her way from a session of shout and prayer.

"Yes, they do know what they're doing," said a young punk, "but they just don't give a damn."

"Son, you oughtn't to use such language," said the Sanctified Lady.

"If you can't get potatoes, buy tomatoes," yelled a vegetable vendor. "Last call! Pushing this cart home! Come on! Fruits and vegetables!"

"I believe I'll buy myself ten cents fruit," said Melinda.

"For ten cents you get half a plum," said her escort. "Ankle on."

At the newsstand everybody was buying the *Daily News.*

"Have you got *PM?*" asked a studious young man.

"No," said the vendor, "but I got *PV.*"

"I want to read about the coal strike," said the young man, "not Jim Crow."

"I can give you the *News* or the *Mirror,*" said the vendor.

"No," said the young man.

"You can't call my mother no names and still live with me," said a little fellow to a big tall girl.

"I did not call your mother a name," said the girl. "I called you one."

"You called me a ————," exploded the man.

"Shame on you, me chile!" said a West Indian lady. "Such language you man use nowadays."

"He just ain't no good," explained the tall girl. "He spent half his money and ain't bought a thing to eat for Sunday yet."

The Blind Too

"Help the blind! Please help the blind!" said a cup-shaker pushing a shut-eyed man ahead of him.

"That man ain't no more blind than me," declared a fellow in a plaid sport shirt.

"I once knew a blind man who made more money begging than I did working," said a guy leaning on a mail box.

"You didn't work very hard," said the plaid sport shirt. "I never knowed you to keep a job more than two weeks straight."

"I am signing up with Uncle for the duration next Tuesday," said the boy by the mail box. "And will the chicks be sorry!"

"I guess the dime store won't have a ball of yarn left in it when they all start knitting sweaters for you," said the sport shirt.

"Hey, Mary, where you going?" called the boy by the mail box.

"Down to the store to get a pint of cream," said the passing girl. "My mama's prostrated with the heat."

"Ain't that a shame!" cried an old gentleman whose eyes followed a fat pair of blue slacks. "Her backside looks just like a keg of ale."

"I never did go for no woman in pants," said a middle-aged shopper on his way in the chicken store.

"It's a shame," affirmed the old gentleman.

Fights Ain't for Children

"HIT ME! Just go on and hit me—and I'll cut you every way there is," yelled a man as another staggered toward him with his hams doubled up. "I ain't gonna fight you with my fists cause you ain't worth it."

"Stop backing up," said the other man.

"Then you stop coming forward—else I'll hurt you."

A crowd gathered. "You children go on home," said a portly matron to a flock of youngsters. "Around here getting under everybody's feet. Fights ain't for children."

"You ain't none of my mama," shrilled back a pigtail.

"I'm sure glad!" said the portly matron.

"And we don't have a go home," affirmed a bow-legged boy.

"You-all ought to be in bed long ago. Shame the way you stays up all night."

"There ain't nobody home at my house," said the pigtail.

"You'd be home if I was any relation to you," said the portly lady.

"I'm glad you ain't," said the pigtail.

"Break it up! Break it up!" barked the colored cop with club in hand. "Break it up!" They broke it up.

The little bow-legged boy said, "Let's go play in 143rd street. There's some ice down there we can sit on and cool off."

"If you can't get potatoes, buy tomatoes," cried the push cart vendor.

A child dropped a bottle of milk on the sidewalk and began to cry.

"When you get older," consoled a hep cat, "you'll be glad it wasn't Carstairs you broke."

"If you can't get potatoes," cried the push cart vendor, "I got tomatoes," cried the push cart vendor, "and you better come and get 'em," cried the push cart vendor, "'cause I'm trucking on home," cried the push cart vendor.

"Here! Buy another bottle of milk," said the hep cat to the child. He gave him a quarter. "Don't cry, sonny! Don't cry!"

Random Thoughts on Nice People

July 1, 1944

One trouble with nice people is that they often go on the assumption that the whole world is made up of folks like them. Unfortunately, it is not. It is made up also of liars, and braggarts, and sneak thieves, and double-crossers, false deceivers, and politicians who sell out.

Another trouble with nice people is that they think if the world is not like them, it ought to be. It should, but it can't, not now. Silk purses never came out of a sow's ear. The world is largely made up of people tainted with mortal sin, some unbalanced and off the beam from birth, others undernourished and hungry—therefore mean and evil and mad. It's made up of people whose mamas had no business having them, or of people whose papas did them wrong.

Another trouble with nice people is that they think all you have to do to be nice is to act that way. They're mistaken. You can be ever so nice on the surface, yet have larceny in your heart. Good manners are only the half—an important half, it is true. But a *good soul* is most difficult to achieve.

Nice people seem to think folks just naturally want to be decent. Nothing was ever farther from many a human mind. Most folks want to eat—cost what it may. They want to have their sex desires fulfilled, come what may—bastards or poverty-born legitimates.

Most folks want to have fun—at whoever's expense. Most folks care less about doing unto others as they would be done by, than a dog cares about a cat. That is why the human race wars so much, battles by hand and by dive bomber, by law and by lynch mob, by polite eviction and impolite imperialism. One of our great American newspaper men returning recently from Europe said, "One of the troubles with the war is that so many men like it."

Nicer to Be Realistic

Liberals who genteelly want to reform the world, are nice people. But liberals don't know that Chicago gangsters are really nicer—because they are more realistic. The Nazis are really nicer—because they don't hide the bad cards in their deck. They mark them plainly marked.

The Nazis say outright that Jews and Negroes are unwanted, and workers swine. They don't underpay with a kiss, or segregate with sanctimony. They just underpay, and kick out races they don't like. No RESTRICTED CLIENTELE with them, or COLORED NOT ADMITTED.

The trouble with many nice people is that they don't know when they're bad themselves. Sweet as anything is Boston, yet evil enough to see evil in *Strange Fruit.*[3] Sweet as anything is the D.A.R., yet prejudiced enough to bar Marian Anderson. A "Great Mother" is the American Red Cross, yet backward enough to separate Negro blood. A marvelous democracy America—yet it segregates 14 million colored citizens.

Another trouble with nice people is that they think everybody agrees with them or ought to. A gang of folks don't agree with them at all, and won't as long as greed and grasping economic competition have the upper hand.

Evil Based on Fear

To make people nice, you have to take the props of evil out from under them. Mammon is one of the main props of evil—that old desire for gold. Give everybody a decent economic base, and folks wouldn't be half as bad as they are. Much evil is based on fear. Much fear is based on the apprehension that somebody else may get more than you possess.

White folks fear colored folks, England fears America, both fear Russia. The Nordics fear the Orientals and the Orientals fear the Nordics. Africa knows that civilization is still making a grab bag out of the Dark Continent.

Of course, this war may change things for the better. People all over the world may wake up and stop trying to exploit each other. The invasion may be more than another evasion. It takes a very hard kick in the pants, however, to wake the average human being up to the point of doing anything very widely constructive in a social way. But since large portions of the human race are busy at this moment kicking other large portions in the pants with shot and shell, bomb and submarine, perhaps it will help.

Maybe this war will jar some decency into all of us, thus making the world become a better world even than that anticipated by Roosevelt, Churchill, and Stalin. Should that be realized, in another generation or so, almost everybody will be nice people—even Southern white folks—and God knows it would be worth a war to make them decent.

On Human Loneliness

November 11, 1944

There are certain places that accentuate human loneliness and how far away everyone is from everyone else. A dentist's waiting room is one such place. Nobody can share anyone else's toothache.

In a dentist's waiting room a dozen people sit, each one nursing his own troubles, and mostly silent, anticipating the drill, the clamps, or the pulling of a tooth. Certainly it is nothing to talk about, and very little talking is done. But sometimes somebody will start talking, and usually on a subject having nothing to do with teeth. Politics, or something removed from the human mouth.

But nobody listens very much. The place for the tongue is not in motion but up against the aching gum, in wonder at how one little tooth can feel like the whole world in pain. Not even sympathy does an aching tooth much good. And when your turn comes to go into that white room where the chair is, nobody can go with you but yourself.

A doctor's office is even more intently lonely, though it may be crowded with people. Each person has his own illness, or his own fear of illness. Even so minor an illness as a cold is enough to cause a person to feel that he is all by himself in this world, and that nobody else's cold is quite as bad as his.

More dangerous illnesses, or the fear of them, generate thoughts of that final loneliness which is death. The men and women who sit silently in a doctor's office find it hard to think about anyone or anything outside themselves, or their own personal problems. The young woman with the cough that has been hanging on now for weeks wonders desperately if the verdict will be tuberculosis. Consumption! The disease that has taken so many folks down that lonesome road to the cemetery.

Death House Like That

The young man who keeps looking silently through the pages of the same magazine, over and over again, awaiting his turn with the doctor, wonders if that strange fester could be the first sign of syphilis, and he is silently afraid of the shots, the long treatments, the blindness and insanity that may lie at the end. So he sits alone in the crowded doctor's office thumbing through the pages of the same magazine, and everybody else seems like nobody else at all.

The death house in a great prison is like that, too. Once I went to visit the Scottsboro boys in the death house at Kilby prison in Alabama. There was a row of steel cells on either side, and at the end of the rows, the steel door to the death chair. The cells were filled with silent men. In each cell were two or three, but nobody was saying anything. Only a few men got up and approached the bars to greet the minister who came to pray with them that Sunday morning. Their loneliness seemed too great for visitors or prayer.

Once in Spain, when I was a reporter there during the Civil War, I went up to the Ebro Front in a truck load of soldiers going back to battle after their furloughs in Barcelona and Valencia. It was for the most part a silent truck load of men. Some made jokes. Once in a while some sang. But they were mostly silent. They were going up a road that might lead to death, or grave injury, and so there was not much to be said on any subject. Speeding up the road toward Northern Spain in the night with the great stars overhead, each man was as lonely as a star. Had the Fascist planes come streaking across the sky, each would huddle against the other, frightfully alone, although surrounded by men. In air-raids, a million people are not enough company.

Facing It Alone

The dentist, the doctor, the electric chair, the battle front, and bombing planes are all things that have to be faced alone. Another may share your anxiety, but not your fear, and not your pain. Fear and pain are essentially lonely things for, at the ultimate end of fear and pain is death. Enough fear or enough pain will kill you. Death is quite entirely lonely.

I keep remembering a story in the *Crisis* where one of the characters said, "You can stand anybody else's dying but yourself." Just like you can put up with anybody else's toothache but your own, or anybody else's cancer, or syphilis, or consumption. You can be kind and sympathetic to the frightened and the sick. But when the man tells you it's your turn, it looks like you are all alone.

Fear and pain build lonely walls. And death is the loneliest wall of all—unless you believe in heaven and are sure you have been good enough to get there—which takes a mighty lot of careful living and sweet assurance. In heaven all the walls of loneliness are broken down, and white and colored angels all get together without even as much as the fear of Jim Crow or intermarriage. On the other hand, if you go to hell, think how terrible it would be roasting all by one's self for all eternity—because it would hardly be possible for anybody else to roast for you. Just as nobody but you can sit in a dentist's chair when the door opens and the man says, "You are next."

My Day

April 28, 1945

This is the time of the year when college students are finishing their term papers, theses, and final themes. Every year, of late, some choose to write about me as an American writer. The wise ones write to me early in the year for biographical information and material. (Most of this they could find easily themselves if they would read my autobiography, *The Big Sea,* Embree's *13 Against the Odds,* or look my life up in *Current Biography.*) The not-so-wise ones, who wait until April to write, may not get an answer in time—since I am frequently out of town on lecture tours for weeks and do not get my letters until I return.

The other day a young lady wrote asking me to describe in detail a writer's day—what I do from morning to night—which is, I must say, a much more reasonable request than comes from many students who ask me to describe in detail my whole life which took me a year to put down on paper in *The Big Sea,* and then I didn't by any means get it all down.

I have now just sat down to the typewriter to try and tell this student about this day of mine today in New York. For her sake, my sake, and yours, I won't go back beyond when I abruptly woke up this morning. The first thing I did was turn off the alarm, and then turn my back to the clock. (It made me mad.)

The Ring around the Tub

I never have much sense when first I wake up, so I got out of bed in a daze, washed my teeth, turned on the radio to hear the news, put my stocking cap on my head to lay my hair down, ran my bath water, shaved, got in the tub and sat and thought about how much I had to do and where to start. When I got out, I washed the tub and thought how wonderful it is that some soap company has announced the discovery of a new formula for soap that does not leave a ring around the tub.

I further thought how all my life I have always washed out my own tub, even when stopping in homes of very rich people with lots of servants—or in hotels. Since I do not like to wash out a tub myself, I imagine most maids and valets don't like to do so either, so I could never allow myself to wish it on them. I wouldn't like to wash away anybody else's ring around a tub. But when that new soap gets on the market, there won't be rings around tubs! With that cheerful thought I dressed.

For breakfast I had some scrapple and eggs and they were good. While eating I talked and ate and read my mail all at once. Some mornings I get twenty or thirty letters (which is why it takes me so long to get around to answering everybody who writes me). But this morning there were only eleven letters and some magazines and some announcements. There were a couple of bills, but no checks. As happens almost every day, someone I didn't know had sent me an original poem they had written for me to criticize.

Invitations Too

There was a note from Muriel Rahn, the singer, inviting me to hear her do an aria of mine from the William Grant Still opera, *Troubled Island,* that Leopold Stokowski is to produce in New York.[4] And there was another note from a pretty girl in Atlanta asking me to have cocktails with her when I come to Clark College to read my poems. Both these things, I thought to myself, I will surely do. But now I have got to hurry downtown to pick up some railroad tickets.

I proceeded to hurry, got down to the ticket office, only to find that the clerks couldn't find hair nor hide of the reservations they had phoned me were ready. I was in the office an hour thinking how much more efficient the airlines are, and how everybody will probably travel by air after the war. Then I got to wondering, since these Pullman reservations were for the South, if maybe somebody had lost them on purpose because I was colored. But finally they were found.

Then I went over to my publishers on Madison avenue and autographed 67 copies of my poems, *The Dream Keeper,* that students at Downer College in Milwaukee had ordered. On the corner I priced a two-suiter traveling bag which cost $22.50. I walked over to Broadway, priced the same bag there, and found it ten dollars more. (My aunt says that's because Broadway is a sucker's street.) Then I went looking for an oval-shaped hat because I have a long head on which a round-shaped hat buckles. I found a hat and bought it.

I stopped by Asch Records to see if my album of poems was ready for release. It was not, they said. But they made me a present of a wonderful set of "Songs of Israel" for the Jewish holidays. I held them carefully in the crowded subway and played them as soon as I got home. I thought how beautiful, elemental, and sad are the traditional Hebrew chants and wails. By that time, it was supper time. We had dandelion greens that tasted like Spring. Thus ended my day.

My Nights

May 5, 1945

Last week a young lady wrote asking me to tell her about a writer's day—my day. Nobody asked me to tell about nary a night, but I feel like doing so anyhow. One night would not be enough to tell about, nor typical, because with me nights vary much more than days. Some nights I do not do anything but write until two or three o'clock in the morning. I do most of my writing and all of my best writing at night. More ideas come, and, when it is late, telephones do not ring, nobody drops in, and it is never meal time.

Some nights, when I am not working, maybe I will go to a show. A few weeks ago, a girl and I went to the opening of Owen Dodson's new play, *The Garden of Time,* that the American Negro Theater put on at the 135th street Library's little theater in New York.[5] We could not get in because it was crowded, so we went to the Elks' Rendezvous instead.

The Elks' Rendezvous is a very dark and cozy little night club that has the best floor show in Harlem. That night Dick Montgomery was doing his famous female strip-tease, which is the funniest strip-tease in the world, and the M.C., Larry Steele, was singing a song he wrote himself about a soldier writing a letter home that had a recitative in it about how the soldiers hope there won't be any color line after the war. It was a very good song, and one of the few I've ever heard in a colored night club that had any social protest in it.

Spotlight for a Wave

The girl I was with is an officer in the Waves, so when the M.C. spied her, she was spotlighted and introduced to the crowd. On the way out two young sailors just back from the Pacific spoke to her and said that although they were only seamen, and barring stripes and all, they would consider it a pleasure to buy her a drink because she was a colored Wave.

I had not been in a night club since the curfew. In fact, I do not very often go to night clubs, or shows either, because I work at night—although I do not always work indoors. Sometimes I take long walks because I can think good walking, and I can meanwhile work out ideas for poems and stories or articles in my head. Then I put them down on paper when I come back home.

Walking at night in New York or Chicago or Los Angeles is often likely to be productive of some colorful incident or bit of sidewalk drama that a creative writer can use to advantage, or that helps relieve the routine of the day. Last night it was a blind man playing a wonderful accordion on the corner of 125th street and Eighth avenue in Harlem, playing and singing the old church songs I remember from childhood. His accordion sounded like the little old upright organ in our church, and I could see in my mind's eye the old sisters in the amen corner on a Sunday morning raising their voices in song while warming up to shout.

One night in Chicago, I saw a swerving car suddenly stop short for the red light, and everybody in it but the driver jumped out as if it were on fire. Three or four men and women yelled back, "We ain't gonna ride with you!" Whereupon the driver jumped out, too, and said, "I ain't even gonna ride with myself! I'm too drunk!"

Misses the Movies

Often, I intend to go to the movies at night, but somehow I never get there. I missed all the good pictures last year, even *Going My Way*. In New York, if I am walking up the hill I may stop in to see old friends at 409 Edgecombe— where practically every Negro celebrity has lived at one time or another, it having been until recently Harlem's tallest and most fashionable apartment house. Folks I know there now include the Walter Whites (his *Rising Wind* is an excellent book), the artist, Aaron Douglas and Alta, the Roy Wilkins, and the Thurgood Marshalls and the Elmer A. Carters, and the singer, Kenneth Spencer and Dorothy, all of whom are at home most of the time to neighbors.[6]

If I am walking down the hill, I might stop by Ralph Ellison's, Harlem's up-and-coming young Negro writer of real ability. Maybe I might look in on Rev. Shelby Rooks who was at Lincoln when I was, and whose wife, Dorothy Maynor, is a wonderful cook. Or I might end up way down past where Harlem runs into Central Park at Margaret Bonds' place where some mighty swell piano is played, and whose husband, Larry Richardson, is a fellow-Lincolnite, too.[7]

Almost always, after I come home I do some writing—maybe only letters— until I get sleepy. Then if there is anything to eat around, I eat it, or drink some coffee, and go to bed. As soon as I hit the pillow, I go to sleep. There is no use trying to read in bed, although I often intend to do so—even going so far as to open the book. I admire people who can read in bed, but sleep overcomes me, book unread. So ends my night. I almost never dream—asleep.

New York and Us

August 31, 1946

New York is not Paris, Moscow, or Mexico City in so far as racial good manners are concerned. But for an American metropolis, it is so far from being Mississippi-minded that, racially speaking, it is almost a paradise.

Few other cities in our United States can equal New York as an example of how well large numbers of people of varied national backgrounds can get along. And few American cities, if any, have less of a color line. Boston, Cleveland, Milwaukee, San Francisco are, of the big cities which I know best, the nearest to New York in freedom from the narrow-minded and cruel color prejudices in daily life that keep Negroes aware of their race in our country.

In the majority of our American towns and cities a Negro is refused service at drug store soda fountains. I have never heard of that happening in New York where I have lived now off and on for 20 years. I have had cokes and sodas at fountains in all parts of the city. In most American cities a Negro can never be sure just what restaurants (other than Negro) will permit him to buy a meal. (I am not speaking of the South where, of course, Jim Crow patterns are set by law a la Hitler.) But in New York it is rare that a colored person is denied service in a restaurant. If it does happen and a suit is brought, the Negro almost always wins the case.

In New York's theaters and movie houses, Negroes may purchase tickets freely and sit anywhere—which is certainly a great contrast to most cities where we are either Jim Crowed to upper balconies or else barred out altogether—as in Washington, our national capital, where colored people may not see any legitimate plays nor attend other than "Negro" movies. In the Broadway theaters Negro patrons are frequently seen in orchestra seats.

Night Clubs

The night clubs are the one area of public entertainment in New York that generally discourages Negro patronage, other than a dozen or so clubs specializing in Negro entertainment—and even some of these give colored joy-seekers the least desirable tables. Barney Josephson's two Cafe Society places have been pioneers in breaking down this sort of discrimination in downtown New York. And the new Zanzibar, built in a sort of horseshoe circle, no longer puts its colored clientele along the side walls—since the new place has no side walls. The little swing and re bop places along 52nd street where Billie Holiday sings, Stuff Smith and Dizzy and Slam play, give Negroes courteous and equal service.[8] But most other New York cabarets would just as leave we kept out. (Which is a long ways from the way things are in Paris or Rio.)

It is a miracle these days that anyone gets a hotel room in New York, since all the hotels report hundreds of requests daily for reservations that they cannot fill. But Negro visitors who succeed in getting into New York's downtown hotels under present crowded conditions, report polite and courteous treatment. In recent months out of town colored people whom I know— not celebrities either—have stopped at the Waldorf-Astoria, the Pennsylvania, the Commodore, the Roosevelt, the Edison, and the Taft. Those of us

who have traveled extensively in America know that very few cities welcome
Negro guests in the first class hotels—so that is one more feather in New
York's cap.

As Harlem's population extends beyond the old borders of pre-war Harlem, interracial apartment houses are less and less uncommon. In the Am-
sterdam-Broadway area that has become increasingly colored in the last few
years, many white tenants have not run away as Negro tenants moved into
the buildings.

Interracial 'Y'

The YM and YWCA dormitories in New York are interracial. Negro girls
stay at the Spelman YW in Greenwich Village and the Harlem YMCA has
some white men residents in its dormitories. Skyscraper International House
on Riverside is really international in that it accommodates students of all
races, white and colored, European and Oriental. Father Divine's Heavens
are interracial, too. When I was a student at Columbia, I lived in one of the
dormitories on the campus. Nobody in New York seems amazed at these
things, which is another mark of its cosmopolitan civilization.

But in spite of these racial decencies I have mentioned, New York still has
its great Negro ghettos, such as Harlem, and in the Bronx and Brooklyn. It
is not a perfect city racially speaking—being American. But compared to
Atlanta, Dallas, Kansas City, or Indianapolis, it is truly wonderful. And every summer thousands of Negro visitors from more prejudiced portions of
our country come to New York to breathe a little of Manhattan's fresh air of
racial decency, dine in good restaurants, and attend non-Jim Crow concerts
and theaters, or pray in churches that won't invite you out for not being
white.

From the International House, Bronzeville Seems Far Far Away

June 11, 1949

Almost up to the sky, my room at International House is the nearest thing
to an ivory tower that I have ever had. It faces North toward the downtown
Chicago skyline and the horizon-blue of the lake off at the right. The eternal Chicago wind whistles by bringing long months of snow, sleet, rain, and
recently a breath of delayed spring. When the window is open even a crack,
the wind blows all the papers off my table.

Chicago's wind goes well with the town because it is a big rough-neck city, a kind of American Shanghai, dramatic and dangerous, one of the cradles of the atom bomb, Carl Sandburg's "hog-butcher to the world" perfumed with stock-yard scents. It is a "Baby" Bell town (whose death by suicide sold out a whole issue of the *Chicago Defender* as soon as it appeared on the news stands). It is a Joe Louis town with a knockout punch in its steel mills and stock yards. It is a Katherine Dunham town, seductive, determined, theatrical and clever. It's a Yancey town with a heart-throb like boogie-woogie.

Heretofore I have always looked at Chicago from the Negro Southside. When I first came to the city as a kid just before the riots, my mother, my brother and I lived on Wabash in one room level with the elevated trains that roared outside our windows.[9] Later, writing some of my early plays, I lived where the el curves to cross Indiana. When I wrote *The Big Sea* I had a room back of the Grand Hotel not far from the elevated's rumble.

So to be living this spring high in a quiet room in International House on the University of Chicago's Midway with green trees and grass below, is like living in another world far away from the Horace Cayton—"Baby" Bell— Etta Moten—Bigger Thomas—Gwendolyn Brooks—Joe Louis—world of Bronzeville.[10] Yet the "Black Belt" is only a few blocks off. But here one cannot hear it. No el trains cut the quiet. No winos mother-foul the evening air. No jitneys blow their horns. No big cars dispensing policy slips speed around the corners. No Bigger Thomases come home to kitchenette confusions. Here in the University's sociology classes students only study about such things, but do not live them. The "Black Metropolis" is a book in the library.

I understand better now what the words, "ivory tower" mean. I understand better how people can live within a few blocks of daily melodrama, yet be as far away from it as one usually is from the news in the daily papers. I understand better how trees, yards, decent housing, cultured neighbors, clean bathrooms and ever-hit water can make people who live clean, quiet, library lives scornful of those whose lives are shattered by the roar of the el trains and chilled by the cold water that comes out of the faucet marked HOT in the kitchenette taps.

When I came to Chicago in February to be a "Poet In Residence" on the campus, I stayed at the Grand on South Parkway, my favorite little hotel. Then, to be nearer my students, a room was secured for me at International House—with the rest of the foreigners. In the "Black Belt" I, too, am a foreigner. In the recent pre-Supreme-court-decision days, Cottage Grove Avenue was the dividing line between Bronzeville and the restricted covenant areas. Japanese-Americans could live scattered among the whites, but not ourselves. Housing in Chicago is still difficult to find for colored persons outside the predominantly Negro section. But, fortunately, International House—being truly international—is open to both foreigners and Negroes, Jews and Gentiles of all nationalities. That is how I came to my quiet room high up in the wind and the nearest thing to an ivory tower I have ever had—since ivory towers do not exist in colored neighborhoods.

International House is a pleasant place to live, to practice one's languages, and to meet students and teachers from all around the world—including Dixie. There are International Houses only in Chicago, New York, Berkeley, and Paris, gifts of the Rockefeller fortune to international friendship and understanding. It would be nice if every major university center had such a house, for it is helpful and good to be able to live for a while with folks from China, Georgia, France, Mississippi, India, Germany, Tennessee, Sweden, Texas, Egypt and Alabama. For white American and Negro American students from the South, it seems to me especially good that there is a house such as International House where they may be together and get acquainted in friendly fashion—because they cannot share the same dormitories at home nor study together behind the Iron Curtains of Dixie.

Notes

Introduction

1. Langston Hughes, "Poem," *Crisis* 28 (Aug. 1924): 163.

2. Langston Hughes, *The Big Sea* (1940; New York: Thunder's Mouth Press, 1986), 40; subsequent references to this work, abbreviated *BS,* will be included in the text.

3. Langston Hughes, "The Negro Speaks of Rivers," *Selected Poems* (1959; New York: Vintage, 1990), 4.

4. Langston Hughes, "The Fascination of Cities," *Crisis* 31 (Jan. 1926): 138–40.

5. Nathan Irvin Huggins, *Harlem Renaissance* (New York: Oxford University Press, 1971), 15.

6. Alain Locke, ed., *The New Negro* (1925; New York: Atheneum, 1968), 5.

7. Margaret A. Reid, "Langston Hughes: Rhetoric and Protest," *Langston Hughes Review* 3.1 (1984): 13–20.

8. Langston Hughes, "The Negro Artist and the Racial Mountain," *Nation* 122 (June 23, 1926): 692–94.

9. Langston Hughes, *I Wonder as I Wander* (1956; New York: Thunder's Mouth Press, 1986), 62.

10. Langston Hughes, *Good Morning Revolution: Uncollected Writings of Social Protest,* ed. Faith Berry (New York: Lawrence Hill, 1973), 50; subsequent references to this work, abbreviated *GMR,* will be included in the text.

11. United States, State Department Information Program, "Testimony of Langston Hughes, Accompanied by his Counsel, Frank D. Reeves" (March 26, 1953): 74.

12. *Chicago Defender* (hereafter *CD*), Oct. 22, 1953.

13. John Hope Franklin and Alfred A. Moss, Jr., *From Slavery to Freedom: A History of Negro Americans,* 6th ed. (New York: McGraw-Hill, 1988), 387; subsequent references to this work will be included in the text.

14. Fred Stanton, ed., *Fighting Racism in World War II* (New York: Monad Press, 1980), 72–73.

15. A. Russell Buchanan, *Black Americans in World War II* (Santa Barbara: American Bibliographical Center–Clio Press, 1977), 23.

16. Quoted in Allen Weinstein and Frank Otto Gatell, eds., *The Segregation Era, 1863–1954: A Modern Reader* (New York: Oxford University Press, 1970), 236.

17. Raymond Wolters, *The Burden of Brown: Thirty Years of School Desegregation* (Knoxville: University of Tennessee Press, 1984), 3.

18. Quoted in Weinstein and Gatell, *The Segregation Era,* 285.

19. Henry Hampton, Steve Fayer, and Sarah Flynn, *Voices of Freedom: An Oral History of the Civil Rights Movement from the 1950s through the 1980s* (New York: Bantam Books, 1990), 17–33; subsequent references to this work will be included in the text.

20. Thomas R. Brooks, *Walls Come Tumbling Down: A History of the Civil Rights Movement, 1940–1970* (Englewood Cliffs, N.J.: Prentice-Hall, 1974), 136–37; subsequent references to this work will be included in the text.

21. Donald G. Nieman, *Promises to Keep: African-Americans and the Constitutional Order, 1776 to the Present* (New York: Oxford University Press, 1991), 170–71; subsequent references to this work will be included in the text.

22. *CD,* Aug. 6, 1955.

23. Roi Ottley, *The Lonely Warrior: The Life and Times of Robert S. Abbott* (Chicago: Henry Regnery Co., 1955), 86; subsequent references to this work will be included in the text.

24. Lee Finkle, *Forum for Protest: The Black Press during World War II* (Rutherford, N.J.: Farleigh Dickinson University Press, 1975), 45–46.

25. *CD,* Aug. 6, 1955.

26. Arnold Rampersad, *The Life of Langston Hughes,* 2 vols. (New York: Oxford University Press, 1986, 1988), 2:53–55; subsequent references to this work will be included in the text.

27. Bob Hunter, "'Simple' Would Call Langston Hughes 'A Writin' Fool,'" *CD,* Oct. 13, 1962.

28. *CD,* Mar. 6, 1948.

29. *CD,* Feb. 15, 1947.

30. *CD,* Aug. 30, 1947.

31. *CD,* Dec. 12, 1942.

32. *CD,* May 12, 1945.

33. *CD,* Feb. 26, 1944.

34. *CD,* May 15, 1948.

35. *CD,* Aug. 6, 1949.

36. *CD,* Oct. 20, 1945.

37. *CD,* Nov. 21, 1942.

38. Amiri Baraka, "Langston Hughes and the Harlem Renaissance," *Daggers and Javelins: Essays, 1974–1979* (New York: William Morrow, 1984), 153.

Part 1: The See-Saw of Race

1. Warren Brown (1905–), educator, journalist, and diplomat, was awarded the U.S. Department of State's Meritorious Medal of Honor in 1965. Virginius Dabney (1901–) was editor of the Richmond *Times-Dispatch* from 1936 to 1969.

2. Henry A. Wallace (1888–1965), Secretary of Agriculture and later vice-president under Roosevelt, was disliked by many white Southerners for his vocal sup-

port of racial integration. Sumner Welles (1892–1961), an advisor to Roosevelt, was outspoken in his belief that the United States needed to develop a tougher policy in dealing with Russia.

3. Mark Ethridge (1896–1981), a Southern white liberal and the first chairman of the Fair Employment Practices Committee (FEPC), made the statement to which Hughes refers to alleviate the Southern fear of social integration.

4. In response to inequitable treatment of African Americans in the war industries and the armed forces, A. Philip Randolph, president of the Brotherhood of Sleeping Car Porters, met with several prominent black leaders and intellectuals to discuss and organize a march on Washington. The march was called off after President Roosevelt issued Executive Order 8802, which was designed to prevent such discrimination.

5. During the "Zoot Suit Riots" of 1943, hundreds of Mexican and African American youths and adults were beaten, stripped, and arrested without warrant on the streets of Los Angeles out of fear that their unique form of dress represented gangster affiliations.

6. Signed on February 19, 1942, President Roosevelt's Executive Order 9066 resulted in the internment of 110,000 Japanese-Americans, 70,000 of whom were U.S. citizens.

7. The Work Projects Administration (WPA)—originally the Works Progress Administration—and the National Youth Administration (NYA) were agencies established under the Roosevelt administration to aid U.S. citizens during the depression.

8. In the Texas primary case of *Grovey v. Townsend* (1935), the United States Supreme Court upheld the use of the white primary in Texas, which stipulated that only whites could vote in the party nominating contests.

9. Angelo Herndon (1913–), a political labor leader and Communist party recruiter, was sentenced to twenty years in prison under an antiquated Georgia slave law that prohibited insurrections. His conviction was reversed by the U.S. Supreme Court in 1937.

10. During his tenure in the House of Representatives, Texas Democrat Martin Dies, Jr. (1900–1972) played a key role in creating the House Committee on Un-American Activities, an organization that would accuse Hughes of being a Communist sympathizer. Senator Theodore G. Bilbo (1877–1947) and Representative John Elliot Rankin (1882–1960), both from Mississippi, were extremists who denounced all legislation that favored African Americans, immigrants, and labor unions.

11. The Daughters of the American Revolution (DAR) was an exclusive group that barred Marian Anderson from performing at Constitution Hall in Washington in 1939.

12. During World War II, the American Red Cross separated black and white blood in the banks that served wounded soldiers.

13. In response to A. Philip Randolph's organization of the March on Washington Movement, President Roosevelt issued Executive Order 8802 on June 25, 1941. The order prohibited discrimination in the defense industry and in government, and led to the establishment of the President's Committee on Fair Employment Practices (FEPC).

14. Paul Robeson (1898–1976), perhaps best known for his performances in *Emperor Jones,* was labeled a Communist sympathizer by the House Committee on Un-American Activities during the 1950s. Marian Anderson (1902–), acknowledged at one time as "the world's greatest living contralto" despite such set-backs as being barred from Washington's Constitution Hall by the Daughters of the American Revolution (DAR) was, by 1941, one of the ten highest paid American concert artists. Dorothy Maynor (1910–), a renowned soprano and founder of the Harlem School of the Arts at St. James Presbyterian Church, became the first African American to serve on the Metropolitan Opera's board of directors. Richard Wright (1908–60), best known for his novel *Native Son,* expatriated to Paris after World War II, where he lived until his death. Hazel Scott (1920–81), a musician, singer, actress, and social activist, was an outspoken critic of racial prejudice and discrimination. Walter White (1893–1955), a writer and secretary of the NAACP, distinguished himself as one of America's leading fighters against lynchings. William Edward Burghardt Du Bois (1868–1963), a distinguished teacher, author, poet, and scholar, argued that an educated black elite, which he termed the "talented tenth," would lead the African American community out of its state of oppression.

15. Hughes is referring to the 1947 lynching of a young African American who was held by police in connection with the murder of a taxi driver. An all-white jury refused to indict the twenty-eight men who confessed to participating in the lynching.

16. Introduced on several occasions by Representative Leonidas C. Dyer (1871–1957), a Republican from Missouri, the Anti-Lynching Bill was passed in the House of Representatives in 1922, but was ultimately abandoned after a filibuster by Southern Senators.

17. Regarded by many as the first great jazz composer, Ferdinand Joseph "Jelly Roll" Morton (1885–1941) began playing in New Orleans's Storyville at the age of seventeen.

18. W. C. Handy (1873–1958) is reputed to be the first man to write a blues composition, and his famous "St. Louis Blues" popularized the musical form around the world.

19. Born into slavery, Booker T. Washington (1856–1915) helped Tuskegee Institute gain national prominence through his agenda of pragmatic, industrial education. Mary McLeod Bethune (1875–1955), founder of Bethune-Cookman College, was president of the National Council of Negro Women and also headed the Division of Negro Affairs in Washington, D.C. James Weldon Johnson (1871–1938), a poet, novelist, and NAACP official, played an integral role in the struggle for civil rights during the early part of the twentieth-century. Countee Cullen (1903–46) and Jessie Fauset (1886–1961) were both leading writers of the Harlem Renaissance, the latter serving as editor of the NAACP's *Crisis* at the time of Hughes's first publication in the journal. Sterling Brown (1901–89), an accomplished poet and literary critic, spent his long career teaching at Howard University. Margaret Walker (1915–) won the Yale Younger Poets Prize for her book *For My People,* a work written during her tenure with the Chicago Federal Writer's Project.

20. As Undersecretary for Special Political Affairs of the United Nations, Ralph Bunche (1904–71) received the Nobel Peace Prize for his work as U.N. mediator during the Palestine dispute.

21. Autherine Lucy was expelled from the University of Alabama in 1956 because of the violent rioting that erupted after the state of Alabama was ordered to admit black applicants.

22. Lillian Smith (1897–1966) is perhaps best known for *Strange Fruit,* a novel that explores the relationship between a black woman and a white man.

23. Born into slavery, John Mercer Langston (1829–97) became Virginia's first African American congressman.

24. Fourteen-year-old Emmett Till was abducted and killed in 1955 for whistling at a white woman in Mississippi. An all-white jury acquitted the men who were charged with the lynching.

25. General Samuel Chapman Armstrong (1839–93) was a white educator who, because of his success in leading black troops during the Civil War, was appointed as an agent of the Freedman's Bureau in charge of a camp of emancipated slaves near Hampton, Virginia. Armstrong helped found Hampton Normal and Industrial Institute in 1868. Lucy Laney (1854–1933), a former slave, founded the Haines Normal Institute in Georgia. Ida B. Wells (1862–1931), a renowned educator, journalist, and civil rights leader, was removed from her teaching post at Fisk University because of a lawsuit that resulted when she refused to give up her seat on a Jim Crow railroad car.

26. Under the direction of George L. White, student musicians from Fisk University went on tour in 1871 to raise money for their school. With their program of spirituals and slave songs, the Fisk Jubilee Singers gained worldwide recognition and eventually raised over $150,000.

Part 2: Jim Crow's Epitaph

1. Instigated by the wounding of an African American soldier by a white police officer, the riot to which Hughes refers occurred in Harlem on August 1, 1943, and claimed the lives of five people.

2. The first black man to receive wide acclaim for his singing both in the United States and abroad, Roland Hayes (1887–1976) was brutally beaten in 1942 by a white shoe store clerk in Georgia, his home state.

3. Best known for his composition "Minnie the Moocher," Cabell "Cab" Calloway (1907–94) was one of the many African American jazz musicians who led groups in New York City during the big band era of the 1920s and 1930s.

4. Popularly known as "Lady Day," Billie Holiday (1915–59) is considered to be one of the greatest jazz singers of all time.

5. Bessie Smith (1894–1937), known as "Empress of the Blues," made over eighty recordings during her short career. The automobile accident to which Hughes refers occurred near Clarksdale, Mississippi.

6. Chiang Kai-Shek (1887–1975) was the first constitutional president of the Republic of China.

7. Pearl Bailey (1918–90), actress and night club singer. Jackie Moms Mabley (1894–1975), comedienne and singer.

8. Melvin B. Tolson (1898–1966) is best known for his collection of poems, *A Gallery of Harlem Portraits.*

9. Made famous by his involvement in school desegregation cases, Thurgood

Marshall (1908–93) was appointed by President Johnson to the Supreme Court in 1967.

10. John Jasper (1812–1901) is reputed to have given his sermon "De Sun Do Move" over 250 times.

11. Edith Wilson (1896–1981) was also an accomplished blues singer, touring on the vaudeville circuit and playing in Broadway musicals. Eartha Kitt (1928–), who gained fame from singing as well as from acting, appeared in the Broadway production of *New Faces* in 1952.

12. Known as the "King of Ragtime," Scott Joplin (1868–1917) invented American folk operas and ballets. Thomas Million Turpin (1873–1922), known as the "Father of St. Louis Ragtime," published the "Harlem Rag," the first by an African American, in 1897. Josephine Baker (1906–75) became a sensation with her performance in the 1920s musical, *Shuffle Along*. Living the majority of her life in Europe, she was awarded the Legion of Honor for her work with the French Resistance.

13. With his syndicated cartoon "Cuties," Elmer Simms Campbell (1906–71) became the first African American artist to work regularly for mainstream publications. Daniel Louis "Satchmo" Armstrong (1900–1971), one of the most creative innovators in the history of jazz, was known for his technical brilliance on the trumpet as well as for his pioneering singing style.

14. T. S. Eliot (1888–1965) and Marianne Moore (1887–1972) were both influential American poets. Arna Bontemps (1902–73), one of Hughes's closest friends, distinguished himself with a prolific writing career that spanned many literary genres.

15. The Mau Mau was comprised of revolutionaries who mounted a rebellion in Kenya when the white minority resisted black participation in government.

16. Clergyman, administrator, and government official, Channing Tobias (1882–1961) served as chairman of the board of directors for the NAACP and, in 1946, was appointed to the President's Commission on Civil Rights. Mordecai W. Johnson (1890–1976), a Baptist minister and a noted orator, was president of Howard University from 1926 to 1960.

17. The Dixiecrat party was a Southern political party formed in reaction to Truman's Fair Deal policy.

18. Ross Robert Barnett (1898–1987), a strict segregationist, attempted to bar James Meredith from integrating the University of Mississippi. Orval Eugene Faubus (1910–94), while Governor of Arkansas, ordered the National Guard in 1957 to prevent the integration of Central High School in Little Rock.

19. Founded in 1890, Daughters of the American Revolution (DAR) is an exclusive national patriotic society that requires its members to descend from an ancestor who served in a military or civilian capacity during the American Revolution.

Part 3: Fair Play in Dixie

1. Ethel Waters (1896–1977), widely acclaimed for her acting, blues, and gospel singing, was popular on the vaudeville circuit in the early 1920s and later toured with evangelist Billy Graham for nineteen years. Edward "Duke" Ellington (1899–1974), a composer, pianist, and band leader, contributed to the Swing Era in American jazz and left a legacy of more than two thousand compositions.

2. John Temple Graves (1892–1961) wrote *The Fighting South*, a book that ad-

vocated the separation of the races. David L. Cohn (1896–1960) was the author of *This Is the Story,* a personal account of the Army Service Forces during the period 1944–45.

3. E. Franklin Frazier (1894–1962), a distinguished sociologist and historian, was the chairperson of Howard University's Sociology department during his long career.

4. Edward M. Almond (1892–1979), a white army officer, was appointed Brigadier General in 1942.

5. Horace Roscoe Cayton (1903–70), a sociologist, writer, and educator, served as special assistant to the United States Secretary of the Interior and later became an instructor at Fisk University.

6. John Foster Dulles (1888–1959), Secretary of State under President Eisenhower, was a militaristic leader committed to wiping out Communism around the world.

7. In an interview conducted by Russell Warren Howe regarding the riots that broke out at the University of Alabama following the admission of a young African American woman named Autherine Lucy, Faulkner made the following statement: "As long as there's a middle road, all right, I'll be on it. But if it came to fighting I'd fight for Mississippi against the United States even if it meant going out into the street and shooting Negroes."

8. Paul Robeson (1898–1976), an African American actor and singer famous for his appearances in *Emperor Jones,* came under fire by the House Committee on Un-American Activities for being a Communist sympathizer.

9. Although he did not publicly support Senator Joseph McCarthy, James Eastland (1904–86), a Mississippi Democrat, was adamant in his emphasis on the threat of Communist subversion in the United States.

10. Richard B. Russell (1897–1971) aggravated racial tensions throughout his career by leading efforts to prevent the passage of an anti-lynching bill in 1935 and by suggesting, in 1949, that Southern blacks relocate to the North.

11. Denmark Vesey (1767–1822) was hanged after organizing a slave insurrection involving approximately 9,000 slaves and free blacks. Gabriel Prosser (1775?–1800), leader of an unsuccessful slave revolt in Richmond, Virginia, was executed on October 6, 1800. Nat Turner (1800–1831), leader of the most successful slave revolt in United States history, was an important catalyst of the abolitionist movement.

Part 4: Nerve of Some White Folks

1. Hughes is probably referring to Thomas Dixon (1864–1946), whose novel *The Klansman* glorified the Ku Klux Klan and was made into the motion picture *The Birth of a Nation.*

2. Katharine Cornell (1893–1974), a popular actress of the period, was awarded the Medal of Freedom in 1946.

3. Instigated by the shooting of a young black soldier by a white police officer following the former's objection to police mistreatment of a black woman, the Harlem riot of 1943 resulted in several deaths, hundreds of injuries, and over $5 million in property damages.

4. Gerald L. K. Smith (1898–1976) was leader of the far right America First party.

5. James Vincent Forrestal (1892–1949) served as Secretary of the Navy from

1944 to 1946 and was appointed as the first Secretary of Defense in 1947. Kenneth C. Royall (1894–1971), after a short tenure as North Carolina senator, was appointed Secretary of the Army in 1947.

6. Norvel Lee (1924–), a distinguished educator as well as a champion boxer, was appointed to the Executive Committee of the World Boxing Association in 1973.

7. Sadie Alexander (1898–1989), a lawyer and civil rights activist, was appointed by President Carter in 1978 as Chairperson of the White House Conference on Aging.

8. Herman Talmadge (1913–) served as Governor of Georgia from 1948 to 1950 and was elected to the United States Senate in 1957.

9. Stridently opposed to the New Deal and organized labor, Eugene Talmadge (1884–1946) organized the Constitutional Jeffersonian Democratic party in 1936.

Part 5: Brazenness of Empire

1. A successful African American business executive, Truman Kella Gibson (1882–1972) was a founder of the Supreme Life Insurance Company. William Henry Hastie (1904–76) became the first African American to serve as a United States federal judge.

2. Instigated by a fight between a black man and a white man, the Detroit riot of 1943 resulted in 33 deaths and several hundred thousand dollars in property damage.

3. One of the great blues singers of her time, Clara Smith (1894–1935) was a star attraction for the Theater Owner's Booking Association (TOBA).

4. Adolphe Felix Sylvestre Eboué (1884–1944) was the first black African to govern a French colony.

5. Benito Mussolini invaded Ethiopia, the only independent black African nation, in 1935.

Part 6: Segregation-Fatigue

1. Joseph Julian (1911–82), a victim of Joseph McCarthy's witch hunts, was a liberal journalist and radio commentator.

2. Robert Russa Moton (1867–1940) succeeded Booker T. Washington as president of Tuskegee Institute in 1915.

3. Hughes is probably referring to Ellis Gibbs Arnall (1907–), who defeated Eugene Talmadge in 1943 to become Governor of Georgia.

4. Lincoln Steffens (1866–1936) was a reporter for the *New York Evening Post* and later became managing editor of *McClure's Magazine*.

5. Boxer Joe Louis (1914–81) was heavyweight champion of the world for over eleven years.

6. Benjamin Oliver Davis, Sr. (1887–1970), was the first African American to attain the rank of General in the United States Army.

7. Roi Ottley (1906–60), journalist and author, wrote *The Lonely Warrior,* a biography of *Chicago Defender* founder Robert S. Abbott.

8. Awarded the United States Legion of Merit for military excellence, Benjamin Washington Johnson (1914–) also holds world records in two track events.

9. George Baker (1880–1965), known to his followers as Father Divine, organized and led the Father Divine Peace Mission and became one of the most widely known religious leaders in the United States.

Part 7: Are You a Communist?

1. During his tenure in the United States Senate, J. William Fulbright (1905–) opposed integration and voted against the Civil Rights Acts of 1957 and 1960.

2. Wendell Lewis Willkie (1892–1944), lawyer and author, argued in *One World* that the American attitude toward the black community was largely imperialistic and impeded the war effort.

3. In October 1949, the leaders to whom Hughes refers were convicted and sentenced to prison terms for violating the Smith Act of 1940, which prohibited United States citizens from teaching and advocating "the overthrow and destruction of the United States government by force and violence."

4. Jack Roosevelt Robinson (1919–72), baseball star and writer. Marcus Garvey (1887–1940), founder of the Universal Negro Improvement and Conservation Association and African Communities League (U.N.I.A.).

5. W. E. B. Du Bois was indicted in 1951 for being a Soviet sympathizer. Although he was acquitted, the incident led many people to consider him a traitor.

6. Charles S. Johnson (1893–1956), the first African American president of Fisk University, co-authored *The Negro in Chicago,* considered to be a landmark in social research. Elmer Carter (1890–1973), an editor of *Opportunity* magazine, was the first African American to head the New York State Commission. Marjorie McKenzie was a respected journalist for the Pittsburgh *Courier.*

Part 8: Beating Out the Blues

1. Hughes's obituary turned out to be premature. Though Josephine Baker was battling paratyphoid at the time, she lived until 1975.

2. George Gershwin (1898–1937), composer best known for *Porgy and Bess.*

3. Mercer Ellington (1919–), trumpeter, composer, and band leader, took over the Duke Ellington Orchestra when his father died in 1974.

4. Pearl Primus (1919–) was awarded the last Rosenwald Foundation Fellowship to study African dance in Liberia.

5. Josh White (1908–69), tambourine and guitar player. William Waring Cuney (1906–76), singer and poet.

6. Lionel Hampton (1908–), vibraphonist, drummer, band leader. Louis Jordan (1908–75), saxophonist, singer, band leader.

7. A novelist and short story writer, Ann Petry (1911–) wrote *The Street* after receiving a literary fellowship from Houghton Mifflin.

8. Pianist and arranger Fletcher Henderson (1897–1952) led one of the most influential big bands of the era.

9. Muriel Smith (1923–85), opera singer and actress.

10. A pioneer of modern writing, Gertrude Stein (1874–1946) developed a personal writing style that stressed sound over sense.

11. During her career as a distinguished educator, Nannie Helen Burroughs

(1883–1961) founded the National Training School for Women and Girls, worked for the Association of Colored Women, and organized the Women's Industrial Club in Louisville, Kentucky.

12. Born Arnold Raymond Cream, Jersey Joe Walcott (1914–) became the oldest heavyweight champion in history after knocking out Ezzard Charles (1921–75) in the seventh round at Pittsburgh's Forbes Field in July, 1951. Syngman Rhee (1875–1965), the first president of the Republic of Korea, received support from the United States for his uncompromising anti-Communist agenda.

13. Eddie Cantor (1892–1964), vaudeville and burlesque performer. Al Jolson (1888–1950), actor and singer. Freeman Gosden (1896–1976) and Charles Correll (1890–1972), better known as Amos and Andy, were popular white comedians who appeared in blackface.

14. Theodore James Ward (1902–83), dramatist and executive director of the Negro Playwrights Company in Harlem.

15. A cabaret and vaudeville performer, Luther Bill "Bojangles" Robinson (1878–1949) is perhaps best known for his movies with Shirley Temple.

16. Stephin Fetchit (1902–77) became one of the most successful black actors of the 1930s with his stereotypical representations of exaggeratedly comic figures.

17. A distinguished dancer and choreographer, Katherine Dunham (1910–) used her training in anthropology to introduce African and Caribbean dance rhythms to her performances.

18. Stephen Foster (1826–64), composer and singer. Harold Arlen (1905–86), composer. James Bland (1854–1911), composer of minstrels.

19. James Reese Europe (1881–1919), band leader, composer, violinist, and pianist.

20. Guitarist and singer Huddie "Leadbelly" Ledbetter (1888–1949) was jailed and pardoned on two occasions for murder.

21. Jazz singers Billy Eckstine (1914–93) and Sarah Vaughan (1924–90) popularized bop music during the 1940s with hits such as "It's Magic" and "Don't Blame Me."

22. Tony Jackson (1876–1921) and Joseph "King" Oliver (1885–1938) were both popular ragtime performers with roots in New Orleans.

23. Blind Lemon Jefferson (1897–1929) and Gertrude "Ma" Rainey (1886–1939) were early pioneers of the blues, while Thomas "Georgia Tom" Dorsey (1899–) played boogie-woogie with a decidedly gospel twist.

24. Rosetta Tharpe (1921–73) was the first gospel singer to record for a major label (Decca Records).

25. James Louis "J.J." Johnson (1924–) and Kai Winding (1922–83), both accomplished trombonists, formed the popular group "Jay and Kai" in 1954.

26. Nelson Algren (1909–81), Ralph Ellison (1914–94), Jean-Paul Sartre (1905–80), Jacques Prevert (1900–1977), and Carson McCullers (1917–67), author of *The Ballad of the Sad Cafe,* incorporate various jazz impulses in their creative writings.

27. J. P. Johnson (1891–1955), rag pianist. J. C. Johnson (1896–1981), jazz pianist. Fats Waller (1904–43), pianist, organist. Willie "The Lion" Smith (1897–1973), pianist.

28. Jimmie Lunceford (1902–47), band leader. Chick Webb (1909–39), drum-

mer, band leader. Ella Fitzgerald (1918–), singer. Tiny Parham (1900–1943), pianist, organist, band leader. Mary Lou Williams (1910–81), pianist and educator. Charlie Christian (1916–42), guitarist. Dizzy Gillespie (1917–93), trumpeter, band leader. Thelonius Monk (1917–82), pianist, composer.

29. An important figure of the free jazz movement during the 1960s, bassist Charles Mingus (1922–79) fused early jazz styles with the new avant-garde that was gaining popularity.

Part 9: Here to Yonder

1. Robert "Bob" Montgomery (1919–) and Beau Jack (born Sidney Walker, 1921–) handed the lightweight title back and forth among each other in a series of three fights during 1943 and 1944. Henry Armstrong (born Henry Jackson, Jr., 1912–88) was the first boxer to claim three world titles during the same time period. Sugar Ray Robinson (born Walker Smith, Jr., 1920–89) won the world middleweight title five times between 1951 and 1958.

2. Pianist Teddy Weatherford (1903–45) traveled to the Far East in 1926 and led bands in Singapore, Manila, and Shanghai.

3. Published in 1944 and immediately banned by booksellers in Boston and Detroit, Lillian Smith's *Strange Fruit* is a fictional account of a love affair between an educated young black woman and the white son of a Georgia doctor.

4. Muriel Rahn (1911–61) was a distinguished actress as well as a gifted concert soprano. William Grant Still (1895–1978), known as the "Dean of Negro Composers," was the first African American to conduct a major symphony orchestra in the deep South. Leopold Stokowski (1882–1977) is perhaps best known for his contribution to Walt Disney's popular *Fantasia* (1940).

5. Owen Dodson (1914–83), playwright, poet, and novelist, is perhaps best known for his version of the Father Divine story, *The Divine Comedy.*

6. Aaron Douglas (1899–1988), known for his colorful murals, was an important figure of the Harlem Renaissance. Roy Wilkins (1901–81) served as assistant executive secretary of the NAACP under Walter White, and succeeded W. E. B. Du Bois as editor of the *Crisis.* Kenneth L. Spencer (1913–64) was a distinguished actor and concert singer.

7. Ralph Ellison (1914–94), a novelist and essayist, won the National Book Award in 1952 for *Invisible Man.* Margaret Bonds (1913–72), an accomplished pianist and composer, founded the Allied Arts Academy for Children in Chicago.

8. Stuff Smith (1909–67), violinist.

9. During the Chicago race riot of 1919, thirty-eight persons died and more than five hundred persons suffered injuries.

10. Bigger Thomas is the violent protagonist of Richard Wright's novel, *Native Son.* Gwendolyn Brooks (1917–) was awarded the Pulitzer Prize for her volume of poems *Annie Allen.*

Selected Bibliography

Baraka, Amiri. *Daggers and Javelins: Essays, 1974–1979.* New York: William Morrow, 1984.

Brooks, Thomas R. *Walls Come Tumbling Down: A History of the Civil Rights Movement, 1940–1970.* Englewood Cliffs, N.J.: Prentice-Hall, 1974.

Buchanan, A. Russell. *Black Americans in World War II.* Santa Barbara: American Bibliographical Center–Clio Press, 1977.

Collum, Danny Duncan, and Victor A. Berch, eds. *African Americans in the Spanish Civil War: "This Ain't Ethiopia, But It'll Do."* New York: G. K. Hall, 1992.

Finkle, Lee. *Forum for Protest: The Black Press during World War II.* Rutherford, N.J.: Farleigh Dickinson University Press, 1975.

Franklin, John Hope, and Alfred A. Moss, Jr. *From Slavery to Freedom: A History of Negro Americans.* 6th ed. New York: McGraw-Hill, 1988.

Hampton, Henry, Steve Fayer, and Sarah Flynn. *Voices of Freedom: An Oral History of the Civil Rights Movement from the 1950s through the 1980s.* New York: Bantam Books, 1990.

Huggins, Nathan Irvin. *Harlem Renaissance.* New York: Oxford University Press, 1971.

Hughes, Langston. *The Big Sea.* 1940. New York: Thunder's Mouth Press, 1986.

———. *I Wonder as I Wander.* 1956. New York: Thunder's Mouth Press, 1986.

———. *Uncollected Social Protest Writings.* Ed. Faith Berry. New York: Lawrence Hill, 1973.

Locke, Alain, ed. *The New Negro.* 1925. New York: Atheneum, 1968.

Naison, Mark. *Communists in Harlem during the Depression.* Urbana: University of Illinois Press, 1983.

Nieman, Donald G. *Promises to Keep: African-Americans and the Constitutional Order, 1776 to the Present.* New York: Oxford University Press, 1991.

Ottley, Roi. *The Lonely Warrior: The Life and Times of Robert S. Abbott.* Chicago: Henry Regnery Co., 1955.

Rampersad, Arnold. *The Life of Langston Hughes.* 2 vols. New York: Oxford University Press, 1986–88.

Stanton, Fred, ed. *Fighting Racism in World War II.* New York: Monad Press, 1980.

Weinstein, Allen, and Frank Otto Gatell, eds. *The Segregation Era, 1863–1954: A Modern Reader.* New York: Oxford University Press, 1970.

Wolters, Raymond. *The Burden of Brown: Thirty Years of School Desegregation.* Knoxville: University of Tennessee Press, 1984.

Index

CHRISTOPHER C. DE SANTIS is a graduate of Lewis and Clark College and of the M.A. program in Afro-American studies at the University of Wisconsin at Madison. He currently teaches composition and literature at the University of Kansas, where he is completing doctoral work in English. His essays and book reviews have appeared in the *Southern Quarterly,* the *African American Review,* and the *Langston Hughes Review;* he is also a contributor to *The Oxford Companion to African American Literature.*